LOVE to ALL

LOVE to ALL

The writings of
Jim Aikens

For Claudia, Barbara Jane, Ashley, Julie . . .
These are the candles that light up my life.

CONTENTS

COLUMNS

(THE ST. GEORGE SPECTRUM)

Introducing the Writers Group

By TODD SEIFERT

We had hoped to get at least 60 responses to our call for a group of volunteer writers. Members of The Spectrum and Daily News editorial board thought that if we would that many, could pick 10 to 20 people to write on a rotating basis.

We passed that number of applicants by the end of third day. When all was said and done, we had 104 entries for our Writers Group.

All five members of the editorial board read every writing sample. Each board member gave writers a rating. After all entries had been read, we compiled the ratings and formulate the top 40. From that list, we selected the 20 writers being introduced today based on writing quality, demographics and length of time in the area.

The goal was to pick as diverse a group of writers as possible.

Some statistics about the group:

- **Gender:** We have 11 men and nine women.
- **Age:** The average age is 48 years old. We have people ranging in age from 17 to 81 on the group.
- **Years in the area:** The average person on the group has lived in Southern Utah for 8.5 years. We have one person who has been here less than a year and one person who has lived in the area for more than 25 years.

You will recognize some of the names because they frequently write letters to the editor. Others will be new to you.

You will agree with some of the writers' political arguments. Others, you will despise.

Either way, we hope you read what they have to write. You agree or disagree with what they have to say? Write us a letter to the editor to share your thoughts with the community.

Now, here is the group, by city:

Cedar City

- **Mary Anne Andersen** in an adjunct piano professor at Southern Utah University and professional accompanist.
- **Joe Baker** is an associate professor of economics at Southern Utah University and is the director of the SUU Center for Economics Education.
- **Jeff Garrison** is a Presbyterian minister in Cedar City.
- **Sharon Palmer** is an assistant speech therapist at Cross Hollows.
- **Karen Pika Lake** is a substitute teacher.

Enoch

- **Caryn Ann Wilhelm** co-owns an automotive repair shop.

Ivins

- **Jim Aikens** is a retired first-grade school teacher.
- **Sandra Williamson** is a retired accountant and semi-truck driver.

Leeds

- **Kerry Hepworth** is the president of the Foundation of Dixie Regional Medical Center.

Santa Clara

- **Paul Roche** is a retired U.S. General Counsel.

St. George

- **Mark Dotson** is a high school senior.
- **Christian Jensen** is a high school student.
- **Raymond Kuehne** is the executive director for national advisory boards for the National Institutes of Health.
- **Barbara Reiland** is a homemaker and hospice volunteer coordinator.
- **Patrick Rodgers** is a youth facilities worker.
- **Patricia Sheffield** is the director of the Children's Justice Center and serves on the St. George Chamber of Commerce board of directors.
- **Randall Smith** is an architect.
- **Tony Van Hemert** is a retired technical writer and editor.
- **Morris Workman** works in the insurance industry.

Virgin

- **Andria Arnoldt** is a secretary.

Starting this week, they will write on a rotating basis Monday-Friday in The Spectrum and Daily News.

We want to thank these writers and the 84 others who applied for sharing their interest and talents.

Probe only turns up a possible accomplice

I love to snoop and pry, but this is an unseemly activity in the best of circumstances. So to have Carte Blanche and a newspaper job is dead and gone to heaven to a nosy person. I even have disguises, although I don't need them. Nobody knows who I am anyway, or cares either, but I like dress ups, so it's fun for me.

I even tried an accent in Enterprise. It was not a success. The woman who I was talking to kept getting redder and redder in the face. I realized that she was trying not to laugh and about strangling herself in the process. So I excused myself and left. I was almost to the outside door when I heard hoots of laughter. I walked very fast to my car and tossed gravel getting out of there. I was red too, but not from suppressed merriment.

I got caught out in one of my disguises in a car lot, of all places. My assignment was to see if I could scam a used car salesman. No! Anyway, here came into the lot Mary, my friend, and sometime co-conspirator in various enterprises, none of which involved disguises.

She spotted me right away, but didn't tip to the salesman, just kept wandering around kicking tires. When she had worked her way nearer to me she whispered, out of the corner of her mouth without looking at me, "You are getting weirder with every passing day." I love Mary. She finished kicking tires and left, as did I.

Later I went to her house to explain, just as I suspected she was delighted. At this time I ran afoul of the law of unintended consequences. Mary got really pumped and told me, excitedly how she had always wanted to dress up like a bag lady. She said it would be so much fun and I could write a story about it.

Well, I really don't want to write a story about bag ladies. I think that they are more sad than interesting and although when I took this job the Editor stressed that we should be accurate but he didn't say anything about truthful. So I guess I could make up a pitiful tale about a Saint George bag lady. Except no such thing exists, and all the kind and generous people in St. George would swarm around with offers of aid, comfort and kindness. How would we deal with that? If they found we were fake, would they laugh or form a lynch mob? When I left Mary was rummaging in the back of the closet for an old pair of panty hose with ladders.

I went home to worry. She was so thrilled by this idea. I couldn't think of how to shoot it down. I didn't want to hurt her feelings, and as a guy who looks out for number one, I knew that if I needed an accomplice in some future adventure, there she is.

It's not over. Mary just called to see if I would go over to Lin's Market and find out if I could lease a grocery cart. She didn't want me to steal one because there could be repercussions if I was caught. Besides, if you steal something, you have to keep it or pawn it. What possible use is a stolen grocery cart except to get groceries or haul bag lady traps? The garage is full of junk already.

Oh boy! What a tangled web we weave. How am I gonna get out of this?

March 1, 2002

Education bill puts all blame on teachers

It has been brought to my attention that most of the people in the writers group write well reasoned, timely columns on subjects of general interest, while I write dorky silliness of no interest at all. I quite often find myself out of the loop, wondering, "Why are they doing that?"

But now I have done some serious research on a timely topic: The President's Education Bill. I was recently substitute teaching at my old school, and I took the opportunity to ask professional teachers some hard questions.

"What do you think of the President's Education Bill?"

Some of the replies were, "Was that in the paper?" and "Anything to do with the feds, means a ton of paperwork. I don't need aid. I need a secretary." also, "This too will pass."

There were a couple of well reasoned replies, but they were presented in such a way as to make them unacceptable in a family newspaper.

For the loyal opposition we have an old friend. Todd is a law student at Columbia with a BA in Philosophy. He is also a Conservative Republican. It is interesting to note that he, in New York, falls into the same category as the Liberal Democrat occupies in Southern Utah. That is to say, suspect and closely watched with narrow eyes.

I called Todd and asked him for his take on this important question. He said that he was taking finals and preparing for an internship at the Supreme Court, and hadn't had time to study the subject. So much for the Conservative point of view.

While I was in class, I thought I would interview a student on this important issue. McKayla came up to the desk so I asked her what she thought of the President's Education Bill. She said, "I don't know nothing about that. I came up here to tell you Dallas just ate a bug."

All forward motion ceases. I repeat the rule to Dallas, "If you eat a bug in class, you must bring a bug for everyone."

Everyone gags and grosses out, elaborately. Some even fall to the floor. The chairs are small so they don't fall far and no one is hurt.

Another busy day in the first grade. It takes a teacher who is alert and quick to slip education in around all this fun stuff, but they are out there and they do it all the time.

My own take on the Bill is this: Telling students that if they do not do well on the test the teacher will be fired could work against you.

Everyone knows the importance of parental involvement in education. This Bill takes no notice of this, instead all the heat is on the teachers. If the parents of failing students were heavily taxed so as to pay for the extra instruction their child required to catch up, this could possibly issue more parental involvement, and it embraces the bottom line, a thing dear to the present administration.

March 28, 2002

The rumors are true: I'm out as a Democrat

When I read a letter to the editor the other day a man admitted that he and his wife were Democrats. My first thought was, "How brave is this man." He was from Hurricane too. Up 'til this time, I had presumed that Tony Van Hemert was the only overt Democrat between Iron County and the Arizona Strip.

Anyway, that man gave me courage. I am a Democrat too. OK. I am out of the closet, but I'm not going to out the few Demos who I know exist out there.

Self-preservation is a strong motive for discretion.

A lady, who shall remain nameless, gave me a T-shirt for my birthday with a patch on the chest that says, "Inauguration of President Clinton and Vice President Gore 1997." When I opened my present (in the presence of the enemy) I almost had a heart attack. How did she know? Why was she ratting me out?

Later we talked on the porch, alone. "How did you know?" I asked.

"You sent off signals that only another Democrat could spot."

"I didn't know that," I said.

"Don't worry about it" she said. "Those 'Dominant Party' people are so full of themselves that they don't notice much. All they ever really see is the bottom line. Those good-old-boys at the Legislature don't take their marching orders from the Angel Moroni. Their handler is the Angel Ezra Taft Benson. The only angel in heaven with two right wings."

I began to get a little nervous at this exchange. "You know," I said, "heaven is right above Utah. What if we are overheard? There could be … um … repercussions."

"Not to worry," she said. "President Hinckley has announced that Democrats are now officially allowed to exist."

I excused myself and scurried out of there. I love this woman and I agree with her — mostly — but I'm real old and not yet perfected. My salvation hangs by a thread and I don't want to screw up worse.

The word seeped out, and I was covertly approached by real "out" Democrats. I felt relieved that my guilty secret was out and comforted by the presence of allies.

They told me that there was to be a gathering of the coven at the Bloomington Hills Country Club. It was suggested that we meet at the soup kitchen — we are Democrats after all — but as it happens, St. George doesn't have a soup kitchen. The closest thing is Chuck-o-Rama, but we eat there all the time already, not because we are Democrats, but because we are cheap. We are out numbered there by Republicans, but just because there are more of them.

It is our goal to overthrow the present tyrant Mikey Leavitt and his White Male Mormon Mafia. "We're gonna make you an offer you can't refuse Bernie (President Bernie Machen of the U of U)" and "Listen up Rocky, 'Loser pays.'"

I haven't been on the barricades since the '60s. If I fall off and break a hip it's over for me.

What have you gotten yourself into now James?

April 26, 2002

Don't give old-timers a bad rap

It has come to my attention that old people around here are getting a bad rap. I feel competent to address this issue because I have always been old. I feel that I have had a pretty successful day if I haven't broken a full jar of mayonnaise on the kitchen floor or dropped my comb in the toilet.

When my son Joshua was in first grade I attended parent teacher conference. I entered the room and after one look at me the teacher, Ms. Burns, said, "Oh it is so nice when the children's grandparents take an interest in their education."

Ms. Burns looked about 14 and probably thought anyone over 30 needed a walker. When I told her that I was Josh's father she looked at me like "this must be one of those miracle births."

One of the things that a decrepit old dad can do with his little children is go to the store. We loved to go to the store, one child in the basket and another riding on the front bumper. They would throw things in and I would take them out. They got pretty smart. They would hide the Sugar Bomb cereal under the crackers. The most fun though would come at the check-out. We always went to a certain lady who never made comments or smiled, but her eyes danced and that was just as good.

There was Similac for them, Geritol for me. Pampers for them, Depends for me. Toothpaste for them, Polygrip for me. One thing that there was a lot of was Macaroni and Cheese. That was for all of us. Anyone who has a child or who has been a child knows that it is the universal food. Of course this was a while back. (I'm a grandpa now.) In those older times the four food groups were salt, sugar, chocolate and grease. With the kinds of food we fed the children (shudder) it is the wonder of the world that they didn't all have pellagra, rickets or scurvy at the very least.

But they have grown up to be robust, healthy and taller than me, which is not saying much. From the time I was 15 years old until I was 60 I was 6 feet tall and weighed 185 pounds. Now I am 5'8" and weigh 250 pounds. My Sunday School shirt looks like a Muumuu, a common affliction among geezers in my demographic.

I have always taken naps in the afternoon. When I got home from school I would take a little nap about 3:30. When my naps moved up to 2:00 and school let out at 3:15, it was time for me to go.

Being old is awful but the alternative is worse, so I guess I'll just go ahead and kill time till time kills me.

Election judge:
Job with inside scoop

I volunteered to be an election judge for the upcoming primary election. I thought of it as a way to infiltrate the establishment and to snoop and pry.

The plan was to reconnoiter and report. A fifth column. I look like a bloated capitalist who grinds the faces of the poor. (Well, bloated anyway.)

The meeting was held right at my nap time so I had to give it a lot of thought. If I don't get my nap I'm crabby for the rest of the day. Then I thought that my wife, Barbara, wouldn't mind suffering for one evening if it contributed to the emancipation and freedom of our country from the cruel dictatorship of the Oligarchy smothering free thought. Turned out she played mahjongg that night thus sparing herself the pain.

You may imagine my chagrin and dismay when I discovered that the election had been jiggered around so that only "those" people could vote.

I listened carefully to the explanation and concluded I didn't understand a word of it, but so what. It was a done deal. We'd been snookered again.

Another thing happened that thwarted my design to creep into the process as a mole. I found that I had been removed as a judge and put in as an alternate to be available in case someone dies. Yeah right.

I have to admire the way these people work. They watch everything and everybody and they know where any opposition lurks and what they are up to. It would be of huge benefit to the country if they would hold seminars for the FBI and CIA who have been having trouble keeping track of things lately. Show them how it's done. It could save the country a lot of grief. No terrorist would stand a chance.

It was a typically "old boy" congregation except that they were old girls.

"Hi Utahna. I haven't seen you since the 'Girls with Guns' rally over at Virgin."

There were a few sorry looking old birds like me, but not many.

The directions were extremely complex. A ton of new rules. Just the thing that bureaucrats love. Many questions were asked. Toward the end there were discussions of pay vouchers. What! I would have made a bigger stink if I had known that money was involved. Well, maybe not. There are going to be many hassles. I don't like the idea of telling libertarians that they can't vote. Those guys will take HUGE exception to that and those old boys are most usually packin'.

I think that I may better serve the public good by setting on my bench over to the side making little paranoid sounds and complaining that the world is not fair.

I know it's a dirty job, but somebody's gotta do it.

<u>July 19, 2002</u>

Going for broke in the 'worst malady' challenge

Don't cha just hate it when your brother-in-law has a better disease than you do? This guy is younger than me, better looking than me, and has this really great disease. How am I supposed to feel?

For many years I had the best disease. I had a total knee replacement, titanium steel and plastic. For a long time I carried around the X-rays. They were cool, showing big screws and bolts through the bone. Wonderful. Everybody loved it but "Sic transit gloria." It got old.

Once one of my nieces asked, "What is it like to be an android, Uncle Jim?" ANDROID, yeh, part human, part machine.

I thought that was cool and told it to everybody.

Uncle Rol usurped the place of glory in the disease category when he got sleep apnea.

He got to go to this sleep disorder place to sleep. He was video taped all night with all these thingies stuck all over and wires. Then he got this fabulous breathing machine. A big plastic thing that goes over your face and a black box that plugs in. We went to England together and he had to get these real cool adapters for the electricity and all kinds of refinements.

The family in England were blown away by this amazing device.

England is not exactly third world, but the place mostly looks like America in 1950. They had never heard of such a thing. "Bit of a rotter," they said, but secretly they were thinking, "Is there no end to the weirdness of these Americans."

Their top misery was ill fitting dentures, "Oh please."

But I do, in fact have a new disease, but it has to do with a malfunction of the waste disposal system. How glamorous is that?

Ordinarily I have no shame. I'll talk about anything, but this is a little too much even for me.

I did try it out once. We had people over to play cards. I started to discuss my new ailment. Suddenly all chairs screeched back. Everyone ran out the back door, over the wall and ran off through the sagebrush.

This alerted me to the fact that perhaps this subject was not going to be popular.

But, not to worry. I'm very old and things are breaking down all the time. Something new will turn up.

Although I despair that I will never get anything as cool as a breathing machine.

August 16, 2002

Reunion shows
I turned out OK

On my way to the "Up North" to attend my 50th high school reunion I spent a lot of driving time reliving all my past high school humiliations. One horror after another passed in front of my eyes. After a while I thought, "What is this? I must have had some fun."

Dredging around for a while I turned up a couple of fun things. All of the major babes were the gang I hung with. We had a locker complex where everyone knew all the locker combinations. In some of the lockers we had orange crates (of course, you remember orange crates!) to hold books. Some were for the long, warm overcoats that we wore in those Arctic Climes. At that time Parkas and Anoraks were in use only by Eskimeux. I was the only male to have privileged access to this inner sanctum. I had hot poop far in advance of ordinary mortals.

All of these ladies were in attendance and looking as good as they ever did. I had good taste before I even knew what good taste was.

I never had a high number in the looks department nor was I a jock of any renown, but I was mouthy, gregarious and treacherous. I was also a male and had access to locker room conversations when women were discussed. I was also able to direct observations and criticisms in directions I wanted it to go, thereby finding out the things that my masters wished to know. Who liked who and if not why not, etc. etc.

Many young men had their heads handed to them on the basis of my information. Most of them are dead now and the ones remaining are too feeble to make a very serious protest, besides it was 50 years ago. If you can't remember the day before yesterday how can you remember 50 years ago? I was in no danger.

I was asked to dance to nostalgic 40's music (remember this was only 52) on the assembly, not so much because I was remembered as a fabulous dancer but because I don't have a pacemaker, wear a truss or need a walker. It was a narrow field. My partner was someone I used to dance with quite a bit, there for a while, and we looked great. I asked her before we started if I got overstimulated and passed out would she resuscitate me. She said, "that didn't work 50 years ago and it won't work now Jimbo. You need a new line."

On the way home I thought more about my mostly negative high school days. I concluded hormonal imbalance (big time), crisis management, poverty, clumsiness, and ownership of the largest zit farm at Ogden High School caused insecurity and at times despair. But, what the heck. I grew up, healed up and to my delight discovered when it really counted, that I had gotten a pretty solid education, which is what it is supposed to be all about. Right?

September 13, 2002

Think today's bad?
Get perspective

The Red Menace Lives!
Every now and then a letter appears in the newspaper outlining how the Red Menace is poised to swallow the world. "Hello." The Red Menace consists of Fidel Castro and Kim Jong-il.

Fidel is sucking up to capitalists more every day. He hopes to get Disneyland Caribbean and Survivor to come to beautiful Cuba and bring money. Kim Jong-il is on welfare. His Koreans are starving and fleeing in vast numbers into China.

China is out on the hustle also. Communism is over there too. China is so vast, fragmented and strange that some people never got the word that the Empress had died (1918) until the late 60s.

Get with the program. The new menace is ISLAM. Not all of Islam, just the lunatic fringe who are getting all the publicity. They constitute an exciting new fright. They are everywhere, lurking and they can get 'cha anytime according to grandmother Ashcroft. Not specifically, but generally. Not now, but sometime.

We can't even take the old couch and ton of old clothes and fruit jars and empty water bottles out of the bomb shelter that grandpa dug in the backyard in the 70s for fear of Nikita Krushchev.

No point, you can't hide.

Another fun thing to be frightened of is the end of the world. Time magazine had a big article on the Apocalypse and related foolishness. Nostradamus, and Edgar Cayce and other deceased nuisances have an oar in the water in this new scare. The Book of Revelations is getting a lot of play as well as some other old wheezes one of which are the Illumanati. These boys have been plotting the destruction of the earth for at least 300 years.

The UN fearers have incorporated these people into their lexicon of terror spreaders. It appears, from the letters to the Editor in our paper, that Hillary Clinton is a "comm-symp" (look it up). "Get Real."

Hillary is far to cool to be promoting some loser Political philosophy like communism. If she intends to rule the world she is clever enough to think up her own repressive totalitarianism cruel and probably fun system. I'm looking forward to it.

For the people out there who "love" terror, suffering, unrelenting misery and death may I recommend a book, "A Distant Mirror" by Barbara Tuchman, my favorite historian. The 14th Century was a hum dinger, plague, war, catastrophe and fear. If there ever was a great time to destroy the world this was it. It didn't happen and things picked up — sort of.

If you think things are awful now, get a perspective.

The silver years suck: Advice on aging

W hy do firemen wear red suspenders? To keep their pants up. Why do old guys wear suspenders? Because their butts have gone flat, deflated like an old balloon.

I am not so very good looking, and the only thing I had going for me in the Babe Magnet Opportunities Department was nice buns. Well, that's gone past too, now. Not that I am concerned about losing the small share that I held in Babe Magneting. I have been married for 35 years and it is the happiest 33 years of my life.

I only bring this up because I went to a class at Dixie State called "aging gracefully." It was three days ago and I only remember things from two days ago. Another benefit of great age. Think about it. Although you forget where you parked your car in the parking lot at Lins, you also forget that you have terminal cancer. That is a benefit, albeit short term.

I am not aging gracefully at all. I am having a terrible time. All of this wisdom and gracious acceptance that the elderly are supposed to feel seems to have passed me by. I don't feel any wiser than I ever did, and when you complain to one of your kids that Aunt Hazel's phone seems to be out of order, because you have been calling her for three days with no luck, they say, "Daddy, Aunt Hazel has been dead for two years."

Your sharp come-back, "I knew that," is really pathetic and just doesn't ring true.

The thing that annoys me most about old age is not the fact that my fingers won't grip early in the morning and that I have dropped a full jar of mayonnaise on the kitchen floor (you can not imagine the mess that makes unless you have lived through it). The other thing that annoys me most is people between the ages of 17 and 32 chirping at me, "You're as young as you feel." I really hate that, especially after a day of dropped mayonnaise jars and of bending over to tie my shoes and falling over on my head. (I could combat this by buying Velcro Tab Tennis shoes at Walmart but that seems like giving up and giving in. I'm not ready for that.) The day also included finding myself standing in the garage and wondering what I was doing there. It is cold in there and I have bare feet. It can really get depressing.

I remember a dear old friend from my school teacher days, Mrs. Hoopes. She was older than me, a phenomenon that I don't often run onto anymore. Sometimes I would look out my door and Mrs. Hoopes was standing out there looking at her feet. Mrs. Hoopes room was three up the hall from me, so she was out of her territory. I asked, "What is up Mrs. Hoopes?"

She would say, "I am thinking about the here-after."

I got a little jolt from this. Mrs. Hoopes was somewhat old, but not that old. "Wha?" I replied.

"I am thinking about what I am here-after."

That was my first brush with memory lapse due to onset senility. It made me laugh. Now when I find myself in the cold garage with bare feet thinking, "What am I here after," I still laugh.

It is a thin line between laughing and crying sometimes, but still there is no going back so you really have to try and have a little fun with it.

Damn little.

Second Alzheimers episode

I'm depressed. Well, not depressed because I take medicine for that, and I have to say I was disappointed in that. It is nothing at all like the depression medicine of the 60s (whoa). It stopped depression, motion, and some body functions. "Groovy" as we used to say.

I guess I was just dismayed when I woke up with a zit on the end of my nose, just like high school. "Please." I'm nearly 70 years old. That coupled with my second Alzheimer's episode.

When it happened the first time I was alarmed, but not terrified. I told everybody and I'll tell you too. I invented this gourmet dining treat. Dip slices of bread in beaten egg and fry in the frying pan. How do you think I felt when I realized that I had invented French toast?

Well the day prior to the nose zit, Katarina, my granddaughter and I were at Joanns getting material for the Dutch Christmas Pagent. (I'll tell you about that sometime.) Anyway, I had strapped her in her car seat (she is three) and went around to my side when I opened the door and saw that the floor mat was messed up. So I knelt down to straighten it when I saw an extra pedal on the floor of the car. I thought to myself, "What in the world is that for? I've never seen that before. I've had this car for five years and never noticed it."

I got in to start the car and my foot went right over to it and pushed. It was the gas pedal. My foot knew it but my head didn't.

I read some where that if you forget where you parked the car don't worry about it. If you forget that you have a car, then you are in trouble. Can that be extrapolated to include a gas pedal? Oh Lord.

I have sort of been looking forward to being old. Being treated with respect and being a figure of calm dignity. I'm not going to make it. They keep raising the bar on me. Old age that is. It used to be sixty, and I made that, except I didn't want to be old yet. I was looking for a job. So I dyed my hair and beard dark so that my prospective employer would think I was 26 years old. It didn't work, but I got the job anyway. I asked him later why he hired me. He said he admired my imagination. (Is that a compliment?)

Then 65 rolled up and I thought I had it locked, but "they" moved it up to 70. I'm almost there again but they are already talking about kicking it up to 80. I'll never live that long.

I have had many surgical operations. More of my internal organs are in the dumpster than are inside my skin. There are those unfeeling few who suspect that I have all those operations so I can get those la la pills. Not so, I just started rotting away sooner than other people. I feel that it is compensation. I won't live very long, but I'll live very happy.

Speaking of happy, the last time I had something taken out and thrown away, my doctor gave me some pain pills and told me if I hurt take a pill. Well, I got the bottle filled on Monday and when I went back on Wednesday for a refill, the pharmacy guy was alarmed. "Did you take all of those?"

"Yea. I don't like pain."

"Well, I'll fill it for you once more, but you had better see your doctor."

I was going in anyway so I told him about the mean pharmacy guy who didn't care if I suffered. He told me to sit down and he sat down and put on his long serious doctor face and told me about all the silver haired junkies staggering around St. George because of addiction to pain pills.

It didn't scare me much. I have an addictive personality and if it isn't one thing, then it's another. Me and the cold turkey are well acquainted.

It has been sort of my illusion that old people are treated with deference and respect and given seats on the bus. Snippy young girls at the dentist don't call old people by their first name, and sales clerks call them sir. When I was young I called every man six months older than me sir. Times have changed. The only persons who call me sir are police officers in the course of their official duties. They call me sir, but it is sort of hard edged and is more scary than differential.

I really don't have that much interaction with on duty police officers. But some.

Arthritis bottle

I would like to take this opportunity to launch into a tirade about the unfairness of life (we have already had this conversation). Being old is alleged to be a reward (excuse me) for endurance and steadfastness (Ha).

We get no respect. When a prescription is filled we get a large prospectus describing all the side effects, after effects and possibly fatal effects. These are included to cover the gluteus maximus (look it up) of the pharmacy, the doctor and all the ships at sea. You are better off to throw the medicine away and take your chances with proper diet and prayer.

The grocery store also colludes with the persons striving to make oldness hard (er). Try opening a bottle of juice (healthy) or milk (not so much). It takes a grip of iron to break the plastic seal. I have to go into the garage for a monkey wrench. Arthritic old fingers just don't have the grip for this stuff.

Speaking of fingers — I got some arthritis medicine once in a child proof bottle, as if children would be interested in arthritis medicine. Grip. Push. Turn. Because I have arthritic fingers I was unable to grip, push, turn. At length I was able to melt the top off with a hot glue gun. When I returned to the pharmacy to get a refill, I explained my difficulty to the guy (you know this guy, a mouth breather with a greasy nose whose glasses slide down). Oh ok! He gave me the same child proof arthritic proof cap again!

Vulgar, even obscene language comes easy to me. After 20 years as a teacher of 6 year olds this aberration has been considerably tampered down, but it is still down there in the heated darkness. I said nothing, I am a gentlemen after all. I just stood there holding the offending object. He stared at me for a while, then got it. He gave an acknowledging grunt, took the bottle back and changed it.

I never went back there again. I don't do too much medicine and I don't like to take medicine from people whose synapses don't seem to fire correctly.

About the prescription aid to old folks. It will happen because a huge block of voters want it. And they all vote, there's nothing else to do and it breaks up our day.

Sympathetic people try to help out by putting the proposal on television. The problem here is the spokesperson (we've had this conversation before too). There is this scrawny old guy with hair in his ears, ill-fitting dentures and permanent frown creases. Not the kind of grandpa you'd like to give a hug.

Then he shows you a table in the kitchen piled high with drug bottles, thousands of them. First thought, he is such a mangy, miserable, disagreeable old coot why doesn't he just let it go. Second thought, even Robert Downey Jr. doesn't take that many drugs. This must be a set up. This is what I think and I'm on his side, what does the opposition think?

We need a kindly looking old gentleman, thin and a little pale, dressed in nice clothes a tiny bit frayed and a jacket just a skosh too big, to indicate how he has shrunk from a robust healthy man to a small and sick one. Holding 3 or 4 pill bottles in his lap with gnarly fingers. A hard working dignified man come on hard times. There won't be a dry eye in the house.

I would put myself forward. I certainly have the scruffy old clothes, and gnarly fingers, but otherwise I don't really fit the profile. I more generally resemble a degenerate Santa Claus, not exactly the image we are looking for either.

Clinton haters

It has come to my attention that everyone is becoming hard and cynical. It is time for a Horatio Alger story.

Once upon a time there was this poor boy with a small brother, a single mother and later a mean step dad. This boy wanted to be somebody. He worked hard in school, got a scholarship to Yale where he met President Kennedy who became his role model (in ways not always admirable). He was a Rhodes Scholar at Oxford, the youngest governor in Alabama history and the President of the United States of America. Who is it? Give up? William Jefferson Clinton, or as he is known around here, Slick Willy or (blankety-blank).

The purpose of this exposition is not revisionist history but an admonition to the people who still hate Bill Clinton.

Attention! Bill Clinton is not a threat any longer. He is over.

He is still out there annoying people, but he can't help that. He made 9.2 million dollars making speeches. Not bad, but remember, he has house payments. He has never had a house payment. He went from the trailer camp to Yale, to Oxford to governor to President. He never owned a home before. He has always lived in subsidized housing.

He presently hangs out in Harlem. Is that cool enough? Toni Morison has said that Bill is our first black President. The black people love him. For the most part, and Harlem is having a resurgence of building and growth due to his magnetic presence.

His wife has a steady job. His daughter is doing fine. The guy is having a nice life. I hope you can live with that. It is a well known fact that hating hurts the hate and is mostly never even noticed by the hated. Keep this in mind when your neck swells up and bile overflows that he is innocent of your pain.

Another reason to get over it is: It is soon to become ridiculous and haters hate to look ridiculous. Example: those poor old red menace, evil empire guys. They can't get out much anymore, so they must rely on old news. They still rail against the communist conspiracy not knowing or not caring, that communism has died a terrible and permanent death.

There is much that needs to be done to make the world a better place. Holding on to ancient grievances and injuries is a lonely and fruitless task. I'm telling you as a friend, do yourself a favor, let it go. "Get over it."

Elder hostel

"And Lois, what do you do?"

"Oh, I mostly lay around and listen to my organs shut down and my synapses click off."

This brought an alarmed stare, but not from me. I attached myself to Lois right away. She is my kind of woman. 82 years old and a retired professor from the University of Ottawa.

We commiserated with each other. She asked the tour guide why were we in a motel with no bar? Why is there no bar in the Golden (Trough) Corral where we eat? (Ask me about the Golden Trough. It is the home of the 5th deadly sin.) Was this trip arranged by the Christian Temperance Union?

The corners of the tour guide's smile really turned down when Lois said, "If I get the D.T.'s in this cramped little bus, you will have to deal with it."

Doesn't she sound fun?

The rest of the people are nice and more or less senile. Everybody forgets things or loses things and wanders around with no apparent goal in mind. So what else is new.

Many are professional Elder Hostelers. They have been all over the earth and know the ropes, such as they are.

We are all packed in the bus when Ann realizes she forgot her sunglasses. Ann is a 300 pounder and so she struggled out of the bus and waddled away. We are still waiting.

Lois' ears really perked up when some people on the bus were talking about going out last night to get a glass of wine.

The place was called the "Class Act." It is sandwiched in between K-Mart and Home Depot in a strip mall behind the motel. The people also said they had Wet T-shirt contests and Boxer Short dancing.

"Sounds like a classy place," said Lois. "We can sprint over after dinner." The visualizations of the Elder Hosteler sprinting made me smile for several miles.

It didn't happen. We got home from Chaco Canyon late. Lois said a bunch of Old Ruins looking at Old Ruins. She claimed that the first time she came here Montezuma had come up from Mexico for a trade conference.

We ate dinner at the Cracker Barrel. This place is way too cute. The waitress was way too perky. The dumplings tasted like library paste. (Yes, you do too know what library paste tastes like.) We were all grumpy and tired so everyone went back to the motel and watched Sex and the City. (dream on).

Guy union

I often find myself on the narrow edge of being ejected from the "Guy Union." I was a first Grade Teacher for many years. That alone rings alarm bells for men whom I have just met. Example: at a Christmas party in my neighborhood, a bunch of the guys were standing around in a circle talking. I came over hoping to join them. They were drinking long necks or whiskey from old tin cans. Here I come with my pussy Silver Goblet. The conversation lagged for a bit, but these macho honchos are also gentlemen, and they wanted me to feel comfortable, so they started talking about the big yarn sale down at JoAnns. (I have tons left from last year.)

The conversation sort of spluttered out, but I'm a gentleman too, so I excused myself so that they could talk about something they were interested in, the Monster Truck rally coming to Vegas.

I am on the cusp of when men were men and when men were human. All the old farts my age, never cooked a meal, (grilling steaks on the back yard grill is about the size of their cooking skills) never changed a diaper, never went to Parent Teacher Conference (my wife took care of that stuff). They took the boys fishing but they called their daughters "little princess" and never took them anywhere or had much of a clue about how their lives were going (my wife took care of the girls).

We hear a lot lately about the "greatest generation." What does that mean? The men went to war to defend our country and protect their families from harm. They came back and went to school, got jobs and "worked hard" to provide for their families. So? This is what men are supposed to do. Being a man has a lot of perks, (ask any woman and they'll tell you). I'm glad, I take advantage of mine. It's a fool who doesn't. However, being a man has obligations and responsibilities. Just enumerated. So any man expecting preferential treatment just because he fulfills his duties and responsibilities can forget it. Expecting to be revered and adulated just for doing your job is vain and arrogant.

The young family men nowadays, "work hard and take care of their families" too, but they do a lot more. I met a lot of young dads in my school teacher days. Some of them were pretty rough cobs too, lots of tattoos, ponytails and teeth missing in front. But they came to parent conference sometimes with their clothes and hair full of cement dust or still wearing their U.P.S. shorts.

These men came to our little programs and playlets, anything their kids were doing, just to support the team. The kids loved it and were very proud when their dads showed up. When they go to a ball game they bring the girls too, and they have a whooping good time. I see young men at art galleries looking at the stuff, and enjoying it. The old fart brigade is sitting on a bench somewhere looking glum and put upon.

I really don't mean to slam the old guys, after all I'm one of the oldest. I just want to point out that the old guys telling each other that the men nowadays have it easy, and they are pretty much a bunch of wimps is not true. The priorities are just different, and I'm glad. "You go boys!"

New hat

At the Dutch Christmas Party my new favorite nephew, who goes to school in Pennsylvania, gave me the coolest hat I have ever seen. An Amish hat made of hand woven straw. It fits me like it was tailor made.

It should become the new must-have, but maybe not. I think cowboy hats are the most manly and correct headgear around, but alas, what you see instead are greasy baseball caps with a plastic strap across the back. Low budget.

I believe part of the problem is that wearing a cowboy hat requires some responsible behavior. It is removed indoors. It is removed when talking to a lady or at the very least, the brim is touched. Men who wear cowboy hats have good posture. Their legs may be crooked, but so what. These hats look dignified and respectable even on very young men. Even old battered and rained-on work hats have a certain aura.

Baseball caps are used mostly to cover bed head or bald head and advertise the wearers favorite chaw.

It was not my intention to go into an etiquette rant here. I was just going to tell you about my new hat and it got out of control. If you give an old guy too much time on his hands and a public venue it can get ugly, and you have only yourself to blame. It could be worse. I am computer illiterate which is lucky for you, otherwise I'd be Bloggin and Spamin till the cows come home (my Grandmother used to say).

So those individuals who have been hounding me to move into the 20th century (that's not a mistake. I'm 200 years behind.) had best give this some thought. I can only get to you once a month now. What if I could invade your privacy every day? That should chill your jollies. (My Grandmother never said that. It sounds vaguely nasty, and gramma would never be that.)

I was getting ready for church. I'm going to a missionary farewell for my Brother-in-law, the one I tease all the time. (He is my only brother-in-law who doesn't carry a knife. I have other Brothers-in-law who are pretty strange too, and I'd love to talk about them, but they are a little bit dangerous. You know, knives and all. So I don't.) I'm going to miss him. Anyway, I am going to wear my new hat and since Amish men wear all black (Dan says the Amana Colonies look like San Francisco.) I have my new black General Authority suit and even high top shoes. But my black vest inexplicably has shrunk right across the stomach part. I need a vest because I got a very fine, engraved pocket watch with a cover that flips up and I need to show that off too.

So I went to look for the duct tape and discovered that I had left it at the party last night and it was Sunday and too late to get more, so I had to wear a grey vest. I hated to compromise because my nephews expect Uncle Jim to be sartorially correct. "If you go to the circus, go to the big tent," my Grandmother used to say. But they are splendid young gentlemen and no one mentioned the gaffe.

I'm going to tell you my new year resolution. I know that you probably don't care but that has never stopped me before, has it? I'm going to clean out my closet. HA HA! Fooled you. You thought I was going into rehab or some other public spirited thing. Well, not just yet. As my Grandmother used to say, "There's always — ok ok.

White trash food

There is all sorts of nutritional information floating around out there now days. I have come upon a whole new food category, "white trash" food. White trash food is easy to spot but hard to describe.

The first thing that comes to mind is probably Big Macs and various other grease burgers with special sauce and super size french fries, "wrong"__

White trash food must at least emulate real food. It should look like a home cooked meal on a plate, but require minimal preparation. Some examples: Manwich, Hamburger Helper and its cousin Tuna Helper. The list is large and growing. Go to the prepared foods aisle in the store and you will find everything you need for a home cooked meal in one box with meatballs/chicken/hamburger included. (What?!) I bought one and checked it out. It did indeed have meatballs included and they were scary looking too.

I did get a shock when my new friends described a "Dolly Parton," white bread with Velveeta and mayonnaise. That took me back. When I was a small boy in Ogden, Utah going to Lorin Farr Elementary in 1940 there was no such extravagance as school lunch. We had an hour, from noon till one, to go home and have lunch. Everybody walked to school and most everyone's mother was a home mom in those days.

However some people in different circumstances had to bring their lunch to school. Since there was no lunch room, lunch was eaten in the library supervised by Miss Umbeck, a thin, elderly benign spinster.

Once in a while I had to take my lunch to school. To take your lunch to school was really cool, but not so much fun for me. I had homemade bread sandwiches with sliced left over pot roast and watercress from the ditch behind the house and a homemade oatmeal cookie as big as a dinner plate. My lunch screamed "poor people."

The real dudes had lunches with white bread and Velveeta and sometimes the major extravagance, a slice of Bologna and a store bought Fig Newton.

I was shocked to discover that the gourmet magnificence that I would have killed for had been brought down in the world, all the way down to become "white trash food."

High end white trash food is to be found at Costco. Huge trays of lasagna in industrial size portions enough to feed a large family reunion or a small prison.

Nutritional value never comes up. Stick to your ribs and ease and speed of preparation is what counts. The "white trash" diet contains nothing that is leafy and/or green. There is no real prohibition for nutritious food. It is just that "nobody will eat it." "The kids hate it."

The last time I ate at a nameless Washington County School they were heavy into white trash food. Corn dog, tater tots, apple sauce "apple sauce?" and a moon pie. "Yum." Children with carry in lunch had "Lunchables" a gastronomic horror at the pinnacle of the "white trash" food pyramid. Processed meat circles (pig snouts), processed cheese, crackers that crumble into dust when touched. It reminded me a lot of "C" rations that we had in the Korean War.

The shelf life of this type of cuisine is about 50 years. Upon perusing the nutrition, nutrition!? label you would discover more preservatives in one box than was shot into old King Tut two thousand years ago, and that old boy still looks pretty good.

'La Boheme' is opera's 'Friends'

Madam and I went to the Opera a while ago. I am a serious opera buff. The Utah Opera of S.L.C. presented La Boheme, not one of my favorites. It is a lot like "Friends." Everybody sits around the coffee house and shoots the breeze. They are all "Artistes" writers, painters, etc. Bohemians (1860 hippies). Nobody understands them and nobody buys their stuff. (familiar?) So they just lay around, hang out and get high (what else is new).

MiMi, the heroine is a milliner which in those days was synonymous with hooker, but they tread lightly on that circumstance so as not to offend the Mormons, and since that is the only thing interesting about MiMi, it's a big loss. Rudolpho, her boyfriend is a pig. Musitta is a bad girl and loves being it. She is the most interesting one of the bunch.

After a long, long time, MiMi dies. Rudolpho is sorry and who cares. It's a little like if Rachel on "Friends" died. You would think, "Well, that's one down."

My favorites are the very grand operas where the music is gorgeous, powerful and moving and the stories are tragic and heart breaking. My favorite of all is Madame Butterfly. It is so sad that I usually start crying as soon as the overture starts and sob away till the end. When we go out at intermission (to the bathroom, you know me) there are other men in there with red eyes and wet lapels.

Generally speaking I don't hate people, especially make believe people, but I hate Pinkerton. The minute that slimeball walks on my gorge begins to rise. When he tells Sachko that he is only marrying Butterfly so he can get in her pants, and when he really gets married it will be to an American woman, by now my rage is murderous. Then he flounces around sweet as pie, lying to Butterfly.

It is sort of a relief when he sails away, except then Butterfly sings "Un Bel De" the saddest song in the history of the world. She really loves Pinkerton and she sings of "One Fine Day" he will sail into the harbor and she and her baby and Pinkerton will live happily ever after, when we all know it's not gonna happen. The theater is awash in tears and choking sobs and sniffles. It is just wrenching.

One time I was talking to the director of the Opera company and told her that one of these days I'll lose it and bounce my Opera glasses off Pinkerton's head and be carried off under restraint. Some poor tenor will have a knot on his head and resolve to be more on the alert for the loony tunes when singing Pinkerton.

She said, "Go for it. It will be good for business. I hate him too."

I felt like I had been given my double-0 number. Aikens, James Aikens.

Another favorite is "Carmen." That is one bad, bad girl. Don Jose is a cocky army officer who thinks he is a hot number. Carmen seduces him, jerks him around for a while and then ditches him for a bull fighter.

He crawls around after her and finally corners her at the bull ring. The desperate man threatens to kill her if she doesn't come away with him. Carmen calls him on it, "OK you pussy. If you are going to do it, do it."

The poor man has had enough and sckkkkkk right in the sternum. Carmen falls down dead and Jose is devastated, but probably relieved that it's over.

During all this action, thundering exciting, fabulous music is pouring out. It is so emotionally draining that afterwards I go back to the hotel for a little nap to recover myself.

That's only two. There are hundreds more. With any luck the kids who love those brutal and vicious video games will grow up to be Opera fans. It could happen!

February 28, 2003

A father's work is never done

Back in olden times, another millennium, in fact, when I was a real person and had a real job, I was a school teacher and had summers off. This caused huge offense to all my friends and family. These people said rude things and made gagging noises when I told them about going on camping trips or to the beach with the children. I bore up under this abuse pretty well. But then, alas, the time came when my children were (shudder) teen-agers.

They attended a large Jr. High School where there were three tiers of students, patrician, bourgeoisie and proletariat. I'll bet you can guess the ones my kids hung with. The Spanish teacher traditionally (tradition has cost me a ton of money over the ages) took the ninth graders on a trip to Mexico to enhance their speaking and swimming skills. They spent three days in Acapulco. Tough assignment. My daughter, Ashley told us that EVERYONE was going.

You know the high minded parents who think that kids should work and save for special treats, and then they will enjoy them more? Balderdash. I got a summer job so she could go. I worked evenings in a factory that made something out of metal that left large quantities of little spirally things all over the floor, mostly in pools of smelly oil. I swept the factory floor and wiped up the grease. I washed the tables in the lunch room and mopped the floor. I also cleaned the restroom sinks and toilets. The work was crappy ("har") but it was easy and paid ok. In fact, it paid for the trip and a few bucks besides. I got myself a new pair of cowboy boots and a used chain-saw in good shape.

The next year it was my son, Josh's turn. His science class traditionally (that word again) went on a science trip to NASA Headquarters at Cape Canaveral to watch a rocket firing. As luck would have it, Disney World was just up the road. Josh's interest in science was just cursory, but his interest in partying was almost legendary even at 13. There was no way he couldn't go.

So I got a job as a waiter. I worked for a banquet and catering service. We set-up large parties and conventions. I learned many skills that were a huge help in later life. I can get the little hard thingy out of the lettuce without cutting it. Cut lettuce is so tacky. Torn lettuce is the way. I can chop onions at warp speed. I did lose a finger tip, but it has healed up.

One time I was pouring water at a table of Eminencies when one of them looked at me. Any waiter will tell you nobody looks at the waiter. Well, she did and let out a gasp. "What are you doing here," she croaked.

"I am pouring water," I replied.

By now they were all looking. "Why are you wearing that curious get up? And pouring water?"

"I am your waiter. My name is Jim. Can I get you anything else?"

It was real quiet for a minute. As it happened the people at the table were on the Board of Directors at the Eccles Art Center. My wife was Chairman of the Board. (She is ever so much more grand than I am.) They had seen me hanging around at parties here and there so they knew who I was. I went back to work, a while later one of the men came over and said, "OK, what's up? Tell."

I did, and he just laughed.

"Isn't democracy great?" he said.

Teaching brought stares, satisfaction

Time magazine recently ran an article about men. In hard economic times, (like now) men will do about anything to get a job, even take what is traditionally considered women's work (whoa). I hardly think of myself as ahead of the curve, but I was once.

Back in the times when "real" men had jobs that produced large biceps and callused hands, I went to work in a factory that made tin cans. The job entailed a lot of heavy lifting and mindless replication. The pay was great and when you punched out, work was over until the next day. It was a union shop with a 40-hour week and time-and-a-half pay for overtime. This sounds pretty heavenly to the young people of today who work 50- to 60-hour weeks without the collateral benefit of large muscles.

In the recession of the 1970s, my factory closed down and I was declared "redundant." This is a term used by my British son-in-law. It is many times more humiliating and scary than the American "laid off" is.

After my initial terror shock and nervous break down, had to think about what to do next.

I was 46 years old. I was married and had two pretty children and a split-level house in the burbs. I had a high school diploma and knowledge of production of tin cans, which nobody wanted. Kind of like the guy who applied for a job with Henry Ford on the assembly line. When asked what his skills were he replied, "I know all about making buggy whips." I was a home dad for a while. My wife worked and supported us all.

As a home dad I had time on my hands. (I could go into how I streamlined homemaking, but that is a different story.) I went to college intently to learn something in the medical field (people always get sick). That didn't work out, but I fell into something that really changed my life. I went to elementary school and volunteered as a helper in first grade. Teaching the little people to read and write was the most fun I ever had. I changed my direction in college and got a teaching certificate — 25 years ago, and I was out in front of the times.

As a man in the first grade, I got looked at and scrutinized, and this was before predatory males and pedophiles were behind every tree. I was unusual, but I was a good teacher (brag). The children loved me and I loved them. I never considered it women's work, but sometimes parents did. After only a few weeks of teaching their children, it was easy to convince them that I knew what I was doing and that their children were safe with me.

We need to redefine women's work. In these times when women are killed in action and taken as prisoners of war, who is the one to define women's work! Look at Annika Sorenstam and Pvt. Jessica Lynch. When I started I was the only man in the school besides the janitor. When I retired there were more men, but still not enough. I talked to the Culligan man yesterday. He is a teacher, but to make a living he has to be a Culligan man too.

How does that make you feel?

RSVP

I look forward to the Writers Group member from Ivins. I love his humor, his sarcasm, his wit. My daughter had him as a school teacher. We loved him then; we love him now. Keep up the good work.

—*Anonymous*

Old folks in restaurants?

There has been much said over the last while about noisy and un-suitable children in public places. Most, all I should say, have been published by, what are referred to by the politically correct as senior citizens, but who are in fact grouchy old f-f-f-folks.

I have taken it upon myself to research this phenomenon. My findings are as follows.

I passed the food court of the Red Cliffs Mall and there were four men of a certain age eating something shiny and covered with powdered sugar. I could tell by the sound of their arteries clanging shut that this was not on top of the health food pyramid. As background let me state I have a friend older than myself, I know this is hard to believe but it is true. So as an older man I defer to his superior wisdom. One of the first things he told me upon attaining first stage old age, 65, "There are two things one must remember in order to be successfully old: #1 Never spill food on your shirt. More importantly don't let it remain there until it turns green."

Well, these old birds had enough stuff spilled on the front of their golf shirts that, if scraped off, you could feed two large hogs for four days. This indiscretion caused no noise, but did cause a serious gag reflex.

Another observation took place in a curious eating establishment, which featured golf bags hanging on the walls like dead animal heads. We were there for a party for a dear friend whose taste is remarkable in all areas but a sweetheart with all. At this place were six older sisters in wrinkles and stretch pants having a party for one of their number. There were shrieks that would shatter glass and squeaks that had men in the gas station up the street come out and look up and down the Boulevard. Other old ladies of that same stripe, who are not tolerant in other ways, might think it was cute that they were having so much fun. Those of us not included in the merriment stuffed bits of napkin in our ears and communicated in sign language.

I observed another class act at one eating-place in St. George with tablecloths, cloth napkins and no booths, where I have never seen a child. The establishment was too expensive and had no children's menu. An old cowboy at the table next to mine whipped out his handkerchief in the middle of his meal and gave a huge honk, which alerted everyone. As it turned out it was not a discreet emergency blow. It was a complete symphony of honks, snorts and vigorous wipes! Eventually everyone present put down their forks and waited a while before resuming their meal.

I point this out not to criticize, but to educate. The kettle that lectures the pot for its blackness attracts closer scrutiny to its own less attractive behaviors.

Of course the vast majority of old people are perfect ladies and gentlemen as are the vast majority of children. No useful purpose is served by calling attention to those few who are not.

Let's quit it.

Say Amen.

On the farm

Once upon a time, a long time ago at a very low point in my life, I was taken to live on a farm. My father and my uncle bought a farm together and fed me and each other a lot of applesauce about liking the clean and healthy life, growing our own food, milking our own cow and a lot of other survivalist foolishness which boded no good for me, but I didn't know it then. The truth was that my dad and my uncle were young (Daddy, 29 and Uncle Jack 30) and thought they could do anything. (Do you remember that feeling? I do.) In fact they were city boys and knew as much about farming as a hog knows about Sunday.

The farm had a huge old house, two sheds, a small barn, an orchard, a large pasture and my nemesis — an enormous garden patch. We also had a water turn on the irrigation ditch whence we watered our place which turned out to be another horror.

We bought a cow, Dolly, and three sheep, Flopsy, Mopsy and Cottontail. After the first year we didn't name the sheep. They were just called sheep. Any farmer will tell you that it is not a good idea to make pets out of animals you are going to knock on the head and eat.

This farm was not a very big farm, and the men thought that they could continue their day jobs and run the farm themselves in the evenings and weekends with slave labor, guess who? My dad had me, 10 years old and Frankie, 6 years old. My Uncle had Janice, 6 years old. According to the perceived wisdom, 6 year olds were too young for slave labor. My opinion was not solicited.

So — I would go to school, come home, pull weeds until it was too dark to see and collapse into bed only to do it all over again the next day. I tried to talk the men into letting me get some friends to help. Uncle Jack countered with, "One boy is one boy, two boys is a half a boy and three boys is no boy at all."

Not that I had three friends anyway. I would have been hard pressed to turn up one and the reason for this is I charmed everybody the first day of school by telling them that they were a bunch of rubes because they wore "over-hauls" and cowboy hats to school. I could have been Poster boy for snotty, conceited, self-important city dudes. Nobody liked me so to get even I made myself steadily more offensive. There ensued a few shoving matches, but no real fights, for although I was a sissy city dude, I was also large and when pushed I pushed back harder. I had no friends and I didn't deserve any.

I had no friends, but I liked to read. There was a little branch library about a half mile from my house. It was run by a beautiful, dignified southern lady who reminded me of Scarlett O'Hara's mother. She recommend books for me. I read them very quickly then sat in a little chair next to her desk and gave reports on them. To encourage my reading further she wrote a note to my dad asking if it would be all right if she selected adult books for me. My dad who really was a pretty good guy, even though he didn't believe in Abolition, came to the library to talk to her with me. He was very pleased and gave his consent. In the long run, this was very good for me. It gave me a leg-up on a really solid education.

In the short run, it served to ratchet up my arrogance quotient to real toxic levels. Even the teachers hated me now. I would ask them, "What do you suppose Eustacia Vye's suppressed desire could have been?"

"Huh" — This was a little country school.

One more short story. (I could go on forever.) One day daddy and Unk had put a rope on Dolly the cow and were leading her up the lane. I asked where they were going and could I come along. It turned out that Dolly's boyfriend was Mastonordi's bull, who lived up the hill a ways. Dolly wanted to go visit with him for a while so they were taking her up there, but I wouldn't like it, a lot of mushy romance. I'd better stay home. OK says I.

Hey. I was 10 years old and this was 1946. Things were different then. It was not the information age. Too damn much information now if you ask me.

The garden

While living in the up-North it was popular to have a garden. I cut out a big patch of lawn, surrounded it with huge, heavy, creosote soaked railroad ties and filled it with dirt. The garden in that particular incarnation lasted two years. When our interest waned, not in a million years was I going to take up the ties, cart off the soil and plant grass — again. So, I had to think of something — this is what I came up with.

I thought, well since weeds are the only things that grow here, lets go with weeds. There are many kinds of weeds and some are really quite attractive, so I kept my eyes peeled and when I saw an attractive weed, I dug it up and took it home. After a while I had a weed patch to die for. (and I almost did) Almost all of my neighbors were gardeners of one kink or another and my beautiful weed patch attracted their ire.

"What the h*ll are you doing with those weeds!? The seeds blow all over into my garden. I have weeds in my tomatoes that I didn't know existed on earth."

This was a time when my incredibly thick skin stood me in good stead.

After a while though, my conscience bothered me so although I really take once to being threatened, these people were my neighbors and friends, so I thought about it again. As it turned out, relief was on the way.

I happened to be in Home Depot one day. This is amazing in itself. I never go to Home Depot. I don't go to Sports Bars either. Well, I did go to Woo Woo Sports bar one time. It was great. I had a lot of fun. It is in San Francisco. The kind of Sports they are talking about are not the kind of sports you are thinking of. Of course, I can never go back again. You can go in one of those places once and claim that it was a mistake, but two times, then you are a Woo Woo. My already tarnished reputation would be completely trashed by suspicion of Woo Wooness.

Speaking of Home Depot and Woo Woo, a gay man of my acquaintance told me that he likes to cruise Home Depot because of all the cute guys in there looking for nuts, bolts and screws.

Anyway, at Home Depot I saw, in the garden section, packets of seeds that were purported to be wild flowers, just scatter and water. Ha! Actually a few scraggly little wild flowers came up among the weeds, but not enough to get me off the hook. So I just bagged the whole operation. It was on the side of the house where there were no windows, so I just pretended it wasn't there.

I was driven out, well I moved out of the neighborhood soon after that and came to St. George to begin life with a clean slate. I screwed that up pretty soon, but oh well, I'm used to it.

Edward Hlavka, artist

The artist Edward Hlavka (HA-LAV-KA) comes from old pioneer stock in Loveland, South Dakota. He has been a sculptor since he was eight years old.

During college in South Dakota Hlavka attended a sculptor summer workshop with Martine Bougel in the south of France. His philosophy for being a successful sculptor is the same as gaining expertise in any field, "Practice, practice, practice." Practice has paid off.

The artist has exhibited in prestigious national shows. The National Sculptor Society's "Masquerade" at the Tower of the Americas in New York City and at the Cheyenne, Old West Museum Show where he received "Gallery's Choice Award" and first place sculptor award.

His work can be found in galleries and collections around the world. Mr. Hlavka's sculptures are sold in Santa Fe, Scottsdale and Naples, Florida. Locally his work is found at the Datura Gallery in Kayenta.

Mr. Hlavka's works cover a whole spectrum. He has a larger than life equestrian monument to Colonel Samuel Sturgis. His life size historical figures are riveting and noticeable for their attention to detail and grace of figurative design. The artists most recent life size commissions include presidents Bush Senior, Nixon, Jefferson and VanBuren. He also makes smaller intimate works; children, fairies and story book characters using an amazing number of techniques and styles.

After coming to St. George to work on a commission piece, he decided to stay for the same reason we all do, the astounding beauty of our surroundings. He has taken an interest in the cultural history of the area and has done extensive research on pioneer figures, Brigham Young in particular and has begun an impressive statue of the pioneer Moses.

Another work in progress is a life size grouping of figures, a stripling warrior and his mother and a missionary and his mother. Not being a native and a newcomer to the LDS culture, the artist is concerned about how the piece may be received. "I became an artist in order to do what I wanted to do. I like to see how my ideas turn out. If others like them, then I am happy. If they buy them, I am even happier."

Mr. Hlavka is a warm, generous, and approachable artist and an asset to any community. Let us make him welcome and hope that he will stay.

San Fran trip I

Sometimes the good life that we in rural Utah are blessed to live, becomes a real drag. You know — fresh air, sunshine, red cliffs, hawks circling in the sparkling blue sky — enough!

The lure of city life calls — crowded streets, millions of people, tall buildings, graffiti, concerts, plays, people laying unconscious in the streets, really good restaurants. I wouldn't want to live there but, boy is it fun to visit.

I visited my children in San Francisco. It was a precarious journey. I drove because I could hang everything I own on a rack in the back and not have to decide what to pack. I always take the easy way, or what appears to be the easy way, but is almost always NOT.

My wife usually drives me everywhere while I look out the window so I thought it would be a breeze. It wasn't. Going down skinny little back roads with thousands of really big trucks can get pretty nerve wracking. Especially when I had to look at the map.

In order to look at the map I had to put on my glasses. With my glasses on, the road and everything further than a foot away from my face was a vague blur. All this at 75 miles per hour. It was a perilous ride.

I stayed in Bakersfield one night and tried to call my kids. I got five dollars worth of quarters and dropped $4.85 cents (no change back) into the phone slot at this creepy gas station where the phone was around the back under some bushes. I dialed very carefully and soon a voice said (the same voice, incidentally, that you hear in St. George when you screw up your call. I hear it all the time so I recognize it). "The number you have reached is not in service, please check the number and try your call again."

All of the coins clanked to the bottom of the box and were gone forever.

$4.85 doesn't seem like much to a guy with a golden parachute, or one married to one of the Rockefeller girls, but to a guy on Social Security and a school teacher pension, both of which, when added together, comes out pathetic — let's just say I didn't try again. The most likely scenario was, either I had punched in the wrong numbers, there were 11 numbers, or I had transposed the order when I wrote the number down. I discovered which one it was, but I'm not going to tell you. It is tough enough to be old and I don't respond well to pity.

San Fran trip II

I got to the city and the fun began. My children treat me wondrously well. Either they like me or they think I have an oil well in Wyoming that'll be coming in anytime soon. (I wonder where they got an idea like that?)

They went to work every day and left me to my own devices. I would meet them in town after work and we would go have fun. I tell people all the time that I can only remember two things at a time. But since I look like a reasonably rational person, they forget.

My son-in-law gave me directions how to get to the train station to get to town. Turn right, turn left, turn right. That's three.

I can turn right and I can turn left but after that it is a fifty-fifty chance I'll get it right. I might end up in the right place, or I might end up in Colma. (Colma is an in-joke around San Francisco, it's the town where all the cemeteries are, not all that funny if you think about it.)

I so long for the old days before convenience when there were human beings to help. As in a ticket agent at the railway depot — tell them where you want to go, they tell you how much, you pay, they hand you a ticket, you go. Not so in these convenient times. You put money into the slots in the wall, punch a bunch of numbers (remember the phone?) then press a button and a ticket will jump out of a slot five feet away (it is hoped).

I tell myself that these potential catastrophes are an adventure. It is the only way I can keep from losing heart and stay in the house all day.

My children's' friends are so cutting edge, inside the curve, and connected that I have to be real careful that I didn't expose too many rube attributes with which I am bountifully endowed.

At the San Francisco Museum of Modern Art, SFMOMA to the knowing, I looked at a big pile of white rocks in the middle of the floor and a pile of red dirt (just like my backyard) with a mirror stuck in it, and I didn't roll my eyes back or sniff.

The hit of the show was a number called "Erased DeKoonig" and that is what it was. Rauschenberg had gotten a DeKoonig drawing and erased it! Put a frame on the erased paper, and sold it to the same lady that recently purchased the Golden Gate Bridge. "Well," says I, peering through my lorgnette, "interesting." But in my heart I thought, boy, there is one born every minute.

I made the cut at the art museum but I about gave myself away when the gang decided to go to the sushi bar. I really don't like to eat anything alive. So I was dubious, but when I whispered to my daughter, "I don't eat living things," she said, "Not living daddy, just raw." Oh Great.

Raw fish, raw shrimp, and other bits of unidentified raw flesh wrapped in what looked like wet black crepe paper and tasted like what I suppose wet black crepe paper tastes like. It is not always easy to be cool.

July 18, 2003

Some events shouldn't be talked about

I had an interesting day today. I went in for my prostate checkup — take it easy. I'm not going to get too detailed. The fact is I really love to talk about my ailments but I never get to.

If I do, my wife gives me one of those 10 pound looks that drive your eyeballs two inches into your head and paralyze your lips.

Anyway, I have been part of a research project by the Cancer Institute to find a cure for prostate cancer. I am doing this out of a sense of altruism and an unselfish duty to my community, but as an offhand collateral benefit, I get a free prostate check every six months and a large jar of expensive vitamins free. I am in cheapskate heaven. I get all this expensive medical attention and free vitamins plus I can elevate myself to the highest moral ground as a selfless benefactor of mankind (sort of like Mother Teresa — well maybe not that high.)

On the way to my appointment while jouncing along in my little car with the top down, an unforgivable breach of senior etiquette occurred. The most important thing that an old person can do is *not* spill food on his shirtfront. I was drinking a mug full of Vita-pro Wheat Germ Protein and Yogurt (this is for another fun ailment that I'll tell you about later). I went through a roundabout too fast trying to beat a pickup going 80 and I spilled all down my shirtfront.

I had to quickly change or I would be late for my appointment. Luckily I have "wipe-ups" in my car. (I have grandchildren whom I take for ice cream.) I cleaned myself off as best I could and then carried my backpack in front.

The second of the small humiliations of my day occurred as I came to the doors of the Oncology Building. I walked toward the doors but they didn't open. All doors open by themselves now days, right? So I stood there for a minute waiting for the doors to notice me. After a while I realized that they weren't going to. I cut my eyes left and right to see how many people had observed my foolishness and were giggling.

The only person I saw was a man far gone in geezerhood like me. He had a baseball cap and a toothless, wide grin, and he gave me a thumbs-up. I was glad it was only him, a compadre. One who, like me, knows all the vicissitudes, snares and traps that the geezer population is heir to. So I smiled back. (I have 11 teeth myself, fortunately all in the front.)

After filling out pages of stuff that the doctor and hospital could or could not tell anyone because of privacy concerns, (Good grief! If I had syphilis I would rather not have it printed in the newspaper but outside of that I am not concerned) the handsome and tall doctor came in and told me to turn around. I heard the snap of the rubber glove and ... here, for your sake, we draw the veil of secrecy over the proceedings.

I left giddy with anticipation. I now have an appointment with an endocrinologist. I wouldn't know an endocrinologist if he was curled around my legs, but if he wears long white coat and works in a hospital, I am in hog heaven. I will certainly keep you posted on all the details — or not.

August 15, 2003

Trip yields new point of view

I was invited to go to Ireland by some internationally famous party animals. I have been to a couple of their parties and they are phenomenal. We dropped everything and took off. If you thought Louis the XIV gave great parties you should see these guys. Between the festivities we roamed around a little.

Galway is a cosmopolitan city — young ladies with multiple piercings, young girls showing their belly buttons. (Just like home.) Harassed looking white men in wrinkled suits and out-of-style neckties. Tourists were easy to spot because the men were wearing money belts under their shirts and were uncomfortable and fooling with their stomachs in sort of a vulgar way.

You hardly ever see toes, at least not men's toes. Sandals don't seem to exist here. Not surprising. It is very cold. Wrinkles don't exist here either, but that is because the air is so damp and cool that wrinkles cannot form. This is what I have been told, but my leg could have been cheerfully pulled by my Irish informant who, as a matter of fact, thought that all Americans are a bit dim. "Look at your politicians Laddy." That's not fair!

On Tuesday afternoon at half four (4:30), I was having a pint of Guinness in a pub with a terrible Irish name. It was unpronounceable in no small part because it had letters in it that had never seen before. The pub customers were talking very fast in either Gaelic or such heavily accented English that I couldn't effectively eavesdrop, something I can usually do very well. It was frustrating.

We wandered through many ruined churches and abbeys with ancient graveyards and mostly Celtic crosses. I talked to a lady who was putting cheesy plastic flowers on a fairly recent grave. Brigit Conner, 2001. She told me that her family had been buried in this churchyard for 400 years. She showed me a gravestone, a Celtic cross for another Brigit and the date was 16 something. Much of the writing had been corroded away — 400 year no surprise.

I told her that I was the great-grandson of a bogtrotter who left at the time of the potato famine. She said that almost every family in the parish had American, Australian or Mexican relatives who left during the hard times and never returned.

Many had "married out." She said this with a wrinkling of the nose. My own grandfather married a Latter-day Saint and was never thereafter received in decent society. Depends on what you call decent society. I didn't say anything. l wanted her to keep talking.

"The Ireland of ancient sadness, poverty and oppression, and the "troubles" when Catholic and Protestants killed each other and it was hard to find a job seem to be over," she said and smiled brilliantly. The men had jobs. The shops were full of beautiful things. The bairns (children) can have their teeth fixed. "These are very good times, very good times."

There is some fun food in these foreign lands. Things I'll bet you have never heard of. Bangers and mash, toad-in-the-hole, spotted dick, steak and kidney pie. The major ingredient in these gourmet treats is offal. You know what that is; you just haven't heard it called that. It is pig snouts and ears, hearts, lungs and other bits that should be fed to the cat. (Stop making those gagging noises and pay attention!)

In America this stuff is used to make hot dogs and bologna and is referred to as "variety meats." I would rather eat a toad than a hot dog, but I chowed down on toad-in-the-hole and asked for more. What can I say?

October 1, 2003

Handiness

Handiness is a skill that has always eluded me. Well, not exactly eluded. I dodged away from every opportunity to learn anything about it.

My Dad tried hard. He could fix anything. He built our house, and I mean built. He didn't pour concrete or lay bricks, but he did everything else. I was about twelve at this time, and only recently emancipated from slavery on the farm. I had no desire to reforge my chains. He tried to teach me plumbing, electricianing, roofing, cabinet hanging, taping and spackling. I remember the words but I forget exactly what it is. I know it was dirty and hard. Everything about being "handy around the house" is dirty and hard.

I was older and smarter than I was when I was lashed into the fields to pull weeds. I had alibis in every pocket. Besides by this time my younger brother who escaped hard fieldwork because he was too young was now old enough to help. A break for me, I thought, "Now he gets his."

The problem was that he loved it. The revenge that I had hoped for was not to be, but still I was able to sneak out of a whole lot of "handiness" instruction.

When I got married my wife had no clue that I couldn't fix the furnace. She had a Dad like mine who could fix anything, so she just thought that it was a genetic thing. HA! When you are dating the subject of whether you can fix a toilet never comes up.

I coasted along for quite a while doing nada because my Dad and Father-in-law scrambled to do all the handiness requirements at our house. It was a long and peaceful time, but then all good things must end and both Grandpas died. I was devastated and I cried for weeks, not because now I'd have to unplug my own drains. I really loved those guys.

But their demise did pose problems. My son was too young. Besides, he inherited my non-handy gene. He went into what appeared to be death throes when asked to mow the lawn. My brother, who knew all this stuff, lived two time zones away. I was on my own. I became acquainted with the yellow pages, a Godsend. When anything broke down a guy in coveralls came and fixed it. Bliss.

Then I retired and moved to the desert Southwest. I gave away all my tools (a hammer and a screwdriver) and thought it was over. NOT. I have friends who are retired and they can hardly wait to wake-up and find a faucet dripping or even more fun a flooded bathroom. Then they get to replumb everything and retile the floor. When we are invited over to see the new bathroom others say, "Great job, or beautiful work!"

I think quietly to myself, "There but for the grace of God go I."

My wife has a favorite television program where this guy, Poncho Villas, or something like that restores houses. He shows ghastly hovels with plaster hanging off and holes in the floor. He walks around showing neat features such as carved moldings around the ceiling which have been painted one thousand times beginning with calcimine (remember calcimine?) and ending with acrylic plastic. You can hardly tell that there is any carving at all it is so gooped with paint, but no worry. You just take it all down and soak it in something and brush away all the old paint (does this sound hard and dirty?).

Why not dynamite the place and call a contractor, but who asks me?

To everyone who disparages my dearth of handiness skills I say, "Can you diagram a sentence with appositives and gerund phrases?"

We all have our gifts.

Festival, 'groupies' give old guy a high

I went into the Great Harvest Bakery and on the bench outside was a man smoking. He was unshaven, not too clean and really sucking on that tiny butt.

When I came out he stopped me, I thought, for a handout. Not so. He explained to me that there was a great shelter up the street, Care and Share, and you could get a meal, a shower and a bed for the night. A real nice place. That seemed to be all he had to say, so I thanked him for the information and walked on.

As soon as I got around the corner I looked at myself, very closely, in the Ace-is-the-Place window. What I saw was an elderly white man with disheveled hair (I'd been driving with the top open needing a haircut — not that bad) and the St. George unisex uniform: shorts, tee-shirt and flip-flops. I was very clean. I am always very clean. I am a clean old man. I didn't think I looked that shabby, but something about me made that nice man think I needed a hot meal, a shower and a bed. It was a bit unsettling.

There is a lesson in this. When you begin to think of yourself as quite grand and above it all, this may not be the impression of others.

I have a point here.

That night I went to the Eclipse Film Festival, a really cool thing put on in St. George every year. We have the Jubilee of Trees for the charitable. We have the Aids Walk for the compassionate. We have the marathon for the athletic. We have Art in the Park for the artistic, and we have the Eclipse Film Festival for the groovy.

I had an "in" to the proceedings. My son Joshua is a TV producer, and he was going to take some film for his TV Station (KCSG). He needed a "roady." A roady, for the uninitiated, is like a donkey used to haul heavy objects to and fro, except there is a lot more status than a donkey. In fact, I even hear that roadies with big rock star tours have groupies. Well! So I was standing around waiting for the onslaught of the groupies and these people started to come up to me and introduce themselves. They were the artists and filmmakers. I was surprised and flattered. I figured that they were nice guys and were talking to an old, distracted old-timer.

I told Josh about this and he said "Geze Pop. You have a black turtleneck, a black leather coat, a VIP pass and a toe ring. They probably think that you are Steven Spielberg."

"Oh really!"

This sort of thing, although bogus, goes a long way toward negating the unfortunate misidentification as a homeless person. I felt really great about that all night.

As a fitting climax to an exciting weekend, I had to drive home after the midnight show. It was 2:30 a.m. The only things moving at that hour were a few sleepy cops and me.

St. George without people or movement is a strange sight. I haven't been awake at 2:30 since I was 15 years old. (I had a brief career as a cat burglar. It came to a bad end. I'll tell you about it sometime.)

I experienced other-worldly feelings engendered by 25 movies in two days besides being awake for 48 hours and driving home alone and exhausted. It was a buzz like one toke over the line.

Siblings forgive but don't ever forget

A while back I wrote a commentary about how non-handy I was. Therein noted that my brother was recruited to do the handy stuff around home. I sent him the column. He sent this reply.

"Dearest Brother:

Received your message and was glad to hear. Since early boyhood I have wondered why it was that you had a complete "pass" on all household and yard chores of any kind and at all times, which thereby fell to me. Now I understand that there is a historical explanation, going back to a time before I became a sentient being, and thus wot not of.

"I learned in school, of course, about the importance of studying history and certainly I have preached much on the topic over the many years of my archaeological career. But to find, in my very own family and experience, such a clear and definitive historical explanation for a previously unexplained phenomenon is a particular delight. I hope to read in a future column, perhaps, an equally illuminating explanation of why you got all the up-to-date fashionable school clothes and I got two pairs of Formosts an archaic brand of jeans from J.C. Penny's and three sport shirts every fall."

Is this guy a hoot or what? Mom always liked me best. Get over it, Bubby.

I had two brothers, Frankie (see above) the epitome of Erudite culture and refinement with a great vocabulary, and Reuben, who was a huge, hairy, scary biker and president of the Sundowners.

I was the only normal brother. I had it made from day one. When our father died, he left a letter for us to read. In it he said, "You guys keep an eye out for your elder brother."

"What does this mean?" I asked.

They looked at me with serious expressions and sad eyes. Then it came to me in a flash. I was not the pampered one because of my beauty, grace or charm, but it was to compensate for being a pathetic loser. This made me feel bad for about two minutes. I consoled myself by noticing that by whatever means, I got the gold mine. They got the shaft. What can I say?

Frankie got scholarships, grants and awards. He had money coming out of his ears. But I had enough sense not to make a fuss. This largesse was due to hard work, diligence and an amazing intellect. We know how I feel about hard work, and am I going to admit to being a dummy?

My second brother Reuben was fifteen years younger than I and in an entirely different biome. Frankie and I were depression babies and poor.

Rueben was a boomer and rich. Papa was the boss now so the kid had all the stuff: car, motorcycle, college, tuition, etc. But my nose was not out of joint. I was happy for the kid. Guess what? I had grown up.

Reuben didn't last a whole lot longer. The life expectancy of outlaw bikers is much less than that of regular people. But he had a great time while it lasted.

My other, much put upon sibling, has buried the hatchet, mercifully not in my head. We have all grownup and can laugh about it now. (Re: the letter from Frankie.)

But we don't forget, do we?

February 27, 2004

Political subversives throw good parties

A while ago I was invited to a really fun party. It was a meeting of the "Under the Radar, Politically Subversive Under-represented Crybabies Marching and Chowder Society." We met at the palatial home of a retired rock star and his trophy wife.

Everyone was there. When we came in, everyone was given a Joss stick to light and place on the altar dedicated to the memory of F.D.R. and the New Deal. It was a moving moment.

One of the guests was the best known liberal between Dixie and the Mexican border. He told us chilling tales of rapacious conservatives who get the huge tax breaks and grind the faces of the poor. "Huah, huah," we all replied as one voice.

One of the fun games we played was a board game called "Tax and Spend." It was sort of like Monopoly. You tax huge corporations and use the money to send welfare queens and drug addicts on Caribbean cruises because they lead stressful lives and need a break. We all learned this game at our mother's knee. It is constantly updated but always the same.

There was a little problem for a minute. Someone said that Barbra Streisand was not the doyenne of the Liberal Party. There were gasps of shock and horror and dire predictions of the demise of the world as we know it if such blasphemies became common currency.

Actually, I wouldn't mind if we cut back on the gasps of shock and horror a little bit. It gets everyone all agitated and really slows down the important business, overthrowing the present regime, and it's mostly B.S. anyway.

There are few regulations, as befitting liberals, but two hard and fast rules:

- If you don't wear your Birkenstocks, you are fined.
- If you have washed your hair in the last two weeks, you are fined.

Sometimes we play "pin the tall on the conservative," which is usually pretty boring except when we capture a live conservative. We use really long pins, then it's a lot of fun.

I'm on the education committee with other old teachers. Our chairman plays golf nine days a week and, when he does have a meeting, it is always at nap time. I am amazed that he gets anyone there, but he does because after the meeting there is drinking and carousing. I love drinking and carousing, but if miss my nap I'm so cranky that nobody wants to carouse with me anyway. Being old has hurt my social life.

The refreshments are pretty good, except for those granola cookies and soy milk slurpies. Yuck. There is usually plenty of sauce. There is a bootleg run to Mesquite before each meeting.

A resolution was passed at the last meeting. No more of those pre-made (in Chicago, last spring) snack trays from Costco.

Disclaimer, in light of my great age (I taught Methuselah in first grade. He was a little slow): Sometimes my memory switches are not all up at the same time, so if you perceive errors in this report, please consider the source and give me a break.

OK?

April 23, 2004

OK, so just one more thing on politics

I know that I promised no more politics, but I went to the guber-natorial debates that were not really debates. It was a political junk-ie's dream.

The fur-licking and hissing and unctuous posturing would have caused Uriah Heep to blush. I had so much fun. But a promise is a promise, so, moving on ...

The St. George Arts Festival was really nice. A lot of nice art. And who cares ...

The debate candidates were mostly 40ish white men in suits.

Some had hair, some didn't, pretty indistinguishable from one another except for the governor at the end of the table.

More fun than the candidates though, were their supporters, minions and accomplices. Signs, banners, flags and T-shirts swamped the patio. I slunk about from group to group, cadging cheese and bits of pizza and doing what I do best — eavesdropping. I heard things as in: "Look at the Two-ton-tessies in the too-tight T-shirts passing out (that candidate's) literature. They must be after the 'McDonald's supersize that' vote (snicker, snicker, snort, snort)."

Some things that I didn't see, although I was not surprised, were Birkenstocks and granny dresses. All but one of the candidates were conservative Republicans with tight belts, tight shoes, tight neckties and tight ... other places.

The only liberal was one of the richest men in the state. How are we going to explain that to the working folks?

Speaking of rich persons, one candidate asked another candidate if he ever had a job. What kind of question is that? If you were the richest man in Utah, would you want a job?

Most of us can hardly wait until we don't have a job. (I am already one of those and let me tell you folks, it's fine.)

The Q & A was pretty interesting. The moderator was kind of on top of it, but he also made what could have been a fatal error. Gov. Walker kept raising her hand to contribute to the discussion, and he kept passing over her until she produced a hard, cold, slitty-eyed, 1,000-pound stare that scared me to death, and it wasn't even aimed in my direction. Mr. Interlocutor must have gotten a clue because he began to pay attention.

Lucky for him.

There have been men who dissed the sweetly smiling, grandmotherly looking Olene Walker and found their head being handed to them.

I have to say that if I were not genetically programmed to vote for the liberal, I might be tempted to jump the tracks and vote for Gov. Walker for no other reason than that her coolness factor is off the charts.

I turned 70 years old a couple of days ago, and you would think that at such a great age I would be delivered from temptation right? Not.

Disclaimer: If you re-read the above you will see that it is not very political at all. It is mostly innuendo and sucking up to the powerful.

Just the usual stuff.

Love to all.

June 18, 2004

Happy to be ignorant on e-mail

As an old person with no technical skills whatsoever, I am mostly immune to e-mail. E-mail, as I understand it, is a means of transporting information of events, which are mean, ugly, shocking and of no general usefulness to anyone. It appears to the dispassionate viewer that e-mail is usually availed of by people with no friends, no confidants, nobody that they can unload onto.

Thus they unburden themselves on the e-mail, as I understand it, of such information as: "Things haven't been good around here. Yesterday the pigs ate baby brother. Mom's back is bothering her, and Cally dropped out of high school because she didn't make the cheer squad. How's things with you?"

This urgent and important information is sent across the whole universe via *myfamily.com*.

When I was a school teacher in a new, high-tech, up-to-date school, every teacher had their own computer. E-mail flew from class to class, with such messages as, "Did you see Mr. Jones' tie today? D.I. reject."

"Mr. Cantes finally got a haircut. Is his head flat on one side or am I seeing things?"

"I got a glimpse of Mr. A coming in this morning. It looked like he was wearing shoes. A miracle! Check it out and let me know."

I was unable to join in the festivities because I didn't know how to turn the thing on.

I had been driven to many computer training classes by my principal, who was sure that computers were the wave of the future. At most of these teaching seminars, the instructor would punch, pour, type and wait and eventually would say, "Well, it seems like the system is down/slow/off/whatever. But anyway, it should do this, that and the other things. All you need to do is Blah, Blah, Blah." All the time we were looking at a blank, blue screen.

I lost interest in the whole project.

The children (first grade) had computer training every other day for a half-hour and instructed by a pro (not me). We used the computer to practice addition such as "6+4=?" If the student got it right (10) I would ask how they had arrived at that conclusion. Answer. Four keys over and two keys down, and the monkey jumps.

My wife gets e-mail. A friend gave her an ancient computer from his garage and they set it up in a small room in the back of the house. She gets messages from our daughter in another country, with messages such as, "The sewer plugged up and spilled all over. I had to stay home from work to wait for the plumber. He didn't speak English. Russell's mother pulled a hair out of her nose and it got infected. When is Daddy's birthday? Love to all."

I say I hate e-mail but in my dark heart I really must admit that this day-to-day stuff is fascinating to me and not at all the kind of thing that you get in a real letter, with an envelope and a stamp.

I know I miss a lot, but I write my letters with a quill pen on parchment and sealed with wax. At least I used to. The post office asked me to stop. It made a huge mess in the sorting machines.

I can't set the VCR, and if on the phone some voice tells me to "Press one or press three or ...," I just hang up. I don't think I'm missing much.

July 16, 2004

Viking funeral is the way to go

I was hanging out with some friends of mine a few days ago. I hadn't been feeling well and looked worse than usual. One of them was prompted to ask me, "What are you going to do for your funeral?"

This inquiry prompted a vigorous discussion. What we came up with was a Viking funeral. A Viking funeral is where the dearly departed is laid out on a boat in his prettiest dress, covered with fagots doused with kerosene. The whole thing is lighted on fire and pushed off into the water to sail, burning, out into the darkness. Is that the coolest thing you ever heard of?

The participants then gather around large bonfires and drink beer and three-buck chuck, eat little cucumber and watercress sandwiches with the crusts cut off and howl and carry on. Everybody is invited. All my friends and my enemies, (If I have one. If I do, don't tell me who.) all the people who like to party, all the people who like weirdness, all the people who are interested in learning about other cultures. It should be a big crowd.

I asked the bishop how the Church of Jesus Christ of Latter-day Saints feels about Viking funerals and he said, "What ever floats your boat."

The bishop is a funny guy.

There was some discussion about getting a permit from the water district. There was some concern that a half-burned rotting body in the Ivins reservoir could constitute a health hazard. But, as is usual in these situations, we decided that it is easier to get forgiveness than permission.

Another discussion was financing. We have set up a committee to go to Mesquite every Friday night to pull those levers. The bigger the jackpot the bigger the party. It is in your best interest to pray for their success. If you are thinking of sending a large check to help defray expenses, please don't. It will hurt my feelings. I'll think that you want me dead. We'll handle it. Thanks anyway.

I do have one concern. I have no interest at all in going to Viking heaven, or Valhalla as they call it. It appears that their idea of heaven is participating in huge battles fought with swords and really big scary axes. I am old and peaceful and chicken.

Another concern: My friends are, on the whole, old duffers like me, so no matter what kind of shakin' is going on they have to be in bed and covered up by 10 p.m. A hairy big bonfire with drinking and shouting in broad daylight loses something, don't you think? Have you ever gone to the dances at the old folks home? Doing the funky chicken at noon on Tuesday is a little surreal. So it needs to be when the days are short. Darkness is required for this kind of activity.

There will be people there who will be sorry that I am dead — My family and a few friends — but I'll talk to them before and admonish them to not get all mopey and spoil the party for others.

It sounds like a great party and I'm very excited, but of two minds. The catalyst that will begin the proceedings requires an action by me — yea, that.

But, what the hey. What happens, happens. It is a comfort to know that everything is taken care of. See you there.

Love to all.

RSVP — To the editor:

I read with great gusto the plans for Jim Aikens' upcoming funeral. (Writers Group, July 16). Now here's a guy that knows how to check out with style. This Viking funeral deal has a lot of merit, and I for one want to be a part of it.

Firstly, I want to attend the party at the water's edge. I will show up with a keg and one big package of horsemeat jerky. Second, I am planning to visit Mesquite on Sunday and will initiate a program to anyone interested to kick off the financing. Third, John Kerry may see this as a photo-op, and I will personally see that he is invited.

I have concerns that the EPA folks may present a glitch. I suggest we invite them to see for themselves that this funeral is consistent with the "dust-to-dust," concept.

Levity would be in order and might I suggest the aforementioned clergyman also be included. We'll see if he really is funny.

Should be a grand affair.

It's up to you now, Jim.

—Lee Robertson, Washington City

August 13, 2004

Finally: Fashion tips for old guys

Fashion tips for old guys is a subject not always clamored for. In fact, I don't think such a thing exists — that is, until now. To be a fashionista in the older-than-70 group is difficult, but possible. You just need to be inventive.

For instance, those tiny buttons on your shirt sleeve, not the cuff button, the other one, you know? The one that arthritic fingers can never manipulate — just leave it undone. I know. GQ will have a hissy fit if they find out, but what the hell. You may leave the teeny-tiny buttons on your button down collar undone too, except when it is your only clean white shirt and you are getting ready for church. Then it is OK to ask your wife (or concubine, if you have one) to button the buttons for you, but mostly we are trying to be self-sufficient.

If anyone notices that your buttons are unbuttoned and remarks upon it just tell them that, "all us metrosexuals leave our buttons undone." They will think that you are referring to another kind of sexual. Their mouths will open slightly and they will scurry away. These people will never ask you impertinent personal questions again. In fact, they may never speak to you again. No big loss.

You must avoid any social interaction with men who say, "When I retired I promised myself that I would dress only for comfort."

These people are not good examples. They mostly look like lumpy bags of rags headed for the D.I. You know the look. A Wal-Mart golf shirt, a shiny blue (plastic?) windbreaker, stretch jeans circa 1970 and, worst of all, white tennis shoes with velcro straps. Personally I would cut my feet off before I would wear such things.

I know it's a pain to bend over to tie your shoes and that you have to sit down for two or three deep breaths before you go anywhere, but think of your image, man. I have personally overcome this obstacle. I just don't wear shoes. This has caused me some grief (at home mostly) but not enough to make me return to suffocating my feet in the stiffened hides of dead animals.

I have the body of a Greek god except for an unsightly protuberance that hangs right out there in front, and cannot be restrained by even the tightest belt. It is there and it is not going away. So wear a large T-shirt and over that a very large (XXL) shirt with the front open and the sleeves rolled up. It looks slightly like a maternity smock but not that much. In this way you can deceive yourself into thinking that nobody notices that you are a big tub of guts and are speculating upon how much beer it took to achieve such magnificence.

Another accessory that is cool is a cane, preferably one with a bronze duck head on the top or one that has been hand-carved by primitive tribesmen on the Amazon river. Those brown metal, industrial strength, adjustable, double uglies that you get at Rite Aid — No. No. No. Those ones with three little feet on the bottom are OK.

Another dude thing is if you have a prosthetic part. Take it off and pin up your pant leg with a safety pin. It not only looks cool, but you get a table right away in restaurants and always get a seat on the bus. Caution: If you are not already so blessed, don't go get your foot cut off. (Hey, it happens.)

Toe rings are optional.

Love to all.

RSVP — To the editor: Writer misses the boat on fashion

Jim Aikens, who wrote the column on fashion tips for old guys, has lapsed into a serious fashion malfunction. He incorrectly stereotypes informal senior styles into two camps: The "cheesy tourist" who dresses only for comfort, with polo shirt, jeans and white sneakers, and the "metrosexual chic," who wear long-sleeve shirts, albeit with the upper sleeve button undone.

Actually there are many versions of sartorial splendor worn by male seniors, a few of which include:

■ The Bowling Beauty: Flowered shirt worn outside of stretch pants, and usually having Velcro straps on their sneakers.

■ The Forest Ranger: Characterized by tan and olive outfits and often topped by a Tilley style hat with brim. A flap to protect the neck from sunlight highlights a serious ranger. Boots are worn as if anticipating a hike in the mountains.

■ The Urban Cowboy: Enough said.

■ Transcendental Guru: Wears loose-fitting clothing appropriate for yoga and meditation, and sandals, with toe rings optional.

As old guys, we need to protect ourselves from being stereotyped. Mr. Aikens' column has caused me to raise the Fashion Alert System from yellow to orange. Someone call the 911 number for the fashion police.

—Paul Campbell, St. George

September 10, 2004

When in Rome, do as the Romans do

For a big time international traveler like myself (yawn) there isn't much that is new.

In Tuscany we stayed in a huge old farmhouse with stone floors and a fireplace big enough to roast an ox. From the Palazzo, across a valley laced with vineyards, is the cathedral of San Pietro. The Campanile rises out of the cypresses and rings the hours. Same old stuff.

As primo fashionista of St. George I went sailing into Roma in all my Old Navy finery and fell with a thud.

All the men in Roma are slim, small, young and dark and they wear pedal pushers. Do you want to hear that again? Pedal pushers and flip-flops. I was on top of it with the flip-flops. I introduced pink with white Hibiscus flowers. People couldn't take their eyes off them. I don't know if they will become all the rage though. The men looked at them, then at me sort of funny.

I had to have some of those pedal pushers, but I was hustled around to see the Coliseum and the Vatican and all that old news and not given an opportunity to look in the shops.

Wal-Mart does not exist here. The shops are tiny, about 10 feet wide and 20 feet deep. There is an exquisitely dressed woman wearing the highest heels you have ever seen or a handsome young man with earrings and his shirt unbuttoned: The harrier the chest, the more unbuttoned buttons. All wear a small gold cross on a chain. Not just the store clerks are unbuttoned. All Roman men are unbuttoned, even those who shouldn't be.

All the shop personnel are friendly and helpful and know about four words of English, but they use their hands when they talk. If you watch their hands instead of listening you learn a lot more.

The sizes are different too. I asked the lady for size 34 and she looked very surprised and shook her head. She got me a size 52 and pointed to my waist. I was incensed. They fit just right.

In Florence (Firenze) it is very hot, crowded, beautiful and NOISY. Thousands of little scooters are zipping around. I saw a very beautiful Florentine lady in a tiny black cocktail dress, Manolo Blahnik shoes and a huge red helmet, gunning her bike at a stoplight. The suits ride too. Everybody rides.

I was further chagrined when in Florence I discovered Dutch tourists wearing pedal pushers. The Dutch are world famous for being out of it (fashion wise). They have only recently tipped to bell-bottoms, and to see them get the jump on me with the pedal pushers was a serious blow to my self-esteem.

Oh, speaking of bell-bottoms, the suits in shop windows and on distinguished greying Italians are so narrow that they resemble dancing tights. Short, close fitting jackets in pin-stripes and Glen Plaids in black and charcoal. Remember, you heard it from me.

I finally got some pedal pushers with zippers, pockets and all the goodies. I wore them very happily all over Italy. I wore them home on the plane. In the San Francisco Airport I began to feel a little uncomfortable. In San Fran you can see everything that ever was and everything that ever will be and nobody takes any notice. People were looking at me. I began to feel a little squirmy.

At home I put them on again in front of the mirror. Then folded them up and packed them away. When in Rome do as the Romans do. When in St. George, don't even think about it.

<u>**October 8, 2004**</u>

Trusted doctor is worth a fortune

R ecently at a party that I went to (I go to a lot of parties. I love parties.) some people there were complaining about doctors: too expensive, rude, make you wait, that sort of thing. I was reminded of my own doctor who saved my life a number of times.

When I was 19 I had a terrible pain right behind my belly button. It was bad. So I caught the bus. In those olden days not every family had three cars and a pick-up, and it was not a disgrace for a 19-year-old man not to have a car. Anyway, the bus took its own sweet time stopping on every corner to get to town.

The doctor, who appeared to be very near my age and just starting out, looked me over. Then he put his arm around me, helped me down to his car, drove me to the hospital and took out my appendix.

"I thought appendix pain was in your side," I said. "Not always," he replied.

His bedside manner was brisk. I returned to excellent health and stayed that way for several years. I had been in and out of the army and was still living at home when one night, very late, I was struck with terrible pain a second time. It was awful. I remember it to this day. My folks called the doctor and he came right over. You must be very old to remember when doctors made house calls.

When he came in he was completely dressed. A grey Glen Plaid suit with one button roll, a yellow knit tie as big as an afghan and brown shoes. His outfit was 10 years out of style and 100 years away from cool, but hey, who noticed. He was saving my life, right!

Again he put me in his car and took me to the hospital. It was a very nice car. He was doing well.

He cut me open and poked around. It turned out to be a perforated ulcer. My stomach had exploded. He told me later what a mess it was to clean up the peanut butter, mayonnaise and pickle sandwich that I had eaten as a bedtime snack. He said that because of trauma (whatever that is) he could only stitch me up and that I should come back in a year and he would take my stomach out. A depressing thought.

But as one of those unintended coincidences, a very attractive young lady, who I knew only slightly, came to visit me. I was very flattered. She came several times and brought me magazines. She was very sweet and kind. Several years later she became my wife. I think we bonded when I was pale and interesting upon my bed of pain. Well, maybe not because now she has no patience with sickness. But that was then.

The fact that I had ulcers was troubling because then it was believed that disposition, wickedness and riotous living caused ulcers. Since I had not been very diligent in keeping the Word of Wisdom, I felt guilty and afraid to face all my old Aunties who would know my shameful secret and would look at me with sad and knowing eyes.

I got the new stomach and that was a drag, but it worked ok, not like brand-new, but ok.

My next adventure with the doctor came many years later. By now I was married and had two children. I was living in the burbs in a split-level and had just started my new career as a schoolteacher of first grade. One night I woke up in terrible pain — again. But by now this was modern times. An ambulance came and took me to the hospital. This time when doc came in, in the middle of the night, he was wearing sweats and a baseball cap.

He looked me over and then he gave me a shot for pain and stuffed a ball bearing up my nose. He said, "When we see this again, you'll be fine," and went home.

I did not give this procedure, as strange as it was, a second thought. By now I had such trust in old doc that if he had put on a voodoo mask and danced around the bed I would have been all right with that.

I didn't have to do the necessary checking for the ball bearing (mercifully). Some poor nurse had to do that. A couple of days later here she came with the shiny ball bearing. I was fine and went home. I had a kinked intestine and the ball bearing pushed through and unkinked it. I have always been sorry I didn't keep that ball bearing. It would have been a great show and tell.

Then there is the cancer story. A lot of cancer stories around. Some are able to tell them. Some are not. I could tell more because I am still here, but I won't.

Thanks doc. Love to all.

Nov 5, 2004

Old age brings
a lot of ailments

My last commentary about all my ailments was well received. People my age (old) love to talk about their ailments. A few don't, but that's because they can't.

I didn't tell you my cancer story, but I will now. As you know, I was a first-grade teacher, and I loved my job. Summer vacation was over, and I should have been excited to go back to school, only I wasn't. I was tired, crabby and didn't feel good.

The last physical I had was when I got out of the army in 1958, and so I went to the doctor (yeah, him, my hero). We went through the physical. When he went around back to do the rubber glove thing he said, "Whoa Nellie." This was on Friday. He made an appointment for Monday to do an operation for colon cancer.

A few minutes before the operation my doctor came to my bedside and explained that because of the location of the cancer there was a possibility that I may end up with a bag hanging on my side. Well, the option was having a bag or trying to get through the Pearly Gates. It was a well-known fact to me and everyone else that I was not quite perfected, and there could have been problems getting in. So I opted for the possibility of the bag in order to give me more time to work on the other problem.

Later in my hospital bed I was still groggy and not all together awake when a beautiful angel came in, hovered over my bed and whispered in my ear, "It's all right. You are going to be fine." She kissed me on the forehead and flew away. I felt wonderful and slept the sleep of the blessed. If an angel tells you that you are going to be OK, then you are going to be OK, and I was.

My next biggie came a long time later. I had moved to St. George when it transpired that I needed to have a bionic knee. The doctor here, who dropped out of the same charm school as Old Doc, said that he could fix me up.

I was all prepped for the operations except I should have been unconscious and I wasn't. I was wheeled into the operating room and there were all these huge guys dressed in those baggy green hospital clothes. But what really caught my eye was the tray of instruments. There was a chrome sledgehammer, a Black and Decker speed drill and what appeared to be a miniature chain saw. One of the men turned around, saw my eyes as big as dollars and said, "OOPS." He came and patted me on the shoulder and I was gone.

This time when I woke up I was quick enough to ask if I could have the old knee. He gave it to me in a cottage cheese container. It was the greatest show-and-tell in history. All the children in the school, the teachers, the cooks and the janitor came to see. The principal came and stood in the door and shook his head slowly. "Your strangeness exceeds all boundaries of imagination," he said. He didn't come in to see. I love that guy.

That's it so far for ailments, but I'm old and a lot can still go wrong. I have no fear. Out there somewhere is a skilled and talented doctor, probably with a personality like a roll of barbwire, who will rescue me.

We have to know when to quit with the rescues. I don't want to be strapped to a chair at Shady Pines drooling in my lap. I have a bracelet on my ankle that says, "Do not resuscitate."

Love to all.

Successful idler

I distrust the perpetually busy;
spinning in tight little circles like poisoned rats.
The slower ones grinding away in righteousness and pain.
Easy does it.

"I think that there is far too much work done in the world." Bertrand Russell was an old nuisance who had a lot to say when I was a young man, and I believed all of it. I became a disciple. I had this really great job where I worked about six months a year and was paid for twelve. (These sinecures do not exist any more, other than political positions, but that would mean that you would be in forced association with people of dubious reputation.)

This largess was provided by the Steel Workers Union. Everytime contract time came up we would insist on these outrageous perks. Some of which defy description. One such was a cultural improvement plan. (We were all uncouth and barely literate factory hands.) My wife and I went to Europe for a month, all expenses paid to become hoity-toity. That worked out ok.

Eventually the union went broke and my company collapsed. No one was surprised. I was cast into the street with a lot of big muscles (most of them in my head) and no skills whatever.

However, by this time I was completely corrupt. No way was I going to work all year. So, casting about for employment I landed on school teaching — three months off. Six hour days. How about that? I loved to be a schoolteacher, but it turned out to be not exactly as advertised. I worked hours and hours and hours for chicken feed, but it was the most fun that I have ever had. The rewards were great.

To return to the subject, the difference between leisure and idleness. That was the subject, wasn't it? Leisure is going on a cruise on a ship as big as Australia, waited on hand and foot, pampered, cosseted and made to feel very grand indeed. It turned out to be the most corrupt exercise I have ever participated in (and corruption is no stranger to me). The idle rich have their own ways, but it is hard to cavil when you are plumped down in the midst of these August personages. Soon you are behaving as badly as they are. I posses a long list of vices, sins and disgusting behaviors; gluttony was not among them — now it is. We were jostling each other at the trough 24/7.

Idleness is another show entirely. To be really successful as an idler it is best to be poor and if possible, uneducated or at least unemployable. Alcoholics and dope fiends have this pretty much covered. Another good cover is to be a deep thinker. In this way you can sit still for long periods of time with your eyes closed — thinking. There is a down side. But food and shelter can be obtained by other means if you work it right. If you don't feel like going the whole hog you can have a job if it is a boring one, but you can't play golf or participate in any other organized activity. When not actively working you must just flop around.

I am writing this in the beautifully appointed reading room of the Norwegian Star with a toddy at my elbow. I have a history of being a sluggard. So, although I am associating myself with the leisure class, I am here under false pretenses. I am an idler and proud of it. I won first prize at the ship's Halloween Party. I was the Sun God. That is so me.

Love to all.

May 21, 2004

Why not honor area's first pioneers?

Today I write concerning the really bilious controversy surrounding the statue of John D. Lee. It would be pretty obvious to a rational person that this touchy subject shouldn't be approached with a 10-foot pole, but, you know me. I have been called many things, but never a rational person.

Who is this John D. Lee person? Perceptions differ. Was he a hearty pioneer who caused Washington to be and after his disgrace went south and dealt with ferries, or was he a homicidal maniac responsible for mayhem, death and destructions and who was executed for his crimes?

There has been a long history of controversial people and statues. Mussolini made the train run on time. He got a nice statue. Hitler cleaned the national debt and solved unemployment (everyone was in the army). He got a nice statue. Attila the Hun introduced the potato to Turkestan. (I was unable to discover if he got a stature or not.)

Saddam Hussein was responsible for stopping the political bickering in Iraq (permanently). Even he got a nice statue.

All of these guys did a nice and commendable thing, which was deserving of a statue. But in the course of events all these statues were knocked down and destroyed for other reasons not connected with do-gooding.

We now find ourselves placed in this dilemma. What to do? We in Utah go on and on about our heritage. Our books and our minds are full of the exploits of these heroic figures and deceased nuisances. We have statues of heroic women on every roundabout. (Well not every roundabout, but some.)

We have pioneer homes, pioneer barns and pioneer Relief Society meeting halls on the historic register. We have Honeymoon Trails, Burr Trails and the Hurricane trail all ossified in history.

Reality check: All this "history" consists of 147 years. I have neckties older than that.

Look around. Everywhere there are signs of people who were here before we ever came, for like a few thousand years (that is real history).

My suggestion is to melt down the John D. Lee statue and make a smaller grouping of real historical figures, a Paiute woman huddling down feeding her baby a plate of bugs, looming over them a man pecking a faintly pornographic petroglyph on a cliff-side. Jerry Anderson, the sculptor, could do this. I've seen it.

Problem solved.

Disclaimer: Since I am not your mother you don't have to do what I say. You may do as you wish, but as a friend may I suggest that you lighten up.

Love to all.

January 28, 2005

Holiday traditions sweeten memories

Family holiday traditions are a lot of fun, but like everything else they can get out of control.

Case in point: My family has enough holiday traditions to fill a large dumpster. Our children and grandchildren come to our house on Thanksgiving and go to the other grandparents for Christmas, so we have to stuff Thanksgiving and Christmas into one hellish weekend.

The subject of running ourselves crazy came up and it was suggested that we modify our expectations. I replied with the wisdom of age, "All right kids, if you don't want to do all the regular stuff, I understand. It is OK that I am real old, and have a frail constitution, and it is probable that I won't be around next year to enjoy the holidays with you all. I thoroughly understand if you want to ch _____." OK, OK, OK. We'll do whatever you want. Can't you just see my smarmy smile? I am grandpa guilt trip. It works every time. Even when they know it is coming they still roll over. It was the most successful child-rearing weapon in my arsenal.

One of our traditions is having our picture taken when we are all together. We have pictures from 10 years back. This year we all wore black and white, and the guy Josh got to shoot the pictures took us out to Santa Clara and posed us all on a mountain of lava. Lava, for those of you who've never touched it, is very sharp. It hurt everybody's bum except mama's; she brought a cushion. She is always the smartest one. The pictures turned out to be wonderful.

My wife and daughters looked beautiful (which they are). My boys looked handsome and strong and the little ones were winsome and sweet, I looked like I was dead and dug up for spite. It is disappointing to be not very good looking but to photograph even worse adds insult to injury, but my family is used to it. When people make comments like, "Why do you have that corpse propped up in the corner?" They don't laugh, and they give the offender a dirty look. Well — I hope they do.

Another fun thing is cutting a Christmas tree. We started very late because the guy who was loaning us the truck forgot to leave the keys. We zoomed up to Pine Valley and en route discovered that we had left the tree permit on the table at home. We then drove the borrowed pickup truck up a skinny little road, where we ran out of gas. We cut down a tree and all piled in my little car to go to Veyo and get gas. When we returned to the skinny, now-dark road, there was a car facing the truck with its lights on, and it could go no farther. They were eating 100-year-old candy bars they had found in the glove box, thinking it might be their last meal.

Just another fun family tradition. On the way home I was telling the little ones a "what if" story. What if the tree-poaching police pulled us over and found we had no permits? Then they would handcuff us and make us lie in the road while TV cameras took our picture and we would be on the 6 o'clock news. They loved the idea, but in the backseat I heard whisperings. "Do you think that it is time to call 'Shady Pines'?" I shut right up then. I don't need a weatherman to know which way that wind blows. Anyway it shouldn't be long before I don't have to associate with no-fun old poops. The little people listen to their old Poppy with an eager ear. I can teach them what they should know. Cheap thrills, here we come.

Love to all.

March 28, 2005

Be careful what
you pray for

Now that things have cooled down and dried up, I feel safe in reporting who is responsible for the recent flood — the Brothers and Sisters of the Gunlock ward.

Are you surprised? I was too, at first, but in thinking it over I see the logic in this conclusion.

Every prayer uttered at the LDS Gunlock Ward for the past five years, give or take, has concluded with, "Please can we have some rain?" or some variation there of. Well! In a discussion with some of the guilty parties one man wryly conceded and quoted this old aphorism. "Be careful what you pray for. You might just get it." But since God never does mean stuff such as washing people's houses away together with their Book of Remembrance and temple recommend, it must be somebody else's fault. The blame has, thence, landed on poor old Mother Nature.

Actually the Gunlockians didn't suffer all that much. The bridges were washed out and they were isolated. (In these hectic times that is something to be envied.) They were on the national news and helicopters brought in medicine and party supplies.

Outside of a little water in a few basements and a few drowned rats floating around, not much harm was done. Everyone got to party hearty, do good deeds for each other and just generally have an interesting and exciting time.

There were a lot of pioneering type things going on I wouldn't be surprised if the Relief Society Sisters were making soap out of bacon grease and wood ashes.

That's how you do it. I know.

I don't actually live in Gunlock. I live in a suburb, referred to by the people in Gunlock as West Gunlock, a.k.a. Kayenta. Of course Kayenta suffered no harm or inconvenience from the storms and floods. Mother Nature wouldn't dare. In fact, Mother Nature has a special affection for Kayenta.

"The rain falls upon the just and unjust alike."

While the unjust were stuffing towels under the doors Kayenta was hosting the "Art in Kayenta" Arts Festival. If this isn't a lah-te-dah doings you've never seen one.

Famous artists from all over the place were here. Even Ermita came all the way from California to make gourmet Quesidillas. While it did rain a little, the drops were warm and sparkling like diamonds. There were rainbows all day long and seven waterfalls in Hellhole. The sky was blue framed in black and silver. It was very beautiful and very classy. There was even a security force (blush). There were no crimes on my watch. The artists loved it. Of course, artists have peculiar ways or they couldn't be artists.

When President Hinckley came down to commiserate with the flood victims (and make a huge cash donation to help the people get it back together) no mention was made of the culpability of the Gunlockians. The Burns arena was jammed to the rafters with people who had come to be comforted by the gentle and funny Prophet. No blame was levied. No mutterings about flood plains and greedy developers. Fault finding just didn't come up. It was pointed out that this is an excellent and beautiful place to live, but stuff happens.

RSVP To the editor:

When Jim Aikens states that Gunlock didn't suffer all that much during the recent flood, I question which planet he resides on. The cost to property and damaged utility systems will place a financial burden on the residents of Gunlock for many years to come. Affected homeowners face financial costs that makes it a stretch to see, much less appreciate, the levity in this article.

Our elected Washington County officials view Gunlock, as does Mr. Aikens, as not being significant enough to warrant any of the $9.5 million dollars allotted to flood loss restoration and the prevention of future flood damage and destruction.

Mr. Aikens' picture puts me in mind of my favorite horse being led away in the dark to escape the flood. All I could see was its rear end.

As for Kayenta being any part of Gunlock, thanks, but we'll pass.

—Jim Heaton, Gunlock

April 22, 2005

Poppy is learning
new rules

Every grandfather suffers growing pains. We're talking real pain here! Tending grandchildren is not for sissies. I may have mentioned that I have grandchildren (about 400 times). They look like stock grandchildren, pretty and sweet, but in fact they are real people, complex, fascinating, endearing and maddening.

I began my grandchild supervising duties when they were still diaper babies. That was a snap. Change their diaper, put them on a blanket on the floor with some kind of noisemaker and read the paper. It became increasingly complex as time went on.

The real trauma began when we first played Barbies. Playing Barbies consists of changing the clothing on these dolls. The clothing varies from vulgar and ostentatious to semi-naked and slutty. We change clothes to go for a walk. We change clothes to go to the malt shop to sashay around in front of a stunned looking Ken and his usually naked buddies. (Ken isn't that much fun to dress.)

Eric is almost three now and has limited interest in Barbie. He does like to throw them at the wall. (He is not often asked to play.) What he likes is to shoot hoops. Just say "park" and he is off like a shot to get his basketball. Hoop shooting consists of standing under the basket, holding Eric up as high as possible (he is a very large three-year-old) while he takes a shot. If he gets a basket we dance around, then I put him down and he chases after the ball, brings it back and we do it again and again and again. Every Poppy of my age (71 last week) does not bend over and straighten up any more times than is absolutely necessary to be a semi functional adult. These basketball games take more bending over and straightening up than I would ordinarily do in two weeks.

We have recently advanced to more sophisticated play. Now we play cards. I love this new phase because we lay on the floor quietly. It is my kind of fun, practically comatose. The game is called UNO. It is basically very simple. The rules are extremely flexible. When I put down an S you are supposed to follow suit. Kat puts down a R. When I say, "What are you doing?" She says, "Sometimes you can do that." Oh!

When I had one card and she had two cards (the object is to get rid of all your cards) on her turn she put down two cards and left me with one. When I questioned this, she said, "Sometimes you can do that." Oh.

I don't win much but I am not required to do anything physical so I feel that it is a fair trade off. Little man plays too, but he puts his cards down whenever he feels like. "I win," he says and gets up and jumps on the couch until the next hand.

Another thing about being a Poppy that is so great, when I say something foolish or make a dorky mistake, Kat gently remonstrates me, "Oh Poppy. You silly goose." I am a fortunate man.

Love to all.

Search for swimsuit takes me back to 70s

The bathing suit season is fast approaching. So a while ago, when I got out of the shower, I looked at myself in the mirror (something that I assiduously avoid) and looking back at me was Moby Dick, the great white whale. It was not so much a shock or even a surprise as it was a disappointment. Something must be done.

I live in a very nice neighborhood with lots of amenities. One of these is a fitness studio. The owner/trainer has a body like Charles Atlas. Remember Charles Atlas, the former 97-pound weakling? Well old Charles must be about 120 by now and probably still looks better than I do. This is a classy place. Only seven people exercise at a time. Everything is programmed and timed. My inner Brad Pitt hasn't emerged yet, but I feel great. I'm the only toxic waist there. The women are all babes and the men have those sinewy, tight, bicycle-rider muscles. I have limp, pillowy, white muscles.

At this gym there are strict rules. If you screw up and get out of sequence there are dire reprisals.

With seven stations carefully timed, sometimes a bewildered and disoriented old guy can't remember if it is chest, curls or lateral raises. The owner/trainer is yelling, "Keep your back straight and get your butt down," and Tina Turner's belting out "Proud Mary" at 2500 decibels. Suddenly the music stops. The owner/trainer says in a severe voice, "You are out of sequence." A chilly and frightened silence ensues. Everyone nervously looks around. Who is it? Then the miscreant is identified and must do 10 push-ups on the floor in front of God and everybody (the women never screw-up).

Speaking of push-ups — when I was in the army (no, not during the American Revolution), at boot camp there was this little Puerto Rican sergeant who loved push-ups. He would greet me with, "Hola, slick sleeve, let's do 10." Then he would dive to the ground and pump out 10 push-ups and you were required to join him. The alternative was the firing squad. For some reason he liked me. I can't say why because anytime I saw him coming I'd crawl under the bed. Over time, however, I could even do push-ups with him standing on my back. He was very small, but still....

I'm no longer in that kind of shape, but my bathing suit dilemma may yet be solved. I was rummaging around in some old stuff and I discovered a swimsuit from the 1970s. You remember the 70s? Madam and I saved all our 70s clothes and dragged them around for years. This bathing suit has legs to my knees, suspenders, a high rise front and red, yellow and blue stripes. But the best part is that it is made of that rubber-looking stuff that bicycle riders wear. It really holds you in. It works out pretty good if I am careful not to turn my profile.

Love to all.

July 15, 2005

Fancy meeting you here!

Ordinarily, life for a man my age is a long, slow slide down the well known tube with pauses for aches, pains, small disappointments and episodes of heavy drinking. But every once in a while, a really cool diversion happens. For my birthday my sweet daughter got tickets for us to go to the San Francisco Symphony Black-and-White Ball. This is rooty-tooty-snooty la-tee-dah at it's apogee. My baby knows how much I like dress-ups and hanging out with my betters in order to poke fun at them. I love this kind of stuff.

I have this really neat tuxedo I have had for years. It is true vintage. I dredged it up for the occasion. It has huge satin lapels and is double-breasted. The pant legs are so wide two people could get in them. But, alas, all that time in storage made it shrink. I couldn't get it to button in front. I loved that suit. I got it from a guy I know who owns a mortuary. It was slightly used but very cool. I found a new tux at a high-end yard sale in Bloomington. It looked like some "same-old-Saturday-night" tuxedo, but I didn't have time to really shop.

At the Civic Center where the doings were held, there were bars with white-coated attendants and huge tables of food every few steps. At Symphony Hall there was a cowboy band. A rock-and-roll band played in the Opera House. The symphony was playing dance tunes from the 30s and 40s in City Hall. Patti Labelle was tearing up the place in the sports arena. I think that she must be a hometown girl. They just love her. Everybody's clothing was black and white and fabulous. One man wore a black cape lined with red like the Phantom of the Opera.

Another man had a beautiful tuxedo with a white satin embroidered shawl with long fringe tossed over his shoulder. Décolletage 'til you couldn't believe it and miles and miles of blazing jewels. I saw one body with diamond rings as big as horse apples on eight fingers.

But, wouldn't you know, the most memorable event took place in the toilet. I may have mentioned the crowd was huge, maybe 10,000 people. The California girls, at least the ones I met that night, don't do stereotypical behaviors: i.e. at most large social events the lines to the ladies room are long and the lines to the men's room are not so long. These ladies chose the shortest line no matter where it went. Some of the older guys looked a little chuffed, but by and large, it went very smoothly. The ladies defaulted to the stand-ups but took their turns at the stalls. Men usually wash their hands and exit quickly not looking at anyone. Women wash their hands fluff their hair, check their lipstick and appear to be in no hurry. One lady at the next sink said, "I love your watch."

"Gulp! Ummmm....thank you, out!"

I would aspire to be far out, but believe me compared to these people I don't even know where "out" is.

Love to all.

RSVP — To the editor:

Jim — you are still an undisputed master at these columns. For my money (which isn't much) you are the best we have. My father (who lives in Salt Lake) also regularly attends the San Francisco symphony and opera and I will make sure he reads this one.

—Geoff Griffin

Journey into the sleeping clinic

Lately I have been amusing myself by supposing that I am in indifferent health. (Indifferent health was my grandmother's word. It means kinda sick but not sick enough to lie down.) Having nothing better to do I hustled over to the doctor. He was very sympathetic. Although I suspect that when he hears that I am coming, he rolls his eyes back, but he never does it in front of me. My most recent complaint is that I can't do all the things that I used to when I was 22 years old. Of course we all know what the cause is, but I rolled right over that. There are pills for everything nowadays.

The good doctor nodded, smiled and listened to my whining. He is a dear man and a good friend or he wouldn't put up with this nonsense for two minutes. One time after he had listened to my long tale of woe he suggested that I had too much time on my hands and that I should get a job. There was a stunned silence while I contemplated that horror. He took that opportunity to hustle me out the door. I was afraid to go back for weeks.

The good doctor devised this scheme to keep me occupied and off his back for a while. He sent me to a sleep clinic.

About a week later, the tech lady lets me in and we go upstairs to a room that looks like, guess what, a hospital room with a bed, TV and a bathroom. I fill out a ream of information papers. The papers were a little creepy. There were pages and pages. Not just name, rank and serial number. The wanted to know stuff like:

A. Do you think that you are ugly and old and people despise you?

B. Do you wish you were dead?

C. Do you often think of killing yourself?

I was afraid to answer because a big iron gate could slam down and the boys in white coats swarm all over me. I was there because I was having trouble sleeping so I asked the technician if I had the wrong list of questions. "No," she said.

Now I have hundreds of small wires glued in my hair and taped to my legs and chest. I am told to go to sleep. This is somewhat anti-climatic.

The only break in the sleeping is one of those small humiliations that dog the twilight years of old men, I had to urinate. I turned on the emergency light and the poor woman had to come from somewhere in the bowels of the building where the sleep watchers have their lair and un-plug all the wires and wrap them around my neck while I shuffled off to the bathroom. She plugged me back in and went away.

In the morning she unplugged me and sent me home. That was it. I had looked forward to this adventure for a long time and it was over. This was surely one of those times when it was better to journey hopefully than to arrive.

Love to all.

September 16, 2005

Life's too short not to enjoy yourself

Now that I am a person of great age and in different health, I have a lot of time to think about stuff. I don't waste my time with regret because that is kind of pathetic and uses up valuable time, and I don't know how much more of that I am going to have.

I don't make long-range plans, not because I don't know how much long range I have left, but because I have never done such a thing, and I don't have a clue how to do it. I have always been a guy who goes with the flow. It has served me well over the millennia so I see no reason to change now.

When talking to my friends who are sitting on huge piles of money due to their facility with long-range planning and financial acumen, I briefly think, "I could have done that."

But my next thought is, "No I couldn't."

I wouldn't know how to do it, and it sounds like a huge drag. I wonder when they had time to do all of this sensible planning and operating. They were like me, with a job and a family with kids and dogs and home maintenance. Where did the time come from for this sort of endeavor? I asked my wife one time, "Why don't we have a nice pile of money obtained from sensible planning and management?"

She tossed off her shoulder, "You were too busy having fun!"

Oh! As it happens she was perfectly correct (as usual). I thought about that for a while and decided that if I had to give up fun time to do sensible anything — forget it. I'm not so bad off. As I am a liberal Democrat, I depend on the largess of the government to send me substantial checks every month — one from Uncle Sugar, one from Gov. Huntsman and one from the Steel Workers Union. Pyramid schemes one and all, and if the politicians will keep their hands to themselves I will be fine for as long as I last. "Apres moi, le deluge" which is none of my concern.

Another thing that I think about is why I don't know how to do guy things.

The men that I know play golf, go fishing in Alaska, go to Phoenix for spring training, play poker at Ed's house, change the oil on the truck and know all of the sports scores from the beginning of recorded time. None of this stuff resonates with me. I tried to play golf once. It was hot, strenuous and boring. No fishing. No automotive repairs (are you kidding). The only sports scores that interest me are the ones at my granddaughter's soccer games. I don't play poker because I don't want to go through the 12 steps again. Not surprisingly, the thing that pulls us all together is party time. It's a thing that we can all agree on.

So if I never made a lot of money pursuing financially remunerative goals, and I never participated in "guy" stuff, what the hey was I doing for all my life? I am going to think about this some more.

Love to all.

October 15, 2005

Career paths not always easy roads

I talked to a young fellow a while back. He had just graduated from a university in his chosen field, was looking for a job and was having a difficult time. There were no openings in his field and he did not want to diversify — yet.

Boy, that sure don't sound anything like my employment history. My parents' idea of solid education was a high school diploma. Neither of them had one although they were very smart and well read. Dad had to drop out in his junior year to get a job. His dad (my grandpa) had blown off a few fingers in a dynamite accident and couldn't work yet. He had seven children at home. Grandma had died in childbirth along with her last child — those were tough times.

My mother made it to the tenth grade, just barely. Grandpa had lost a farm in the Great Depression, and the family had to move from Altonah (find that on the map) to town (Ogden) to find work. Well, he didn't find much, so when the rent came due they decamped. This was about once a month. Mama would enroll into the closest school and very soon have to leave, so she chucked the whole deal and got a job cleaning rich ladies' houses.

Their truncated education made them very eager for their boys to get a diploma. So I buzzed right along. I worked on Saturday at the laundry where Dad worked. (He eventually became the manager.) I cleaned the greasy machinery. It was a nasty job but I got $5 a week, which was a magnificent sum for a boy of 13. I had to put one dollar in "savings" but I could blow the rest on anything I wanted.

When at last I graduated from high school, my parents were delighted. I had never worried about getting a job. That was all taken care of.

My dad took me down to the American Can Company and introduced me to the general manager for whom he had worked some time back. The warehouse foreman was my uncle. The chief of personnel was my scoutmaster. The paymaster was the husband of my aunt's sister. I got the job. This is called nepotism. It was how things were done, but I had to work hard or it would disgrace all the men who had given me a boost.

I did work hard, but advancement was *slow*. Somebody had to die first. It was a Union Shop and all that counted was "whiskers" or longevity. All the old guys had the good jobs, which they sometimes did poorly, but this was assuaged by giving them a "helper." I was the carpenter's "helper."

After Old Coy had shown me the ropes, I don't think I saw him more than once or twice a week in the breakroom. There were many helpers in many fields.

Nobody squawked. It was the way it was. It was a great job with lots of "bennies." I had a perforated ulcer and a gastric resection (a new stomach) at the age of 25. I was in the hospital for two weeks. It didn't cost me a dime. Also, I was paid full salary.

I worked there for 25 years until the company went under and I was 45 years old with a wife, two kids and a mortgage. I was skilled in the manufacture of tin cans, which was about as much in demand as buggy whips.

I turned out OK though. If you wheedle me, I'll tell you about it.

Love to all.

November 11, 2005

Baseball with the ladies left its mark

There has been a ground swell of interest in my fascinating and ongoing health problems (yeah right). So I am going to tell you a tale of cultural interest and woe all in one.

At the end of the year in the public school system, almost everywhere you go, the oldest class challenges the faculty to a baseball game.

It seems that it was a given. There was a lot of sexist foolishness in the old days, which was taken as a given.

There were two men at Municipal, me and Jack the janitor. Jack knew all about baseball and was the pitcher. I knew nothing about baseball and was the short stop. The younger women were pressed into service at the other positions. The sixth grade team was all male. We won as many as we lost. Anyone paying attention would see that the "ladies" played as well as the men but nobody said so.

In the new times, at Bloomington Hills, there were six men — five teachers and the principal. On this team the pitcher was a woman as were the first, third and short stop positions. I was way out in the left field or on the bench. Since I was older, the lineup looked odd to me. The younger male teachers saw nothing odd in the fact that the best pitcher was the pitcher, sex not withstanding.

One fateful day I was up to bat. I took a mighty cut — and missed by a mile, spun around and fell down. My arm hurt like the blazes. I was dazed and couldn't get up. It was very funny and everybody laughed and laughed. But after a while, as I lay there unmoving, the laughter died down and my first graders who knew me best began to cry. Some jumped up and ran onto the field. This alerted the faculty that something was amiss.

Everyone rushed to my aid. One female teacher unbuckled my belt and began to unbutton my pants. This caused me to forget my pain (briefly) and pay attention. She learned this lifesaving skill in a Martha Stewart magazine.

At last the ambulance came roaring onto the field with all lights blazing and siren shrieking. This further terrified my poor students, who saw me packed away and hauled off. At the hospital it was discovered that my arm was broken too near my shoulder to be cast. So I was given a sling, which held my arm close to my chest. I was also given a powerhouse shot of something. Not only did I not hurt anymore, I thought I could fly.

I insisted then that I go back to school and show the children that I wasn't dead. It was the last day of school and they wouldn't see me again. I didn't want them to worry all summer.

So we had (gentle) hugs all around. Everybody went home, and I passed out. I woke up at home, in my bed, in my underwear. For many years afterward, I endured inappropriate remarks concerning certain physical anomalies that could only be seen if I was unclothed. I appreciated the ride home and the tender loving care — but jeez ladies! (Can you imagine my explanation to my wife?)

January 6, 2006

Army days taught tolerance

A long time ago I was drafted into the Army. I was a cosseted and coddled child of privilege — never had to do a lick of nothing. Never been out of the city limits of Ogden, Utah 84403. A rube and a boob and boy was I in for a lot of surprises. The first clue was when they shaved off my greasy duck-tail and made me wear really un-hip (un-hip is an archaic term superseding cool) green canvas uniform, one size fits all, combat boots, and a really dorky looking round hat with a beak. I also wore a nametag over my left front shirt pocket that was misspelled.

I could complain about a lot of things but you'd expect that. Instead I am going to tell you about an important lesson that I learned. Where I was stationed in South Korea it was way back of beyond in the D.M.Z. (This is Army talk.) We lived in little shacks. 200 men in very close quarters all day and all night. I am a pretty sociable guy but I really need a little solitude from time to time. All the soldiers were offered R & R (more Army talk). So I went to Tokyo. A salty old Sergeant told me where to go.

I stayed at an old traditional Japanese hotel. The bed was a mat on the floor. The chairs were cushions. The door was paper. Just like the movies. It was a great place but best of all I was the only one there. The hotel guy would leave a jug of hot water outside the door every morning so I could wash and shave. This was all right for a couple of days but I am an American and I shower everyday. I was beginning to feel a little funky. The hotel guy sensed my problem. He got me a kimono, a towel and a bar of soap and pointed me down the road to the public bath.

It was a cool place. It was about seven o'clock and all the people in the neighborhood were trooping down to the bathhouse with their soap, towels and children. You hung your kimono on a nail and sat on a small stool. The bath attendant (a middle aged lady) poured hot water over your head, shampooed your hair and washed your back. Then you washed the rest when she moved to the next customer. Later she came back and poured more water to rinse off. Then you stepped down into the bath and soaked for a while.

Now we come to the educational part. Japan is a small country with a jillion people all squeezed in together and they get along just fine because they are courteous, polite and accommodating. The bathhouse was small and jammed with people. I was the elephant in the living room. I was large, white and hairy. The only ones who gaped at me were the little children who could not believe their eyes, but that only lasted until their mother caught them. There were a lot of people having this warm, toasty bath and enjoying it because everyone let everyone else have their space. It was great.

After a while we dried off, put on our kimonos and headed back up the hill. I noticed a lot of the men peeling off and heading into a little teahouse-looking place. Well it wasn't a teahouse. It was a bar. Very unlike an American bar but a place to get a drink nevertheless. The limit of my Japanese was ohio, gosiemus (hello), asahi (name of the beer), domoni gato (thank you). That was all I knew and all that I needed to know. Life was good. Moby Dick the Great White Whale sitting in a nice bar with a bunch of small, polite men who minded their own business and didn't have stinky feet.

I was a happy man.

Love to all.

February 3, 2006

Political awareness is
an eye opener

I had decided to pay attention to politics (I've told you before, I have no life.) I have been getting a little annoyed with the low intensity whining all around me and the increasing paranoia of the ... how shall I put it, people out of power, and the truly incredible Utah State Legislature. I had to begin somewhere so I accepted an invitation by the Democrats to attend a lunch on Martin Luther King Day at the Dixie Center.

My first observation was that a great many of the cars in the parking lot were Hybrids. You know the ones that run on gas and electricity or at least that's what I think they do. (I love being an investigative reporter but I hate to investigate. It is time consuming and boring. I'd rather just run my mouth and assume that I know what I'm talking about.) Anyway, there were very few semi size SUV's in the lot, what does this indicate? I'm still thinking about that.

The Dichotomy of the Democrats was very obvious as always. The lunch was fabulous, served by waiters in tux shirts and cummerbunds, very elegant and high end. Then for a fundraiser they sold t-shirts that had been misprinted for five bucks each. Big bucks there. I bought one just to be nice. The sales guy said that he would be looking for it around town. I told him, "In your dreams." Nobody in their right mind would wear "Southern Utah Democrat" printed on their chest in rural Utah. It would constitute a bullseye.

Speaking of targets. I was at my health club in the locker room getting dressed. Three old guys came in together. All the old guys come in about the same time after breakfast but before naptime. They were friends and often came in together. They were getting dressed and I wasn't paying any special attention until one guy pulled a shiny silver pistol out of his locker and put it in his jacket pocket. The next guy had a holster and put his piece in under his armpit. The third guy shoved his in the back of his pants. I had never seen such a thing and

I guess I made little gasping sounds. They all turned to look at me. Nobody said anything. Their mouths didn't smile but their eyes did. They knew that I was not dangerous and would not be a problem. They could tell this because I had a SpongeBob SquarePants gym bag and was stunned and helpless. They left. I saw them again from time to time but I look special care not to be in the locker room when they were there. I'd see them around town once in a while, but never at Democrat functions.

I don't like guns. Guns give me the fantods, not due to my religion, politics or ethnic origin. I am ok with police officers, soldiers and hunters, but walking around with a glock stuck in the back of your pants is scary.

Anyway the Keynote speaker was a lady who talked about sexual diversity and how Dr. King believed in equality for everyone no matter how different they may appear. There was some sensible and dignified disagreement on the way the gay marriage subject was proceeding and I loved that. The general perception of Democrats is that Hillary points, Howling Howard Dean barks and all the sheep run in that direction, maybe not.

The meeting was high minded and courteous, but in the lobby afterward the tone changed perceptibly. I was reminded of the wise old saying, "The people who appear paranoid are people who *really know* what is going on."

Love to all.

March 3, 2006

Not athletically inclined?
Go fishing

To say that I'm not very athletic is to minimize the situation. My eye hand coordination is so bad that my parents worried that I had neurological damage. I still stab my face with the fork at least once every meal. I took at a tennis lesson once. After five minutes the instructor, who had been making gasping, snorting sounds the whole time, told me that maybe I should try hopscotch. Hysterical laughter followed me out to the car.

I recall vividly my most humiliating athletic experience. The 19th Street Gang was playing the Oak Street Gang a game of touch football on the church lawn. We were short a man so they lent us Dunland Newey. The game was going along and Newey and I were running down the field. I was in the clear, so I called "Open Dirt!" (He called himself "Dirt" because it sounded tough. If my name was Dunland Newey I would call myself something else too.) Had I given it one minute's thought I never would have said it. I knew what was going to happen, and it did. The ball hit my chest and bounced away. Someone got it, and the runner scored. I was criticized for this mistake long and severely. It really hurt my feelings and I went home.

Remember the fat, clumsy kid with glasses who was chosen last? I am him.

I did learn from this. I was no athlete and never would be so I quit trying. I have never since involved myself in anything that required throwing, catching or running. I did try golf once and after about five minutes it was relegated into the category of boring, time wasting, silliness that encompasses fishing, skeet shooting and taxidermy.

Without athletics I have a real good life, due to good friends, the fresh air and sunshine that surrounds us all, as well as various —um substances, designed to cause happiness.

When I became a parent I became a serious person. Comparatively I am practically grim. I loved being a parent and wanted to do it correctly. Someone told me that if you do not take your children fishing they will become juvenile delinquents. Not mine. I overcame my revulsion; bought small fishing poles and we went fishing. It was horrible. It took forever and the whole time the kids (age 5 – 7) were shrieking and screaming and jerking those slime balls out of the water every ten seconds. Taking the fish off the hook was like manipulating a handful of snot. Then put on a new worm and "bang" doing it again.

When it was over (at last) I took many pictures of the children and the fish. When they were teenagers I would take out the pictures and make them look. "If you have any ambitions of criminal behavior, forget it. I paid the terrible price and juvenile delinquency is not an option."

I never had to fish again and my excellent children never did one minute of jail time.

I give my children child rearing tips from time to time but they don't seem to be terribly responsive. Compared to some others their upbringing was a little strange and off center. But everything turned out all right and that's the point, right?

Love to all.

March 31, 2006

Is what you see, exactly what you get?

What goes around comes around and the conspiracy theorists are out there again peering through the tall grass and warning us once more of the ancient enemy "the media" who are the running dogs of the (Left — Right, choose one). Vile and corrupt they are (attacking — defending) the president as he (Does his best to bring democracy to the world — Drag us all on a screaming spiral into hell). I'm sure that you are getting the picture. So the remedy for this blatant misinformation has been suggested. Turn off the T.V., stop the paper, don't listen to the radio, instead go online and stalk the bloggers.

Informational aside — Bloggers: people who get on the machine and expound upon subjects of their choice sometimes at great length (mostly) these people expose Utah, information gathered, for the most part, from a place we all have access to "the top of their head."

As a general rule by the time that you are half way through the blog you either have steam coming out your ears or puking in the wastebasket. If you do get a grip and go on you may discover the source of the aforementioned information. "A guy I met while hiking on Utah hill. He was very good looking and his shirt was ironed and he had nice manners. So he was probably gay. However this in no way diminishes the validity of his information."

"One other thing, he was sort of pale greenish color. When remarked upon he said, 'Oh it is genetic. All the people on my planet are this color'."

This should replace The Wall Street Journal and The New York Times and of course our beloved Spectrum?

A thumbnail guide to reading columnists and letters to the editor is: If they contain words like ignorant, traitor, liberal, collaborator, or disgusting you will know there is foam on the writer's mouth even though you cannot see it. If, on the other hand, you see words like stupid, draft dodger, liar, or incompetent then you can feel the warm glow of a halo, even though you can't see it. Times change and vituperation changes. In another life I was called a long hair, weirdo, red commie, freak. Well now suddenly red is blue and I am a blue man in a red state. Still weird but I have gotten a hair cut.

My point is, "Everybody is just as nasty as everybody else and if you aspire to the higher ground forget it." Your true colors (whatever they are) will bleed out and you will be in the steaming swamp of despair just like the rest of us.

If you don't find this all very depressing then you are missing the point (or have access to drugs).

Love to all.

April 27, 2006

Segregation and racism do not blend

D id you know that in a time within human memory (mine) it was illegal for black people to drink out of white people's drinking fountain?

Can you get a picture of a crusty old lady skulking about at the bus station hoping to catch a black person sneaking an illegal drink of water from a white people's fountain, springing out of the shadows with her accomplices and snapping pictures of a startled illegal drinker? It could have happened.

In another incident that you may remember, if you are old enough, it was illegal to be Japanese. If you were ethnic Japanese, that is to say if you looked Japanese, whether your family had been Americans since the gold rush, you were packed off to the concentration camp with great alacrity.

I can just see the present day minute men squatting in the creosote bushes with their camo pants tucked into their army surplus boots waxing nostalgic over the good old days when they could have been shoving illegals into boxcars and sending them off to Topaz and Manzanar and other beautifully named concentration camps (excuse me, detention centers). After all they were illegal and if you have the misfortune to be illegal any unkindness, cruelty or injustice that you suffer at the hands of legals if your own damn fault.

One last example: I've got a ton of them but I don't want to get too shrill. My brother was at school at the University of Utah where he met an attractive young lady and fell in love. They wished to be married. Both families were delighted at the prospect. In the course of events the "to do list" noted "Get a marriage license." So he trooped off to city hall for the necessary papers. There the couple was told such a thing is not possible because they were of different races and it was illegal for the races to mix. Wasps must marry wasps, Chinese must marry other Chinese and Mexicans must marry other Mexicans (female only) etc. So they slunked out into gathering darkness guilty and ashamed.

Those bad old days recede from memory until something brings them sharply to mind. Even as we speak the president has decided that he can tap phones and spy upon whomever he wishes, even detain people (nearly all of whom are a different color from himself) because it is a time of war. Sixty years ago the constitutional rights of American citizens of Japanese decent were trashed and today the rights of American citizens are being trashed, again with the same alibi. There is a wise old saying, "Who ignores the lessons of history is doomed to repeat them."

I love wise old sayings, especially when they bolster my own opinion.

To sum up, all the discrimination and unconstitutional laws noted above are gone now and everybody is embarrassed and ashamed that they existed at all. This newest flap about illegals will blow over too for the same reasons. So my suggestion is that since in the end we will all have to live together it will be best in the interests of everyone if we don't say a lot of nasty things that we can't take back. (Except present company.)

Love to all.

RSVP — German internment is often forgotten

Just once, when someone is wringing their hands about Japanese internment, I'd like to see mention that people of German heritage (mine) were also interned. Many of them, unlike the Japanese, remained interned after the war. Try reading a history book someday.

The Writer's Group comments were just as racist and offensive to us as any anti-Japanese comments are to them.

—Ron Olroyd, Ivins

Immigrants

With your permission I am going to begin an assault upon one of the unhappiest conditions now existing in Utah, indeed in the whole country. The harassment and unkindness shown by a segment of our population to the people who are just trying to get along. By this I refer to the illegal immigrant criminals/undocumented workers (choose one).

Let's begin with a little back-story. My grandfather, James O'Houghlahan Aikens, an Irish Bogtrotter (a derogatory term), fled the Irish potato famine, impelled by the indifference of the government who didn't give a sh..(hoot) and the specter of starvation. Black Jim got on a boat destined for either New York or Vera Cruz. Whatever, anywhere he could have a chance. He landed in New York. Resultingly I am an American. If Vera Cruz, I would be a Mexican. (Either way I would still be in your face.)

At this time (1860) the Irish were not exactly received with gladness. There were too many and it was supposed that all they could do was raise potatoes and get drunk (how little things change). Black Jim toughed it out, resultantly two generations later I have a brother who is a Ph.D., a daughter who has an advanced degree from Cambridge University and a son with a thriving business which he began from scratch. Personally I am not nearly so exalted but I have always had a steady job with only negligible jail time so I feel qualified to comment. (I only bring this up to illustrate how far an immigrant family can go if given an opportunity.)

My wife's parents are F.O.B. (fresh off the boat) from Holland and melded smoothly into the population. They were white, which may or may not resonate in this discussion.

One of the more unlovely tactics of the no immigration contingent is, "Be sure that nobody can get a job" by fining anyone who employs undocumented workers. This way there is a possibility that, since there is no job and no money for food, the designated targets could starve to death, thus eliminating the problem. A sort of slow moving final solution.

May I take the opportunity to propose an alternate solution?

These people had a hard time getting here and now that they are here they are here to stay. Get used to it. If you think that writing snotty letters to the newspaper complaining that "those people" are sucking up all the social welfare and breathing all the air is going to make them feel so bad that they will huff, "Well if we're not wanted we'll just go home" you can forget about that too. Rather than harass these people and make us all feel secretly guilty whether we participate in the stoning or not, let them have a job. Let them have a driver's license so that they can get to their job. Let the children get the same tuition break that we all get.

If you live in St. George, Utah and your great grandfather was not a Piute then you have a lot of nerve challenging people who only want the same breaks that you have. Politically, socially and realistically it is in our best interest to help them fit in and contribute to society. Think about it.

Love to all.

I'm just not cut out to be the community scold

I was very gratified by the response to my last commentary into the realm of public discourse and away from the mostly morbid remembrances of an old turtle about things which probably never happened. (Who remembers?)

It was in response to my Editor's suggestion that we (the Writer's Group) stretch ourselves, try something new and see how it goes. Well, it went very well. Thank you Editor.

I have been casting about (I read a lot of English detective stories and they always say "casting about") for a new venue. I have decided to become the village scold. I am eminently suited to this work. I can find fault with anything and I certainly have the vocabulary for it. A "scold" is a person who goes around finding fault, errors and mistakes, foolishness and minor crimes in the village and excoriating (bawling out) the guilty parties. I thought it would be a blast. As a general rule a scold is a mean, skinny, frustrated old lady with too much time on her hands and not enough to do. I qualify on all counts except for being a lady and being skinny (I wish).

I thought I would start with the town drunk (an easy target). At a party with several of my friends I told them about my quest and asked if anyone could direct me to the town drunk. There was a deafening silence for a few moments and then everybody began to laugh like maniacs. I tried further inquiry but all I could get was hysterical laughter, choking and gasps. I finally gave up and went home. Further research is needed.

I thought about developers, a common enemy, raping and pillaging the landscape, scarring the hillside, building tacky tract houses and ugly forbidding walls, but really that is an old horse that has been flogged to death. The chance that a scolding would make any difference was slim to none.

But I did, in fact, corner a developer and before I could crank up, he disarmed me completely. Talk about your silver-tongued devil. After a couple of glasses of really good wine and an earnest explanation of his motives and actions I was about ready to jump on a bulldozer and scrape off the desert. I'm not ready to deal with the pros.

To be an effective scold one must have a very narrow focus and the self-assurance that they have never made a mistake. I fall very short in this category. I was about to chuck the whole process when I had my first success. A person stopped me in a public place and asked me to write about a serious problem at the "Care and Share." This person saw a bunch of illegals getting food and school clothes for their children and felt that this should stop.

Now I must admit reluctantly that the people who squawk about the illegal use of their tax money have a leg to stand on (a shaky leg), but whatever the Care and Share has, has been given to them by people of good heart who care and who could possibly be hurt by it? At first I thought that they were cutting into this person's territory, but this person has very obviously never missed a meal. Anyway, I listened and gave what I thought was good advice. GET A LIFE.

Eventually I conceded that I would have to give up the scold business. The field was too crowded with amateurs and I really wasn't cut out for this kind of work. I'm nicer than I thought I was.

Love to all.

June 23, 2006

A new suit, a few truckles and a grand wedding in England

We were invited to a wedding in England this summer. My daughter is married to an English person and his brother was being married. We were very excited.

The first thing to do was buy a new suit. In keeping with my reputation as a fashionista it had to be a really great suit. I saw the one that I wanted in a catalog. Black and white striped seersucker. Very cool indeed. Of course the handsome man modeling the suit wasn't 72 years old and 40 pounds overweight, but I blew that off, measured myself with string and sent it off.

I was leaving to the country in two days when it came at last. I put it on and it was not what I had pictured. I looked like a fortune-teller's tent. An added complication was that the pants were too big. Pants that go around my waist are very big and when they go around my waist and then some, they are way big. I needed a tailor and fast. Do you know that there are only two tailors in the St. George phone book?

I hotfooted it over to this nice lady's tailor shop. She had enough work already to last her till Christmas, but when I told her my long tale of woe and looked sufficiently pathetic she said that she would squeeze me in and have it done by Monday.

The pants fit around the waist but they were still mighty big. I looked like a 1940's zoot suiter with a long coat and very baggy pants. Anyway, I didn't need to worry about standing out. The groom and groomsmen all wore the sort of thing one would wear to Buckingham Palace: striped pants, a swallowtail coat, a weskit (vest) and a really big cravat, which is a sort of a necktie only not really. Nobody knew how to tie one, so there were as many variations as there were men.

The bride is Canadian and the three bridesmaids were Canadian also. In America, as we all know, the bridesmaids all wear the same dress no matter what size or shape they are, usually something shiny with poofy sleeves. These bridesmaids wore dresses that were a little bit the same but not altogether. Two wore shawls. One wore a vest. Two were short. One was long. They were the same colors, black and red, but in different combinations. They looked great just not uniform.

The reception was held at the Squires Pile in Yorkshire. In America the first question would be, "A pile of what?" In England everyone knows that it is his country house. A marquee was set up in the sheep meadow and the music was a Celtic band called "Dogsbody." (There is a story there, but it would take too long to tell it.)

In the marquee were two firkins of beer. A firkin, is like a keg, and any American who was ever a teenage boy knows what a keg is. Firkins serve the same purpose as kegs only much larger. All young British men of my acquaintance know a lot about beer. These young men were as thin as whippets but had a capacity for beer that is beyond belief. I am no slouch as a beer drinker, and I have a belly to prove it, but they put me to shame. Plus they could dance every dance and go outside to smoke. They still smoke in England. Aside from lung cancer the evil weed costs five pounds a pack, which is about eight dollars in American two packs a day — do the Math. This combined with gas prices six bucks a gallon. These boys and girls have good jobs or else they live in refrigerator boxes under the carriageway and eat at the Salvation Army.

The snacks provided at the dance were delicious and exotic. There were truckles (what's a truckle?) of Wensleydale cheese, pork pies, sausage and mash. I have to tell you about the sausage. There is a place in Sedbergh, the village close by, which makes its own sausage. Since the bride was Canadian, and Canada is known for its maple trees and syrup, the sausage makers were prevailed upon to make a special sausage with maple syrup. It was fantastic. In fact, Mr. Steadman, the sausage man asked if it would be ok if he made and sold this special sausage to his general customers. How cool is that?

The illusion that Americans and Englishmen speak the same language has been propounded for years. There is no truth to it. Examples abound otherwise. However, understanding is not a problem. How about that?

Love to all.

July 21, 2006

First graders taught this school teacher to roll with laughter

I am going to tell you a story about when I was a school teacher. — Don't be that way. It's either that or another bulletin on my declining health and you <u>know</u> how boring that is. OK?

One day the children were doing seat work (seat work is what you give the children to do when you have been tap dancing as fast as you can to keep the students attention and on task, and just need to sit down for a minute) a little girl came up to my desk and stood there quietly and politely. Tiffany was pretty, had blonde curls and a very sweet smile.

"Do you want to hear a joke, Mr. A?"

"Yes."

"What do you call a mushroom that buys all the drinks?"

"I don't know."

"A fungi."

The combination of that sweet face, the funny joke and being really pooped caused me to laugh like a maniac until tears ran down my face. I think it scared Tiff a little bit because I laughed too loud and so vigorously. Soon everyone jumped up and ran to the desk to see what was going on. I was able to stifle myself long enough to explain and asked Tiffany to tell her joke again.

So she did. A couple of the kids guffawed politely but mostly they looked blankly at each other and me.

"What the hell does that mean?" this inquiry was from Dirty Darwin a boy with a very bad mouth for a six year old. I have been on him all year about it, but in my dark heart I was in sympathy with him. We were both fighting the same battle. I was raised in a family whose talk was salty. I worked in a factory for 25 years and had been in the army. In neither of these jobs was delicacy of language necessary for advancement. Though I'm ashamed to admit it Dirty Darwin's remark and all the blank looks made me laugh even harder. This was the signal for chaos to erupt. Everyone began to run around laughing and hooting and it took me a long time (after I had recovered myself) to get everyone back to work.

Another incident was handled in a more professional way. We were doing a special project that entailed the use of glue. First graders love glue and its use must be carefully monitored, so I had a mother come in and help. About half way through the project Daffodil (not her real name) took the lid off the glue jug and announced, "This is the way volcanoes work" and squeezed hard. Glue flew through the air and came down on everybody and everything.

When the screaming began I was across the room but I quickly scoped out the scene. Then I ran out into the hall, shut the door, leaned on it and began to laugh. After I was able to quit laughing and get a grip I went back in to view the devastation. The mother helper viewed my hasty retreat and commented on it. I explained that I had learned long ago not to let the first graders see me laugh at any sort of disaster because it then became an epidemic and was repeated by copycats forever. To deal with this problem I would just run outside until I quit laughing and thus thwart endless repeats of the incident. I learned a lot in the first grade.

Love to all.

August 18, 2006

Babysitting grandkids merits a few stimulants

When I arrived at my son's house to take up child minding duties the two page note on the refrigerator advised: If Buddy (a child) wakes up before 6:00 (what?) give him a sippy of water and put him back to bed (HA).

"Buddy can watch TV, channel 7, 11, or 32 until breakfast."

Buddy watched Oscar the Grouch (an old friend, his dad and I used to watch Oscar when he was three years old) a real OLD friend. I staggered around trying to get it together, opening and closing cabinets when the horrific truth fell on me. My son is potential bishop material and they don't keep artificial stimulants in their house. My already frayed nerve ending began to convulse and I knew I couldn't make it without stimulants. Resultantly I made Buddy a peanut butter toast and we jumped in the car in our jammies, bare feet and bed head and roared over the gas station for a HUGE cup of coffee. A calmer Poppy resulted.

I thought I might stick out at the gas station coffee pot. Not so. All the men there, and there were a lot of them (no women) were generally as raggedy as I was although they seemed to be dressed for work, as least they all had shoes on. I was the only one with bare feet and a peanut butter smeared baby in his arms, but still no one blinked.

We were able then to proceed with the business at hand. Breakfast was a gourmet delight. I looked all over for oatmeal, which was on the preferred list. I looked high and low. Finally I asked for help. Kat showed me an odd looking square box. I had been looking for a round can with a smiley guy in a blue hat. I had no clue that other oatmeal existed. The microwave directions seemed fool proof. When I was making oatmeal for my children microwaves did not exist. I had my usual confrontation with modern electronic torture devices. The breakfast blew up and covered the inside of the oven with sticky oatmeal.

I was able to scrape enough together to make a bowl. Then I cut up fresh strawberries on top and for added appeal I gave it a squirt of whipped cream. It looked great. He ate a few of the strawberries. The way this kid eats he should have pellagra or scurvy or both, but he is big for three, sturdy and strong as an ox (a small ox).

The language barrier seems to be slipping away. I can understand more and more. Before it became a matter of life or death I guess I listened with half an ear. His conversation and thought consisted of "No" and "I want." There is some informational stuff in there as well. The word "potty" brings me to my feet. "Oh no" really loud and somewhere out of my sight makes me move swiftly. All this jumping up and moving swiftly takes a lot out of me.

My son and daughter-in-law were on a river-rafting trip with friends. Big Foot and Mrs. Foot were river rafting guides in another life and invited them to go along. Working hard and raising small children is difficult and exhausting work (tell me about it) and they needed a break. So Poppy volunteered to help. It has been fun and rewarding, however, I have the cooler packed, a pile of books, and my spiral note pad and the minute they get home I am gone to the cabin in the pines for R & R. I may not come back till the snow flies.

Love to all.

RSVP — Aikens' columns good for the soul

Keep Jim Aikens coming! He started the day out right for us with a good laugh.

In a day where most news is gloom and doom, it's great to read something in a lighter vein.

Maybe it's because we also are a couple of the elderly boys and girls.

—*J.D. & Gloria Jones, St. George*

<u>**September 15, 2006**</u>

The upcoming election is the time to declare your position

Well, the mid-term election politics are beginning to bubble to the surface. It is time to declare your position. It is well known that I am to the left of Mother Theresa and although I will try to be fair and balanced, I probably won't.

One might suppose (I have English relatives, and as I like to put on airs, I say, "one" as opposed to the American "you") that I could care less as I am an old retired person living in the lap of luxury. I should no longer give a hoot about congressional politics or their effect upon the great unwashed — but I do.

The president whose ratings are in the toilet and deservingly so, has begun a new series of hustles speaking to the NAACP, whom he never gave a minute's notice before, and championing the "Voters Rights Act." Well, big deal. The "Voters Rights Act" is something that should be as usual as breathing. Does he expect extra points for allowing us to breath?

There was a recent jeremiad on the Editorial page accusing Bill Clinton of every crime, excess and depravity in the world since the destruction of Sodom and Gomorrah. When Old Bill was President nobody was "shocked and awed to death" and there was a healthy surplus in the national treasury to name a couple of things. Old Bill did a naughty thing. Let me be very clear here. I am seriously opposed to adultery and lying. These are heavy charges. I do not do adultery and I have the same problem with lying that everyone else has, but — these are personal disasters, mostly none of our business. To suppose that while President Clinton screwed up his personal life and that therefore he screwed up the country is a real leap. It sounds a little like rounding up a scapegoat for all that has gone on before. A lot like the old "Red Menace" used to cover all the sins of omission and commission and anything else nobody wanted to take responsibility for.

The new guy, Bush, had all kinds of erroneous information i.e. weapons of mass destruction "not," Collaborators with Ben Laden "not," Saddam Hussein (the excuse that they finally landed on,) "yes." He was a bad guy. There are bad guys all over, but not many who will sit on a huge oil reserve. "Get rid of him and the Iraqi people would throw flowers at your feet." It didn't happen did it? Bad intelligence was the culprit — actually, intelligence and the Bush administration in the same paragraph is an oxymoron (look it up).

Sometimes one must stand up and be counted. As an old guy on shaky legs living in the desert, I have no exhaustive, well worked out plan except "stop killing people." It is expensive (as we know) and fruitless (as we know). The perverted wisdom of "taking out" Iran and Syria and North Korea would have been a laugh at any other time in American History but now, it seems, a blood bath of that magnitude appears to be a considered objective by some elements.

Attila the Hun and some of those guys killed everybody that strayed in their path and it worked o.k. for them. But then was then and now is now. If the world has not ramped up a little in compassion and reason and enlightened self interest then we have not come a long way baby.

Listen to one side, listen to the other side and make up your mind. That's the American way. (My side is best, but I don't want to influence anybody.)

Love to all.

October 13, 2006

Mainstream of information offers few alternatives

After a long spell of untrammeled merriment traveling around, hanging out, associating with my betters I realize that I must come down from all this frivolity and silliness and attend to my real mission in life, which is whining and complaining. I hardly know where to start.

Let us begin with the "Pointy-headed Eastern Liberal Media Establishment." (This is all one word.) We are inveighed to ignore NBC, CBS, ABC, CNN, BBC and everyone else, except for "Fox News" wasn't on the list so it must be ok. From whence does our information come? The dope fiend Rush Limbaugh? The lizard with the comb over O'Reilley? The charm school drop out Ann Coulter? Winners one and all.

As is generally the case, the advocates of ignoring the mainstream information do not offer alternatives, other than the afore mentioned. It is implied that the internet is a feast of conservative's true facts. Indeed. My observation is that the internet is crowded with teenagers bent on hooking up, perverts bent on hooking up with teenagers, lavish porn sites bent upon illustrating what hooking up looks like, and bloggers with agendas.

Among political conservatives the bottom line is the only line and newspapers who don't make money do not survive. If conservative papers are a feast of truth, how come nobody buys them? Why don't they sell tons of advertising and make tons of money? Can you say "Lunatic fringe?"

Next!

There are untrammeled and sometimes vicious attacks on the educational system. This is an especial interest of mine. It has been suggested that the children couldn't find Syria on the map. Really? The complainant is a contemporary of mine. I would ask, "Could you find

Tobruk or El Agheila or even Normandy on a map when you were in the fifth grade?"

Maybe, maybe not. More importantly, "Who cares?"

The adult obsession with war is out of the range of 5th graders. Why should they know? There are a lot more subjects of force and moment than who is killing who.

If education has fallen into such disrepair who are the people who have been curing horrible and deadly diseases, have discovered new and distant galaxies, and sent people into space? The "no child left behind" is an excellent start. I am in complete sympathy with children who need extra help. But what of the children who could soar?

In an elegaritian society everybody is the same — well they are not. You know it and I know it. What effort is being made to assist the children who do not fall under the category of needy?

Love to all.

RSVP — We do not need another hack writer

In response to Jim Aikens' column of Oct. 13, he uses the same sort of rhetoric used by most of the media with phrases like the, "comb over O'Reilly," buzz words meant to ridicule not enlighten. We have enough partial reporting of news in all forms of media; we do not need another hack comedy writer.

The education of our children is important. We may not have known where Syria or Iraq was when I was in the fifth grade, but we did know all the states and capitals in America. We also knew the three R's. Today, we spend more money and get less education in the basics.

Being politically correct on what to teach our children and in what language sounds nice, but does nothing. This country is falling behind in most of the things we used to excel in — science, math and physics, and chemistry.

Jim, do you really believe the moral fiber of this country is being subverted by the likes of the "evil O'Reilly's" of this world? We need to get rid of the ACLU, not "In God We Trust" and maybe, just maybe, have unbiased reporting from all sides.

—Chuck Vavrek

November 10, 2006

Red light district memories of childhood stir chatter of old

I am going to tell you a story of high and far off times when I was a clean towel boy at the house of ill repute. Do I have your attention?

In the village where I was born there was a red light district. It was called "2 Bit" Street (25th). At one end was the railroad depot. Half the men in town worked there. From the depot for about five blocks on both sides of the street there were bars, pool halls, restaurants and more bars. Above several of these bars were hotels, only they were not hotels. They were cat houses.

I was sixteen years old and had just gotten my driving license. My father was manager of the laundry which provided sheets and towels to these "hotels." Through fortuitous circumstance I was given the job on Saturdays of delivering the linen to these places. Papa told me "Mind your manners, keep your mouth shut, and don't tell your mother." I was so excited that I could hardly breathe.

I bundled up the stairs with these huge packages of linen only to find that most of the places were crummy dumps with a desk in front and a lot of closed doors. One place, however, was a little higher end and had a parlor of sorts with a few tables and couches. Sometimes the "ladies" would be sitting around drinking coffee. After a while they got used to me and asked me to sit down and have coffee with them. "Now's my chance." Well, maybe not. They talked about things like "Too long hours, too little money. No place in this hick town to buy decent clothes. My boyfriend went to get the car fixed and got hosed."

This is the same conversation my mother and her sisters had when they sat around the table and had coffee. All the things that I wanted to know never came up and I was to scared to ask.

One day when I was just outside the door chattering with two of the ladies, a carload of kids from my school cruised by slowly. Driving up and down 2 Bit Street was a popular recreation. As I was starting up the stairs one of the ladies gave me a playful smack on the butt.

Monday morning the school was all a buzz. "Old Ace is in so tight with those ladies that they get physical with him!" I played it to the hilt. With the girls that I wanted to impress, I denied everything vigorously. With the boys I wanted to impress I did a lot of guilty smirking and eye rolling. I dined out on that incident for weeks.

There was another incident that got a lot of publicity. One morning I was having coffee with my lady friends when Ralph, the cop, came up the stairs in uniform. He looked around and came over to me. "How's it going Ace."

"Fine, thank you."

"How come you're not in school?"

"It's Saturday."

"Does your Dad know you're here?"

"Yes, sir." I pointed at the laundry.

"Have a nice day," he said and went down the stairs.

Ralph went home and told his wife. His wife told her mother. Her mother told everyone in four states, one of these being my mother. Mama said nothing to me about it, but the next Saturday I was wiping grease off machinery, sweeping out behind the dryers and shaking farts out of shirt tails. My sojourn in the tents of wickedness was over. Small tatters of my racy reputation lingered for a while and faded away.

Sic Transit Gloria.

Love to all.

Adventures take toll on old and exhausted man

I recently returned from an adventure. I don't like adventure. It is hard and scary. I am old and exhausted. All I want to do is lie in the warm sun with a good book and a toddy and wait to slip into Valhalla.

It all started with a Halloween party. I live in a community in the desert of great beauty and apparent peace. Appearances deceive. This is party central. There are parties going on all the time and with the advent of Lee's Discount liquor in Mesquite the parties have increased in volume and sound.

For Halloween there was a costume party with an old timey rock and roll band. The lead singer was a very pretty girl whose costume was practically nothing. A nun with a five o'clock shadow on the guitar, a scarecrow on bass and other assorted non-humans played like crazy.

As I am genetically disposed to party I was compelled to attend despite my great age and numerous disabilities. We danced the night away big time. My varicose veins were twanging like guitar strings. I didn't win a prize for my costume. I suspect voter fraud. I was a gay Arab vampire. Nobody else thought of that!

In the morning I was unable to rise. At first I thought I had polio. It turned out to be not so, but it took three days to recover. I was barely on my feet when I was hauled off to Whitmore Canyon and hiked down to the Colorado River at the bottom of Grand Canyon. I made it down to the bottom, but was not able to make it back up. My new best friend came back down, got behind me and pushed me up. I love that guy.

Another long convalescence was in the offing. Time was when I could dance the night away, hike to the bottom of Grand Canyon and go to work the next day. No more.

As usual when I want to rest up and dry out I repaired to my families cabin above Zion Canyon. As it is always summer in St. George I forgot that this is not always so in places above 9000 feet. I got to the cabin, unpacked my gear and took a nap. When I awoke it was snowing. I ran out and got all the wood I could find, stacked it in the kitchen and battened down the hatches. I probably should have packed-up and run for it but it was cocktail hour and you know how that goes.

The cabin consists of two rooms and a path. The path wanders through the pines to the outhouse. A very long way. You know about old men and toilets (at least old men know). After several trips through the blizzard I didn't get much sleep. I started the fire in the morning and the place filled with smoke. I had to open the doors to breath. The smoke went out and the cold came in. I was pretty discouraged so I thought, "I'll just go ahead and die."

I lay down on the couch to wait. I went to sleep and when I woke up I wasn't dead (a good thing). So I gathered up my gear and drove slowly and carefully home.

As a present on my last birthday I was given a nice ceramic wall plaque which read, "It may be that your sole purpose in life is simply to serve as a warning to others." Oh boy.

Love to all.

Bad crowd

I have recently fallen in with a bad crowd and haven't had such a good time in years. The type of bad crowd I refer to here is the "bad crowd" your grandmother warned you about when you started Junior High School.

We are all retired guys with way too much time on our hands. We drive around in our pickups, spit out the windows, whistle at the chicks, glower and make rude gestures at other pick-ups that cut us off or are offensive in other ways. We also shout, "What the — Heck — are you looking at?" Although not very loud and with the windows rolled up. (We're silly, not insane.)

We like to hang around in low dives and drink beer. Actually, I should say dive, singular. There is only one low dive between Hurricane and Mesquite. We drink beer, talk loud, and tell really coarse jokes remembered from our first Junior High lives.

We bum cigarettes from these thistly ladies of a certain age who go there. We make sort of improper suggestions to which, if the women said, "Well, ok" we would drop dead from terror, but they are playing the same game we are. Hanging out and having naughty fun, so they don't try to corner us. They even laugh at the fart jokes.

Something I noticed too, as a 70 year old Junior High wannabe, well brought up even against my wishes, the conversations never get nasty, cruel or mean, as sometimes happens to people who drink beer in dark bars during daylight hours.

I can hear the soft voice of my sainted father telling me, "You will show courtesy and respect to women at all times. If I hear otherwise I'll take your face off."

My Daddy never threatened or bribed but what he said he meant and he never gave me a bum steer.

My quasi-adolescent buddies seem to have had much the same kind of upbringing. In our other persona as fathers and grandfathers we lament the fact that the almost holy decree that women should be treated with respect seems to be eroding away due, at least in some part, to the women themselves. (However — that is just a fight that I won't get into right now.)

The Bad Boyz recently went camping at the Grand Canyon. We did all the teenager camping out stuff. We built a huge fire. We drank beer and sang dirty *** songs. Then squirted beer on each other, ran around in our skivvies and had a spirited debate on the **** qualities of boxers vs. tighty-whities. We peed in the Grand Canyon, but we didn't throw in beer bottles. Just like old times except for the fact I had to get out of my sleeping bag and go to the bathroom behind a juniper tree six times. Just like usual.

You can pretend away some things and some things you just can't.

Love to all.

Runaway hits the road, learns about Vegas — and carrots

A long time ago, and I mean long, I was 17 years old and smothered by work, school and parents. The entire world just didn't understand me, so I ran away from home. A friend had a car and the same idea that I did, and away we went.

This was 1950, and the world was different then. There was no freeway, and Highway 91 wandered its torturous way through every hick town in Utah. Gas was only 25 cents a gallon, but the speed limit through the tiny villages was about 20 mph. It took forever to get to St. George.

No one drove across the desert at night. Everyone going to Las Vegas and beyond backed up in St. George and waited for sun down and cooling of the desert. Then they ventured out in small caravans — safety in numbers. Everyone also had a canvas water bag with a cork, which hung in front of the radiator. The water was used for the radiator and to drink.

Frannie and I got to St. George in the early afternoon, so we had to kill time. We went swimming in the Santa Clara River just below the reservation. This spring did double duty as a bath. We had been in the wind for two days in a hot, sweaty car (air-conditioning did not exist). We slept in the car. I remember that, but I can't remember what we ate or where.

So we crossed the desert in company with other pilgrims to Las Vegas. Its reputation for debauchery was already beginning to grow. The Desert Inn and the Sahara were tents of wickedness in the desert. All the gangsters wore tuxedos, and the ladies were in evening gowns. It was very classy.

The two runaways couldn't get past the doorman, so we just peered in at the glittery temptations. We thought that we would get a job, stay there and be debauched and ruined. We could hardly wait.

But it was not to be because we didn't know anything. We didn't know anybody, and we were minors. Nobody was clamoring for our services, so we were forced to move on.

We moved to San Diego. Why? I have no clue. There we found the YMCA. We had been told that they would help poor, wayfaring strangers to find work, and they did. At the YMCA there were men wearing eye shadow and holding their cigarettes with their thumb and index fingers. We had heard of men who did that but had never seen any. It was thrilling.

We went to work for the Rideout Produce Co. delivering vegetables to grocery stores at 4 in the morning. We were paid under the table (not much) and had all the raw carrots we could cut. We slept in the car on the beach. It was no fun. After a while we telegraphed our parents and asked for money to come home. My dad said, "No, I can't bail you out now. You will be ruined for life."

He did, however, send me $5 for a carton of cigarettes. What I wanted for my 17th birthday was permission to smoke in the house. I got it. Were these old times or what?

We worked, ate carrots and saved up enough to drive home. That was it. I was glad I did it, but I sure as heck wouldn't do it again.

Love to all.

I am in charge of my life and not a slave to addiction

Every once in a while I sit down and count my blessings so that I have something positive to report when I say my prayers instead of endless whining and complaining because the listener (you know who) probably gets as sick and tired of listening to that crap as everyone else does.

One day I had a little time left over so I thought that I would list my personal faults.

It was appalling.

The list was as long as the Chinese phone book. That didn't even include faults that I had overlooked and were eagerly pointed out by my alleged friends.

Which bad habits do I love the most? Sometimes you don't like your bad habits any better than anybody else, but sometimes you love them more than life itself. These are the two that I chose. Part A, stop watching T.V. I love T.V. All the crime shows and action thrillers and especially the five o'clock news. It was easier than I thought it might be because my wife doesn't watch those kinds of shows. It is like quitting smoking when someone in the house is sucking fire and blowing smoke all over. Been there.

Done that. Barbara doesn't smoke or watch violent T.V., a perfect spouse for me — in other ways as well.

Part B was the really hard one. I quit drinking beer. Approximately one-third of all my body fluids are Pacifica or Negro Modelo so it was a real wrench to my systems. I had to drink water (gag) and you know how much fun that is. Also there was a problem with my drinking buddies. They were not supportive in this endeavor.

These guys are really Butch. You pull the cap off with your teeth and drink out of the bottle. If done otherwise, you are a sissy. They would mutter darkly among themselves about mental evaluation.

Concerning this matter during the time that I was drying out, we had a party at my house catered by Lee's Discount Liquor. There were lots of beverages but ____. The first guys to arrive said, "I'll have a beer."

"Ok," I said and asked the hostess where the cooler with the beer was.

"Beer?" she said. "I thought you didn't drink beer anymore. There is no beer."

My life flashed before my eyes. These guys were going to kill me. It was too late to run to the store and I was cornered. There was a lot of huffing and puffing and working themselves into the necessary rage so they could lynch me. My reprieve was engendered by a large Polish person who lives next door to me and keeps a case of Coors Light in his refrigerator at all times. I am eternally grateful. He saved my life but more importantly, my reputation. I endured the depravation of television, the taunts of my friends and dreams of dying of dehydration in the desert, but I made it.

My objective was to prove to myself that I am in charge of my life and not a slave to my addiction. I think that I did that. Now I feel confident and gratified so I may return — to the dark side.

Bottoms up.

RSVP — To the editor:

I need to vehemently deny the allegation in the Writers Group article about addiction, that I always keep a case of Coors Light in my refrigerator. It is actually regular Coors.

—Anonymous

February 21, 2007

Father's influence in boyhood carries over into adulthood

This is a moral tale, which may be read to children if you leave out the naughty words. One day my father came home from work. I was probably lying around reading a book, which is what I mostly did. He said, "Sister Leavitt has been sick and her garden looks like the Wrath of God (whenever something looked really awful this is the way my father described it). Would you like to go over there after school and clean it up?"

'Tis a wise child who knows his own father, and I knew mine. "Would you like?" could be interpreted as "You will go."

"Sure Pop," tumbled from my lips, the only acceptable answer.

Any whining, shuffling or excuses would be swiftly dealt with. Of course I didn't want to go pull Sister Leavitt's weeds. What thirteen-year-old in his right mind would? But obedience was important to my father and in my own best interests. The next day after school I knocked on Mrs. Leavitt's door. "I am here to pull the weeds in your garden."

I did a good job because back in my mind was the memory of the woodpile. A long time ago (long time in kid time) there was a big pile of fire wood logs and kindling just thrown against the cowshed. I was directed to sort and stack it up neatly. I didn't want to and was rebellious, so I just stacked a single layer over the jumble and let it go at that. It looked pretty good, but only a fool would think that they could get away with that. This fool didn't. After surveying the work my father said, "I am amazed that you would enjoy that heavy, slivery job so much that you would want to do it twice."

No further discussion was necessary. I did it again, right this time. It took three days. There were no time limits on my father's projects.

All the time that I was working on these service projects my younger brother did nada — which fueled resentment (hidden for my own safety). It didn't register with me that he was only six years old. I was working and he was not. But time marches on and we had moved off the farm to the city. In the city were no chores. Make your bed and help with the dishes once in a while. But something else was going on that I didn't see. My little brother was getting the joy of labor and obedience training right under my nose. I had done my time in the barrel and had been set free.

I wrote to my brother a while back and referred to this phenomenon. His response was, "I often wondered how you got a complete pass on any and all household chores. On the subject, I learned the value of hard work and perseverance. You missed these instructive occupations. Resultantly, I am rich and famous and you are, as we know, a total loser. How are Barbara and the kids?"

He didn't realize that I had undergone the same training. He was too young to notice.

The moral of the story is get a father like we had. His gentle insistence that we be hard working and responsible, his sharp eye and careful guidance assured that we would be confident, responsible and happy men. One rich and famous and one a total loser, but that is a different story.

Love to all.

March 21, 2007

Geriatric tips go with my departure from Writers Group

It has recently come to my attention that I have been declared redundant and cast out upon the dust heap of history. To be possibly more precise, I have been canned and am myself, history.

As a charter member of the Writer's Group I have had a long and interesting tenure. Many of the people who began with us have dropped out and new people have come in, but a few old warhorses, like myself have endured.

With my departure goes the popular "Geriatric fashion tips." I feel I have had some success. I believe we have seen the end of those nasty white plastic shoes with the Velcro straps. One hold out exists. (You know who you are and please know that I'm not through with you.)

It is my hope that you old birds have been educated enough so that when you need a new jacket it will not be one of those blue, vinyl, Wal-Mart numbers. And when you make some wardrobe adjustments remember you have enough golf shirts, for God's sake no more. Toe rings never caught on. I am really surprised.

Depending on who is recruited for the new guys in the group, you may be seeing the last of the bleeding heart liberals. We are a rare breed in Utah. We are out there like the elusive puma, seldom seen except for a few tracks. Seldom heard except for an angry scream once in a while, but there, never the less. Quiet, watchful, dangerous.

What was the conservative reaction seeing Nancy Pelosi sitting next to V.P. Cheney on the dais? I'll bet your jollies were chilled by the sight. Wait till president Clinton comes in waving and smiling to deliver her State of the Union address. "Oh Boy."

The thing that I will miss the most is the attractive ladies who stop me in the aisle at the store or on the hiking trail, or at the concerts. "I know you! You are a writer for the Spectrum."

"Yes," I say.

"I love your column. I read it all the time."

"Thank you," I say blushing modestly. That's about it. Then we go on about our business. No man ever gets so old that he doesn't appreciate the attention and compliments of beautiful women. Sic Transit Gloria.

If I have ever given offence by any word or deed or inadvertently caused hurt feelings or embarrassed anyone, please take this opportunity to get over it. I certainly never intended to make anyone unhappy. I'm a good guy. This is my last chance to make it right. I'm sorry.

I want to thank my Editors, Todd, Jennifer and Julie. They have let me say anything I felt like saying. (I did try a time or two to sneak in bad words or double entendre but they caught me every time.)

It is a very liberating feeling to be able to say anything you want to say in the land of the free. Please remember that and defend the right of free speech. I have had my thoughts published but yours are just as important and don't let anyone stifle you or tell you that your opinions don't count — bull shit.

Well I have had a great old time, made some friends, and had some laughs. Thank you.

Love to all.

Goodbye.

Jim Aikens, go in peace my old friend

Just a quick note to say, "adios," to Jim Aikens whose writings have inspired me for several months now. They have been a refreshing departure from all the heavy stuff usually found in that group.

Jim, I want you to know that should you beat me to "The Great Reward," I will be on the shore, hat in hand, as you sail away on that Viking ship. And I wish to add here, that although you obviously have a shaky grip on the game of mumblety-peg, it is still nice to have someone mention that pursuit. (I was the Plat A Champ during the 30s in Springville.) I know all the rules if you need an update.

So, go in peace old friend. I saw you once driving home in that little red car of yours. I waved, but you ignored me. I forgave you for that indiscretion because I know what it's like to be an antique. I will miss your prattle. God speed.

—Lee Robertson, Washington City

I'm proud to wear Velcro-strap shoes

My friend and neighbor and Writers Group correspondent Jim Aikens, in his final article, left some of his readers wondering: Who is the one person remaining who continues to wear shoes with Velcro straps? Well, let me solve the mystery — it is I. What Mr. Aikens could never quite comprehend is that in my geriatric years, I have totally forgotten how to tie shoe laces. Therefore, I will continue to wear those comfortable and incredibly attractive Velcro strapped shoes that I purchase locally.

I also could solve another mystery as I know which founding member of the Writers Group wears toe rings. I won't disclose his name at this time, but he lives near me and has a white beard and mustache. And, I do believe Mr. Aikens, that when the next President Clinton waves to us at the State of the Union address we will see the middle digit of a hand — or maybe even of both hands.

Love to Jim.

—John Curry, Ivins

Reconsider Jim Aikens' retirement

Awakening this morning to the beautiful sunlit vistas of St. George was suddenly changed on reading of The Spectrum's Writers Group columnist Jim Aikens' retirement. No longer can I look forward to his wit and use of seldom employed language, which drove me to the dictionary and thesaurus for interpretation.

His stories of misspent youth and hardships made me appreciate his rise to the stature that he has attained with senility.

Forget his personal peccadilloes, such as toe rings and social hiccups, which were performed under the guise of humor.

Please reconsider his persona non gratis status and return his wit and remembrances of the past that only a true Curmudgeon can harbor.

—Norman Shore, Ivins

Publish Jim Aikens' column on Saturday

I would like to join those wishing for the return of Jim Aikens' column. If he can be persuaded to re-enlist it would be preferable if his column could be run on Saturday. Then you could have two flaming liberals on the same page.

The contrast in intellect, common sense and humor would be enlightening!

—*Fred Osborn, Ivins*

Substitute Aikens column for Barry's

I, too, must say a fond farewell to Jim Aikens of the Writers Group. Even though he and I are of a different generation, religion, political persuasion and gender, he never failed to bring a smile to my face or even the occasional chuckle!

Maybe The Spectrum could substitute a Jim Aikens article for a Dave Barry article once a month. Just a thought!

You will be missed, Mr. Aikens. Love to you, sir.

—*LuAnn Dotson, Hurricane*

Add my name to list of Jim Aikens' fans

I want to add my name to the growing list of Aikens' fans that would like to see more from Jim. From Jim's fashion tips, toe ring and Viking funerals, he always had something interesting to share. Even though I am not a liberal, he expressed his points of view without name calling or idle threats.

Jim, my friend, keep the upbeat, common-sense advice flowing.

—*Scott Lewis, Ivins*

OTHER WRITINGS

Kayenta

In the place where I live a lot of fun things go on. It is a little bit restrictive to live here, there are a lot of rules and regulations.

In order to buy property here you must sign an affidavit which states that you have never ever heard of the W.P.A., and you have to be good looking. I had some trouble with that but my wife is so good looking that she gave me some of her points.

It is a conforming community. All the houses are square and brown, referred to as "mud huts" by the lower orders. We are deprived of the joy of rural Utah yard art. Rusty old car carcasses tastefully arranged in the sage brush are off limits. Also we may not have a clothes line to hang out clean underwear (remember Doonesbury?).

The required zero scape attracts many desirable as well as undesirable creatures. We have multiples of rabbits (bunny and Jack), lizards, raptors, quail, coyotes, road runners and an occasional tortoise. There are also Sphernothines, rattlesnakes, scorpions, tarantulas and Mormons (a few).

The only place that you will see more white faces is at a Ku Klux Klan rally. We do have cultural diversity of a sort here. First there are the people who work for a living, every day. How ghastly! Not too many. We don't want them to get organized and make trouble. They are young and vigorous and pay huge social security taxes so that the rest of us may live in the style we deserve. They are pretty good about it. They grumble a little from time to time, but I don't think they are planning an uprising anytime soon. There is this one guy that I kind of worry about, but I'm keeping a close eye on him.

We also have hidden celebrities, a retired rock star with a beautiful house and a trophy wife who dabbles in radical politics.

Last of all we have famous writers (besides me) and artists. Near the main office lies a beautiful art gallery queened over by elegant ladies who sell elegant art objects to well heeled (and padded) clientele from the fat farm.

I hope that my friends and neighbors don't get mad at me, but if they do form a lynch mob I am assured that I won't be hung with a nasty old Home Depot rope. I will be hung with a nice rope from Abercrombie and Fitch.

A.D.D.

I feel that it is time that the controversy concerning Ritalin in the classroom be put to rest. I know all about it. Listen to me and you can't go wrong.

I was in the first grade for 20 years and I figure about 500 tiny totlets passed beneath my benign gaze in that time, and there were all kinds too. The ones we will be discussing are A.D.D. children. Let me first say that although A.D.D. children and Dyslexic (another term I hate) children do exist on the earth, in my personal experience I have met maybe four or five of the former and none of the latter.

Also in the Halls of Legend are the teachers who are too lazy or incompetent to deal with rowdy little boys so they insist on having them drugged so their life will be easier. I don't know any of them either.

Let me tell you about a couple of children who really needed the medicine. Daffodil (not her real name) was one of the sweetest little girls you could ever know, but her appearance didn't give a clue. Her hair stuck up every which way. Sometimes she would take off her dress and put it on backward and put her shoes on the wrong feet. Once I inquired why she did this. She looked down her nose and in haughty tones replied, "Why do you ask?"

—Why indeed.

But since my job was to teach reading and writing and addition and subtraction to 18 and not to give fashion tips, I just let it go. Things came to a head the day of the volcano. The class was doing a project (I don't remember what) that had to do with glue. Gluing is an exciting and dangerous occupation with first graders and sharp-eyed vigilance is required.

On big project days I would have a mother come in and help. On this day it was the mother of the Chief Blue bird. (In the class we had three groups, the Buzzards, the Turkeys, and the Bluebirds.) Well the Bluebird and Daffodil, the least Buzzard, were seated together with the mother Bluebird hovering near.

Before anyone could react Daffodil got the very large glue bottle and squeezed it hard. As about half a gallon of glue was flying through the air she said, "This is the way volcanoes work."

Everyone within ten yards had glue in their hair. It was on the ceiling, on the floor and on everyone's project. There were howls of dismay and fury and very bad words (This was an inner city school.) I was no help what-so-ever because I had to run outside into the hall. This was a reflex I learned early in my career. If I laughed when some terrible disaster occurred then it would happen again and again with all kinds of copy cats and variations. As soon as I could control myself I went back in to help, but by trying not to laugh my snorts and strangled wheezes alarmed the mother even more.

The shake down was that we had to get Daffodils parents in and have a talk. They were good parents and they understood the problem. So Daffodil got the medicine.

She was still the same wild child, but she was able to sit still and concentrate for ten minutes at a time, about average for first grade. She was very smart and she blossomed. She moved out of the Buzzards into the Bluebirds, but she never really fit in. She thought they were a bunch of snots. She hung with her old Buzzard buddies.

Daffodil needed the medicine. She benefited from it. Without the medicine she could not have learned to read or write or do sums to 18. Not her fault, not my fault, just one of those things.

Another case and not so amusing was Bobby. Bobby was no wild child but he was wound up tight and closed in upon himself. Every once in a while he would explode usually on the playground or in the boys bathroom. He would begin screaming and swearing and swinging on anybody, even the big third graders.

I would have to catch him and hold him tight and croon into his ear until he could decompress and get a grip. Bobby had a sad history. His biological parents were devil worshipers and whatever they had exposed their child to had scared him. His adoptive parents were very young and kind and had been told that medicine was not good and that it was only used to make zombies out of difficult children.

I had to talk like a Dutch uncle to these parents, and talk and talk and talk. The advantage that I had was that I was old enough to be their father, and they had been brought up to be respectful to their elders.

At last they agreed to try the medicine. Well, it worked. Bobby was a bright boy. These children often are, and with his demons suppressed, he could concentrate on things like long a, short a and syllables and all that stuff. He very soon caught up with the other children and turned out to be quite an artist. He still was no social butterfly, but he did have a couple of friends to play with and although he was still a little scary, he was learning and having some success and even having a little fun. Something he knew nothing about before. This kid was six years old. The medicine saved his life.

Then there was Amber J. This was my first clue. School hadn't even been underway for a week when one morning Amber staggered in dragging her book bag and collapsed in her desk. She fell across the desk and in a voice that you would swear was Bette Davis she declared, "This is the worst day of my life," remember, Amber is five years old (six in two weeks).

What could I do? I knelt beside her chair and patter her hand. (There is a rule that teachers may only touch children on their hands and maybe put a hand on their shoulder. HA! I'll tell you about that sometime.)

It seems that her father had yelled at her because he was going to take her to school but she was too slow. (Boy did he have that right.) Her sister had ratted on her because she hadn't made her bed, and she had the wrong shoes that didn't match her outfit. Her dad had just grabbed any old shoes because he was mad.

Does this sound like six years old in two weeks? — No.

Amber's father had asked that she be placed in my class because she related better to men. Not really. He confided in me later that he thought that I would be more patient and understanding of Amber's peculiar ways.

Amber was a smart little girl with flashes of real creative genius, but she also had her own agenda. Most days she was far away in la la land while the rest of us were learning boring stuff like letter sounds. She would morph in out of our world a few times each day.

The two kindergarten teachers and the special ed teacher all recommended that Amber take the medicine, but I wanted to watch for a while.

One day while the rest of us were doing the lesson on the board and sound cards and whatever more, Amber was drawing (in her Spelling tablet) pictures of what appeared to be a dissected lizard with little arrows showing things like hart. This was significant because she could also spell leg, fut, and toz. Nobody else in the class could spell anything at this point. When we went back to reading circle Amber zipped through the text like she had listened to every word I said.

Amber levitated around through the first grade about a foot off the ground, but she was one of the best readers and comprehenders that I had that year. Math she didn't do so hot, but anything creative she was first chair.

We did a little play about "Rabbits and the long thing." She swooned through the part of the Rabbit with panache that Meryl Streep would die for.

Amber didn't take the medicine. Her little brain could encompass two things at once, what she was doing and what I was doing. This is an important skill and some people are never able to do it. Now, Amber was annoying and aggravating sometimes, and her shenanigans were time consuming, but I'm not running a charm school here and Amber was learning what I was teaching which is the bottom line. Besides, she was such a sweet child and so fun and full of surprise. I loved her dearly. I also consulted with one of the second grade teachers down the hall who had pretty much the same philosophy as I had, and warned her of Amber's imminent appearance. After about a week in second grade Mrs. T came to my room to ask, "Are you sure?"

"Yes," I said, "Just give her a little time."

She did and it worked out. Amber is gone now. She is all grown up and graduated. she passed through our school in her own special way and everyone loved her.

Sometimes it looks like they need the medicine but they really don't. A case by case careful study and evaluation is necessary with a lot of leeway given to the student. Sometimes it makes the teacher's work harder, but so what. if you want it easy go work at Walmart.

Another success story was Boomer. Boom came into the room like a rocket. He circled a couple of times, checked all the tables, the book cases and everything else and was whirling like a small tornado when his harassed mother came into the room towing two more children, a toddler and a carrying boy. I guess that you have noticed that Boom is an inquisitive child. We both laughed.

Boomer had been spotted in pre-school but the doctor didn't want to give medicine to so young a child. They had recently moved into the school district so I couldn't consult with his kindergarten teacher, but I was assured by his mother that she was still alive, but just barely. A mother with a child like Boom really needs a sense of humor. There was not a long observation because one look could tell you.

Liberals Conservatives

For a substantial donation at the Clinton white house you got a cup of coffee and a sleep-over in the Lincoln bedroom.

In the Bush white house you get a substantial tax break and a nickname.

Except in the case of Enron where the President forgets your name altogether.

Or if you are an oil man you get a tax break and the phone number to Dick Cheney's alternate universe.

What liberals do on TV:

A wispy bearded man so thin and white that he looks to be made out of pipe cleaners, and who has been outdoors twice in his life. This is the second time.

He is on the Jericho Sand dunes pointing to a scraggly weed and explaining that this is the endangered "redundant milk vetch" and he wants the dunes shut down to any human presence for at least twenty years.

Off to the edge of the frame are several large, sweaty, pissed-off looking men on ATV's waiting for him to tippy toe out of camera range so that they may explain to him how it REALLY is.

Cut to the Conservatives:

Outside the Navajo Power plant at Lake Powell a nice looking young man with a good haircut and a Versace shirt open at the collar looking into the camera and earnestly explaining why you can't see Navajo Mountain.

"So there is a little smoke, what's the big deal? If you've seen one mountain, you've seen them all."

Cut to the liberals at Klamath Dam Reservoir:

A greasy haired woman with brown teeth and birkenstocks defends cutting off the water to the farmers in Klamath Valley.

"We must protect the Extranious spotted suckerfish."

"What about the farmers?" she is asked. "Without water they will be forced to leave their homes.

"What's the big deal?" she asks, "If you've seen one farmer you've seen them all."

It is really difficult to know which side to come down on. At present I have my nose under the liberal tent. I would like to suggest that we get more attractive spokespersons. Wan, spaced out looking faux hippies with metal piercings do not engender either sympathy or confidence.

Even if the conservative front persons do look anal retentive it is still less off-putting than a ring in the nose.

Politics are so difficult these days. Where is Attila the Hun when you need him? He would cut through this extraneous nonsense right away.

With a sharp ax.

Running for office

Since my Political affiliation has been reported in the newspapers, people have been sidling up to me in public places and talking out of the corner of their mouth.

"When are we going to get together and throw off the cruel yoke of oppression?"

There are more of these people than you might suppose. Does your neighbor get the Bulletin from the John Birch Society? It could be a beard. There are many opportunities to drag red herrings across the trail.

A man at my church told me that he would pay the $15.00 filing fee at the city hall if I would run for the next available political office because "everybody knows everything about you." That gave me a jolt. If I thought that everybody knew everything about me, I'd be on the next bus out of town.

I told him that it was very generous of him but that I am constrained from running for political office by my Editor at the newspaper. This is the only restriction upon the writers group, as you have found out.

I really can't quit because I am the voice crying in the wilderness exposing corruption and greed. I am the voice of the oppressed, depressed, suppressed and bewildered. Without my wise council, civilization as we know it would disappear. Modesty has never been a problem with me.

I aspire to be humble, but I can't figure out what that means.

Anti Immigration

Letter to the editor:

It was bought to our attention on Thursday that the anti-immigration forces are still at work.

They certainly know, as do we all, the new immigration law will feature mostly amnesty with maybe a small fine and admonition that the new citizens should learn English. The difference between "legal" and "illegal" is the dash of a pen, which is easy. Are these people going to say, "Well, we took our stand and we fought the good fight and we lost. We will shake hands, let bygones by bygones and live in peace and harmony."

I suggest that this is the most sensible attitude to take. If you do not like the new law and make a big stink about it you will be setting yourselves up for the new citizens to say, "What part of "legal" don't you understand?" and they will say it with a Spanish accent and you will hate that.

Changing the law requires pencil and paper, changing an attitude from pious selfishness and righteous anger to, at the least, compliance and respect, won't be so easy. People who nourish the feelings of injustice and paranoia will discover that it can burn small holes in your stomach lining and give you big headaches. Don't do it.

Election
illegals vent

When I discovered that the Citizens Council on Illegal Immigration, the Defend Dixie Pac and the Republicans had endorsed the candidates Nickle, Baca and Swan, I knew that it was the kiss of Death for the fear and loathing party and I was delighted.

The candidates came out after the election to whine and complain that "the rich kids bought their way in." It never dawned on them for a minute that civilized people do not buy in to hatred, fear, unkindness and cruelty.

The political platform is as follows: Don't allow people a place to work, a place to live or a place to get medical attention if they are sick. Then they will go back to where they came from and (hopefully) starve to death and no longer be a problem.

Why would decent people support this?

Let me ask you. Would you quit your job, take your children out of school and go back to a place where there is no future, no hope, no life? All because a bunch of rednecks and bigots were rude to you? I sure as hell wouldn't. And they won't either. Get over it.

April 13, 2008

Utah's education system is fine

Letter to the editor:

The writer who declares "we are insane to accept mediocrity in public education" should reword that to say "we are insane to refuse school vouchers," which is really his point. All the touchy feely nonsense referred to is a loser's excuse.

Parents (me) and teachers (also me) who have been in the system or paid real attention voted it down overwhelmingly for good reason. The writer states, "In Utah we spend the least nationally and are consistently ranked among the top 25 states, which is a credit to our parents and teachers" (who voted down the vouchers).

He could have stopped right there but went on to say that Washington, D.C., spends $14,190 per student and is in the toilet. Ditto New York. So? We don't live in Washington, D.C., or New York. We live here. The teachers and students skimp along on a low budget, work hard and do OK. Utah's system is not perfect, but we do pretty well.

Why try to fix something that is not broken? Does Washington, D.C., or New York have a voucher program? Probably.

Feng Shui

The room where I mostly exist is so not fung shui that it looks deliberate. Under the bed is a lot of crap, boxes, pictures, frames, large pieces of cardboard and lint balls as big as cantaloupes.

There are two windows, one obscured from the outside by a huge grey bush, alleged to be ornamental. The other obscured from the inside by a huge potted plant. The patio door slides open. The bathroom door swings out. The place is a death trap. It's a wonder that I don't have leprosy or dementia praecox (what the hell is dementia praecox?) It is a mental disease which has fallen out of fore. It is really un-P.C. to be demented nowadays so it is probably erratic nerve syndrome or some silliness.

I brought a thermometer to the cabin this time, a nice one that I got at Home Depot and I nailed it on the back of the cabin. I have been coming to this cabin for 40 years and there has been no thermometer. There was no need for one. For most of my life I took no interest in the temperature. It was either hot or cold, that was all I needed to know. Now it is important to me to know if it is 72 degrees or 46 degrees or whatever. Why? I have not the faintest idea.

My thinking has always been slightly off center for all my life, but not so off center as to cause problems, well not too many.

Adventures in getting a passport

Have you ever rented a Villa in Tuscany, bought your ticket on the big bird, bought some new (modest) shorts and some real shoes (why? You tell me.) then, when you get to San Francisco and the plane leaves tomorrow, then you take a look at your passport and behold, it has expired?

After a sleepless night, I got up very early to catch the car-pool into town (I'll tell you about this sometime. You won't believe it.) I stood in line at the passport place with numerous other losers and we tell each other wretched tales of misery and woe, missed connections and bureaucratic fu---ups.

Light then appears at the end of the tunnel. "Come back at 3:30 and pick up your passport." Thank you Jesus.

But it is now only 9:00.

The tale now segues into an ill wind that blows somebody a lot of good — me. A whole day of roaming the streets of San Francisco waiting for 3:30.

What I saw: A homeless person with yard art. A large urn and plastic gnome. Must have weighed a ton.

At the end of a long pier, (I was at the ferry building, known locally as the Clock Tower.) There were six Asian men, tiny ones, and between them there were eighteen fishing poles hanging in the water. One guy caught a fish. He whacked it on the head and chucked it in a big cooler.

Also there was an alarming warning posted. It was oddly worded. "Pregnant women should eat only one fish a week if caught in this bay! Two at the most." It then listed all the reasons why not's beginning with mercury and continuing with a whole bunch of toxic substances. I'd skip that first fish if I were you, mother to be.

Across the embarcadero from the ferry building is a large plaza with a huge and interesting fountain and a stage. On the stage was a children's choir from the Baptist Church singing somewhat religious songs for the lunch crowd with a lot of enthusiasm but not much skill. But on a beautiful sunny day, and with all your sins recently taken away they sounded great. (Thank you Jesus.)

Choosing a restaurant for lunch in San Francisco is a daunting task. Everything looks so great. I finally chose the "Hog Island Oyster Bar." Seafood, right. 12 oysters Rockefeller and Organic Wheat Beer (everything in S.F. is organic.) I'm also thinking that low-carb diets don't fly in San Fran. The bread is to die for — Acme, Boudin and who-ever-else. The oysters weren't as garlicky as I like them but, sitting on the pier, the Bay Bridge over my right shoulder, some sort of monument to dead people across the bay, and bright sunshine and really healthy beer, I'm in (hog) heaven.

Out the back door of the ferry building in a big parking lot is a statue of Mohandas K. Gandhi, along with his better-known mantra, "My life is my message." Very appropriate for San Francisco.

Coming out of the ferry building after lunch on the outdoor plaza was a bagpiper in full regalia playing for whatever reason. San Fran is so much fun.

Notice. Everyone in this city wears long pants, men and women. I watched carefully. The only adult made in S.F. in shorts was moi. Not everyone wears black, but just about. No fatties, carbs not withstanding.

I am hesitant to point out that people, other than white Anglo Saxon Protestant exist upon the earth. Living in St. George you would never know it. There were people of shapes and colors that I have never seen before. I can't say that they are peculiar to San Francisco or just that I am a rube from Utah who doesn't know much. In the huge loser line at the passport office there were two white guys, a dazed looking twenty-ish guy and me. At the Hog Island, there were more whites, but they were tourists.

Another un-St. George-like thing, all the black women have their hair done in cornrows in very exotic configurations. The black men mostly have shaved heads. (Lotta white guys too.) Some people look great with shaved heads, but more do not. They look microcyliphic. Look in the mirror guys.

At 2:30 I wended my way back to the passport place. This place has metal detectors, armed guards and dogs. I told the guard that I would like to wait in the lobby until 3:30—No Dice.

I can come in at 3:15 and not one second earlier. I used my time wisely. If there are a plethora of fine restaurants in this city, there are an equal number of nice bars. I thought I would seek out the coolest looking one for the cocktail hour and success celebration. That would mean the cocktail hour was moved up about three hours, but I can handle it.

The only caveat here is that in order to get home I have to find the B.A.R.T. station and aim myself in the right direction, not something I am good at, even when unimpaired.

As luck would have it, after cocktail hour at the Hyatt, where the bar revolves like a merry-go-round only much slower (thankfully) I caught the correct B.A.R.T. train. Except, I went past my station and had to double back. (Hey, only being lost once in a whole day that is a record for me.)

Growing old gracefully

I would like to take this opportunity to file a grievance. (This is union talk; I used to be a union goon in another life. In order to complain about conditions, harassment or some other B.S. it was necessary to file an official grievance.)

I wish to grow old with grace and dignity. This is being denied me! I have been trying to grow old for some time now. I had always assumed that 65 years was old age. It proved not to be true. Every Tom, Dick, and Harry was 65. So I set my goals at 70. Well, everybody that was 65 was now 70. Some were a little dilapidated but still hanging on. So I aimed at 75.

At first it looked pretty good, I had become hoary with years and ponderous with dignity (well sort of). This is where I ran into a snag. Nobody seemed to be in sympathy with my goal. I desired to lay on the chaise on the patio in the warm sun and read my book. Then, when it got dark, go inside and watch unsuitable T.V. and go to bed at 10:00.

I could not imagine a program more benign and less offensive to anyone, mostly because it affected only me, but objections began to pour down like rain. A large and noisy bandwagon formed and a boisterous crowd jumped aboard.

"Poppy you must exercise and eat proper food and do crossword puzzles."

I don't want to exercise; I am fat and arthritic and exercise hurts. I was given a gym pass and I went a few times, most of the patrons were scrawny pathetic old farts who appeared not to enjoy it any more than I did and didn't seem to improve much over time. The only ones who seemed to enjoy it and make any progress were these huge inflated looking guys with really cool tattoos. I quit going.

"Well maybe you could walk briskly through the desert?"

I don't want to walk briskly through the desert.

"You must eat correctly."

Eating correctly consists mostly of large bowls of grass, leaves and twigs and sliced tomatoes. Ugh. I hate sliced tomatoes. What's wrong with a peanut butter and cheese sandwich?

I have always been a good citizen, innocuous and compliant. I did my duty. I have a plaque, which states that I did civically responsible stuff. I have another plaque, which states that I am first loser as teacher of the year. I paid my taxes and got regular haircuts.

Now I am 75 years old. My house is paid for. My children are raised and educated and doing fine, thank you, and I have some old age pensions that cover expenses. I am a problem to no one, why won't they leave me alone?

"Because Daddy, we want our children to have the joy of knowing you and the benefit of your hard-earned wisdom."

Applesauce. When I complain that they are laying a guilt trip on me, they reply, "Damn right, what goes around, comes around."

By this they refer to the fact that I relied on guilt trips as one very effective weapon in the arsenal of child rearing practices. It worked for me, but it won't work for them because…well, I hope it won't work for them. I don't plan to die or anything that serious. I just want to disintegrate at my own pace.

Eating leaves and twigs and sliced tomatoes (ugh) and walking briskly through the desert will only delay the inevitable and annoy me greatly.

I have pointed out to those concerned that my friends have planned a fun and exciting funeral for me, which they can look forward to. They seem not to be impressed.

I am in a dilemma. I don't want to piss everybody off but I want to do what *I* want to do. Maybe I make too much of this. I am going to do whatever I wish and always have done so why should anyone be surprised that I'm still doing it?

I hear whispers about the rest home and that chills my jollies.

I have lived a long time on the Aikens diet of salt, sugar, chocolate, and grease. Leave me alone.

Terminal condition

To Whom It May Concern:

I am suffering from a terminal condition. I am not alone. There are many, many others. Some view it with alarm, some with equanimity, some just ignore it. I am watching and taking notes. It is something that is only going to happen once and I have always been interested in how things work, not things like machinery, toilets, rocket booster engines or the internet (especially not the internet), I'm talking about the human condition.

I am an old man. I have grown old with grace and dignity, or not, depending on who you ask. I think so. There are others who do not share this opinion, lots of others. Which is neither here nor there. I have done pretty much as I please since my father decided that I was too old to be taken to the wood shed. (There will be archaic references, swearing and startling confessions in this dissertation. Not rated P.G. nor for the faint of heart or anyone under 60. You won't know what I am talking about.)

I have not grown old without problems, problems for others mostly. I ride pretty much above the fray. Life clips along at its usual pace but I don't. My movement is slower. My reaction time is slower. (If I am driving don't get in front or in back of me. You are warned.) My mental acuity, despite infusions of Ginkgo Biloba, Merlot, Cabernet, Pacifico, et al is slower and for short periods, non-existent.

After 5pm my hands no longer grip. In cold, damp weather Arthur (ritis) clamps me down until I am rigid. I clump around like "Lurch." (I told you.) I go to yoga twice a week. It is the only thing that keeps me on my feet and ambulatory. My point here is, through no fault of my own, I have become difficult, cranky, recalcitrant and a big pain in the ass. Not to myself of course, but to others.

I started writing this a week ago. I must have had an idea, but whatever it was it is gone now. This too is a learning experience. When I have a good idea "begin at the beginning, go straight through to the end and then stop." Always a good policy to follow the advice of the

Red Queen. Don't stop and put it (the story) aside and hope to pick it up later. See what happens? Moving right along—

My children have read some of the vignettes from the olden times and have suggested that I write something about my own personal self. Something about my childhood. OK. I have already gotten as far as being born and living in a little shotgun house at 1035 20ᵗʰ Street, Ogden, Utah. Why do I remember my address from 70 years ago? For the same reason you remember yours. In case I got lost I could tell a policeman my address and he could bring me home. To my knowledge, at that time I didn't know what a policeman was, or where to find one, but my parents insisted and I was an obedient child, so I remembered.

I also learned my Aunt's phone number 2185J. It was the only phone for 10 miles in any direction. This was 1939. Aunt Dora was the telephone exchange for the whole neighborhood and was glad to be it. Anyone could use her phone and she could listen in thereby learning everybody's business and having endless topics to share at Relief Society meetings. This was reward enough.

My Dad worked as a washman at the Model Laundry and my mother was a home mom. She did mom stuff. Also, as I remember, she "put up stuff" (canned), actually bottled all manner of fruits and vegetables for the winter. She washed our clothes on a washboard. (Do you know what that is? It is more often seen now days as a musical instrument.) Around this time I acquired a brother, four years younger than myself. He was named for my grandmother's drowned brother, Melvin.

We had a coal shed, which in a different life had been a "dry house." My father had scrounged it from his work. The original function of a "dry house" I never discovered.

I was not required to split kindling. Axes were dangerous and I was six-years-old, however, I did have a job. I filled two coal buckets each everyday, one for the kitchen stove and one for the parlor stove.

As you might suppose any kind of continuity is difficult for a six-year-old. I remember events.

One day my Grandma and Grandpa and all my mother's myriad sisters came to our house. Everyone was crying and hugging each other. My cousins and I were watching. I don't know what the cousins thought, but I thought, "What the hell is this?"

At our house we laugh a lot, we don't cry much. My father was crying. This scared the shit out of me. Fathers never cry. Something very bad was coming down. As it turned out my mother and Aunt Bessie were diagnosed with T.B. At this time it was a death sentence. Almost nobody made it through. Mama and Aunt Bessie were locked away in the T.B. sanatorium in Ogden and Melvin and I were looked after by hired girls. I was in school in the first grade, but Melvin was still little.

April 2010

The Relativity of Peace

It has occurred to me, upon much reflection, that peace is relative. It is not just flat-out peace, readily recognizable. It is incremental bits and pieces coming together, and one man's peace is not always another man's peace.

Back in olden times, I was in the army. (No, I wasn't one of the men rowing George Washington across the Delaware, but close.) I was in Korea, I had been drafted, but as luck would have it, by the time I had finished my training, the war was over. Except that it wasn't a war; it was a police action — whatever the hell that was. But it was a war, all right, with serious death and destruction, swept by confused alarms of struggle and flight where ignorant armies clashed by night. As it happened, we won, thus saving us for another day. All of the armed conflicts since then have been with small, poor countries, and they've really been none of our business. But I digress.

When I got to Korea, Seoul, the capital city, was blown to bits. The war had been over for about a month, and not much had been done to repair the country or its infrastructure. People I came in contact with lived in lean-tos and shacks in squalor and poverty, but many of them were happy campers. I couldn't believe my eyes, but they were smiling and cheerful and trying to get themselves together.

"Truly, are you not furious and bitter about your condition?"

"No, because peace is wonderful," was their response.

"Huh?"

"We can go to sleep at night and not worry about bombs falling on our heads. We can walk the streets without fear of someone shooting at us. We can concentrate on the rebuilding of our lives. It is hard, and we are having to scrounge up enough to eat and a place to keep warm, but we are at peace."

Fear of a violent death was finally gone, and just having hard-times paled in significance. I can't say that I understood it at the time, but I can understand it now: Safety for myself and my children. The opportunity to rebuild shattered lives. It was a great feeling I realize that now.

Another kind of peace is the relief experienced when you have completed a job that, when first began, seemed an insurmountable task. I use myself for examples because I know myself better than I know anyone else. Once, a long time ago, my life was smooth sailing. I had a lovely wife, two sweet children, a split-level in the suburbs and a good job. Then, quite suddenly, I had no job. Through no fault of my own, the business that employed me for 25 years closed down and put me on the street. I was, by now, 46 years old, had a mortgage and car payment, two children in school — second grade and kinder-garten — and no education. I had gotten this good job right out of high school (with a little help from my friends; it is called nepotism). So I knew all about the manufacture and distribution of tin cans...and who cared? I was like the guy who applied for a job at Henry Ford's new automobile manufacturing plant and noted on his job applica-tion his expertise in making buggy whips.

After the initial terror at my plight, I realized that I had good backup: a caring family and a wife with a good job. I had to start over. I became a 48-year-old college freshman. You didn't see that everyday in those old times.

Now, we come to the peace part. I completed my courses, which weren't as hard as I had imagined they would be. I got a degree in Elementary Education and a job in the first grade at Municipal Elementary, all in one day. I can tell you what I was wearing and the chair that I was sitting on when the peace that I had long sought — and feared would never come — descended on me, and I knew that every-thing was going to be okay. And it was.

I don't want to suggest that I achieved Nirvana and became a bodhisattva. Not a bit. Shit happens. But I have learned over time — a lot of time — how to deal with it. I practice yoga. That is a pathway to peace. I have achieved great age, and not much bothers me as I could drop dead anytime. So why sweat the small stuff?

This column is provided by World peace Gardens, a nonprofit orga-nization promoting oneness, inner peace and world peace. The World Peace Gatherings take place every Sunday at Green Valley Spa in St. George. The gatherings begin at 11:00 a.m. and are located at 1871 Canyon View Drive. For more information call 435-703-0077 or log on at www.worldpeacegardens.org.

Opinion: A.D.D.

I would like to second the opinion of Amy Bates of the Writers Group. I was a teacher in first grade for 20 years, and I know whereof she speaks. In ancient times, ADD was just coming into vogue. Every squirrely or too-quiet kid was suspect.

I knew from the get-go that there was no "standard" child and one size fits all. Careful observation and a little tweaking of the curriculum and everyone gets, at last, where you want them to go.

In all my years as a teacher I had two little boys who were, in fact, ADD and would benefit from the medicine. I had to talk like a Dutch Uncle to get the parents to agree, but at last they did. Both boys were smart as sheep dogs and soon were head of the class. Remember these were two boys out of approximately 700. Now we have ADHD and Asperger's and God knows what all.

Be careful. Be very careful.

Cherry Picking

Once upon a time, not your time nor yet my time, but one time there was a gang of boys who all lived on Eccles Avenue in Ogden, Utah. There were Joe and Lee Taylor (brothers), Scott and Cook Chapman (brothers), Mike and Jerry Hogge (brothers), Benny and Terry Sadler (brothers), and Jim and Ronnie Aikens (cousins). We were all within two or three years of age of each other. Mike and Bennie were freshman in Ogden High, the rest of us were in Central Junior High, except Ronnie and Lee who were at Lorin Farr Elementary.

We hung out together all the time. We played flag football on the church lawn. We played Miggz (marbles) and Mumbly Peg. Occasionally we would promote a track meet with the Oak Street Gang who lived a few blocks over. I was not much of a jock so I was chosen last every time, however I was not traumatized by this because I knew I was a klutz and I also knew that I was smart. I had better grades than anyone, so I considered myself an intellectual. I did play as good as I could which wasn't very good, but I was one of the gang so my shortcomings were overlooked (mostly).

For several summers we all went down to Winnie Badgers Cherry Orchard and worked during the cherry season. Eccles Avenue ran right to the edge of a cliff. It was called the "Clay Hill." I'll bet that you can guess why! It was a neat place with trees, bushes and hidey holes. We played there a lot, building huts and throwing clay balls. Down at the bottom of the hill the Ogden River came rushing out of the canyon. Across this river were miles and miles of fruit orchards, mostly cherries.

We were special friends with Winnie because he had been a friend of my grandfather, whom I never knew. He died when my Dad was a teenager. My Dad took us all down to meet Winnie and he told us he expected us to do a day's work for a day's pay. Winnie was as old as the moon and slow going, but a sweet man. My Dad promised us, all of us, that if we screwed around and took advantage of Winnie we could expect a seriously kicked ass. We were basically good guys but like all teenagers noisy, erratic and strange, but we liked Winnie and we worked hard.

He paid three cents a pound for cherries. We could scramble up and down the ladders but the buckets were huge, so when they became too heavy to carry we would dump the cherries in a lug (a big wood box) with our name on it. Winnie would come around with a wagon and take the lugs to the shed and weigh them. He kept a notebook with our names and how many cherries we picked. At the end of the week we would get a white envelope with money in it. I really don't remember for certain how much it was, but it seems like it was a five-dollar bill and some change. In those olden days five dollars was big bucks.

For a quarter we could catch the bus both ways. Ten cents was the cost of the movie at the Paramount Theater and it was always a double feature: a Tom Mix Serial and many cartoons. We would get a ten-cent popcorn and have a whole days entertainment for two bits. Five dollars could last forever.

One day we fell into work and Winnie said, "From now on the stem must be on the cherry."

We all frowned at this. It was harder to pick cherries with stems. It took a long time to fill a lug. Nobody had very many lugs that day. We were disappointed and mad about that.

But when the cherries were weighed Winnie said, "Oh, by the way, stems on pays five-and-a-half cents a pound."

OK!

The next morning we were ready to start when someone sang out, "One-and-a-two-and Winnie wants the stems on."

Everybody picked it up and it went on all day. One-and-a-two-and Winnie wants the stems on. Winnie probably got sick and tired of the singing, but he didn't say anything. He was a good old guy.

We never took a lunch to work. We ate so many cherries that we couldn't hold down a lunch. When Winnie went into the house for his lunch we scurried through the orchard, over the fence and down the hill to the river. This river was a typical Utah river, shallow with lots of rocks. However at one particular spot there was a very deep hole, deep enough to dive into. It was called "soapy" because against the bottoms of the rocks was this white gooey stuff that looked like soap bubbles, hence the name.

We would charge down to the river throwing our clothes all over and dive into the ice cold-water. The Ogden River was mostly snow-melt and way back in the mountains the snow was still melting. There was a device that was much fun. Someone in ages past had tied a rope to a tree limb that hung out over the water and tied a tire on the bottom. In order to partake of the cheap thrills you had to climb up the tree a ways and hold onto the rope with your feet on the tire and let go. The tire flew clear out to the middle of the river, and then you let go. The ride ended in either a cannon ball or sometimes a dive. It was a hoot.

At the cherry shed Winnie had a big Iron Triangle and a steel bar. When he whanged the triangle it could be heard for miles. That was our signal to go back to work. So we gathered up our clothes, got dressed and trudged back to work, cool and refreshed.

Birth of Rowan

As the long train of ages glides by there be events which alter and illuminate their times. This is one of those times and the birth of Rowan is one of those events. There is no such thing as a small miracle. All miracles are large and important. And those for whom this miracle was made will solemnly attest to this fact.

Rowan is a re-affirmation of the ties of love and respect that bind two families and two countries. Separated by space but connected by affection and concern. Rowan is the future, a lock that assures the cooperation, love and respect of two nations sometimes at odds but never enemies.

A child conceived in love, raised with love, surrounded by love is a fortunate child and when he grows older and responds in kind he will be an ornament on the tree of life, a consummation devoutly to be wished and the answer to all of our prayers.

Belly Buttons

I would like to take this opportunity to settle another community problem. One of my esteemed colleagues wrote about young girls' belly buttons and suggested that there was something incorrect about this.

If a man my age reports that he is looking at 16 year olds' belly buttons, his circle of acquaintance shrinks and he is never invited to homes with children.

Let me hasten to state that I am remembering belly buttons from 50 years ago, except, come to think about it, I never saw a belly button 50 years ago. In fact the way the young women dressed in those days made the burka look positively lascivious.

The girls bought their skirts at Omar the Tent Maker Boutique. They were huge and long. Between the white ankle sock rolled down and the bottom of the skirt was about an inch and a half of skin. On top they wore one sweater on top of another sweater with long sleeves, and a scarf or a little white collar around their neck.

Of course there were those old busy bodies for whom an inch and a half of skin could send you skidding into hell. Those people have always been around.

But don't feel sorry for me. For after the 50s came the 60s and with the 60s came Hot Pants. Hot pants were pants but they were short—very short. A young woman I knew at that time had legs that went clear up to here. When she wore hot pants it would make my hair sweat.

We would go dancing (a lot of dancing went on in those days. The monkey, the surf, the funky chicken) all kinds of very vigorous dancing. We would go to the Elks Club and other low dives and carry on. The other men there would try to cop a peek at my hot pants lady when they thought that I wasn't looking. HA. Eat your hearts out lads.

An interesting thing about these dancing venues was the smoke. Everybody smoked a lot. Sometimes it was so thick that you could hardly see your partner's face. If I went into a place like that today, four breaths and I would be terminal.

I loved the 60s. The culture shock would blow you away.

My favorite song of that era went like this: "Eating Rueben sandwich and sauerkraut, don't worry about it baby, let it all hang out," and did we ever.

There were two completely different cultures circulating then. The long hair hippie weirdo freaks (me) and the razor cut hair three-piece suit and woolly sideburn guys (you).

We coexisted pretty well. We had different interests and didn't get in each other's face except for the war—that got ugly and I'm so sorry about the way we all behaved. I hope that never happens again. But for the most part it was great.

Now for the moral of my tale. We can glean from this three things. 1) Nothing's forever and time flies away. 2) The only thing that men should say about women's clothes is, "It looks great, honey." 3) Minding other people's business is exhausting work. It required eternal vigilance (somebody may get away with something). It pays nothing and you never get a day off. Give yourselves a break?

Love to all.

Car

Once not too long ago I had this little car that I loved a lot. I am not ordinarily a person who has any sort of affection for inanimate objects but I really loved that car. Well it got old and began to fail in many ways. It was in the shop a lot of the time as things wore out and things broke down until at last, Jim the car fixing person said, "This is an exercise in futility, these endless and ever more expensive repairs need to stop. Let me put a bullet in the crank case and I will pay the towing fee to take it to the junk yard."

Harsh. Time passed and this was accomplished. I then decided that I wanted another car exactly the same.

Excuse me

Excuse me? Can I talk to you for a minute?
Sure.

I'm a reporter for the Spectrum, do you know it?
Yes.

I notice that you left the key in the ignition of your Tracker and the top is off and anyone can see it.
Is there a point?

Don't you think that is dangerous?
I don't think about it at all.

What if someone stole your car?
What if five minutes after that an asteroid struck the earth at Bluff and Tabernacle, I'd be dead, the car thief would be dead, and you would be dead. So what is the big deal?

Don't you think it could happen? (Not the last part.)
It could happen. But the St. George police would soon find my car. They have a very good record of finding things. They would catch the thief and put him in prison where he would be serially buggered by large ethnic men with bad temper and huge equipment. He would decide while in prison that a life of crime is not all it is cracked up to be. So upon his release he would get a job and work hard and by doing this he would get money and self-respect which he never even knew existed but found to be very pleasant.

Although he walked funny he would meet a nice girl and get married and even some day join the P.T.A. Becoming a decent, hard-working, tax paying citizen with a good life that he would not have had if he had been denied the opportunity to steal my car. I feel that by leaving the keys in the car I am being socially responsible.

You have interesting, though strange opinions.
I am retired an often at liberty. If you would like to hear thoughtful, well-reasoned opinions on almost all subjects by a person hoary with years and ponderous with dignity please contact me. I am able to discourse on any subject rationally, amiably and interminably. Please contact me.

As the child of immigrants

As the child of immigrants, the son-in law of immigrants and the father-in-law of an immigrant I think it is time to make it clear to all where I am in the (so-called) immigrant problem—just where I usually am, way over to the left.

There is a movement afoot to give prizes to businesses that do not hire Mexicans. This melancholy idea is propounded by a newly formed group of California move-ins who are reluctant to take the blame for the trashed economy and disastrous school system (once the envy of all) and various other illnesses and complaints besetting California and instead choose to blame it all on the Mexicans. Or in our case, flee the sinking ship, come here and continue to blame the Mexicans.

Are you aware that "what goes around comes around"? Back a ways and not that far California belonged to the Mexicans. Remember that? They were driven out with shock and awe and an overwhelming swarm of boomers, miners, fortune hunters, prostitutes and plain white trash. They were overwhelmed and fled. Well, they're baaaaaack. In the necessary overwhelming numbers. How does it feel?

The plan as outlined seems to be, starve them out, give prizes to people not to hire them and take away their driving licenses so they can't get to their job if they have one. This nasty little progrom together with other schemes and manipulations designed to cause worry and discomfort to already poor people is called, I believe, "family values."

If you were a poor man whose children may be hungry and for sure have no future, no education, no doctoring when they are sick and you see just through the fence, a land of silk and money, and a history of people who worked hard and kept their nose clean and had a wonderful life, why just them? Why not me? You would be through that fence and into the desert in a New York minute. You couldn't call yourself a man if you didn't. Why shouldn't your children have the same opportunities as the little Anglo children? No damn reason at all except an accident of birth.

When my old grandfather came here to escape the potato famine in Ireland some old settlers said there were too many of them and the country couldn't hold them. Those Irish men would use up all the welfare and breathe all the air. It was an acute and terrible situation. We are now hearing that same story in the same key. It was B.S. then and it is B.S. now. Any society who closes in on itself, builds high walls and shuts its gates to new ideas and new blood is doomed to stew in fear, incest, paranoia and despair. That ought to scare the bejesus out of you.

Now before you get mad at me let me explain something. If a coyote comes down out of the hills and eats your granddaughter, you can't really get mad at him because he is just doing the coyote thing. You shouldn't get mad at me either because I am a genetic liberal democrat going clear back to the Roosevelt administration so I am as helpless as the coyote. I have to be how I am. Of course you are within your rights to shoot the coyote even though you understand his motivation, so that he won't eat your other granddaughter. I have no intention in the world of eating your granddaughter. Devouring granddaughters and having different opinions are not in the same category of crimes and should be viewed with differing severity. But if still you plan to retaliate, be a good sport and give me a little heads-up so that I can run for the border. (Beat you to it!)

Child discipline

There are times in every life when things become difficult and you feel that everything is conspiring against you. At a certain age (mine) when you begin to lose function and rot away, when your fingers won't grip and your feet hurt and you are unable to do the tortoise position in your yoga class, and a dog has pooped on your driveway. You might feel that it is time to curl up in a fetal position in the back of the closet for a few weeks. That is not an option for me because I take expensive drugs, which preclude that type of action. The best thing to do is to try to cheer yourself up by counting your many blessings.

I posses a gazillion blessings and it took me most of one day to count them all. Then I came to an especially dear one. I didn't invent a cure for cancer or how to get rid of Donald Rumsfeld, but the star in my crown of accomplishment is: I am an excellent parent. When my children were young they were so perfect that people came from miles around to ask me how I did it. I became giddy from so much praise. Nobody has asked me lately, but I'm going to tell you anyway in case you need to know. It is basically very simple. Guilt and fear. These are not new concepts. They have been around for years. I just polished them to a blinding sheen.

I am prepared to take ALL the credit for my perfect children. Well, except for a couple of things. They are very good looking. One glance at my picture here and you will see that I didn't contribute much. My wife, however is very beautiful. So she took care of that for us. My children are very healthy. They never missed a day of school in their lives. They had the chickenpox and some other childhood ailments, but they always did it during summer vacation when I was home to tend them. This too I must attribute to my wife, who is never sick and sickness makes her very nervous.

Ordinarily calm and efficient, at the sight of sick children she became unglued and behaved strangely. As a result the children never got sick because their mother became so strange and alarming and they were afraid she would either blow up or run away. So they would forgo illness with the attendant perks such as staying home from school and having sugar tea and little squares of toast with the crusts cut off and ice cream for every meal. It just wasn't worth it.

Everything else I took care of myself. Through the dim haze of memory I sort of can't remember too many specifics.

They did well in school. I was a schoolteacher so they dang well better.

They were outstanding jocks, baseball, basketball, soccer. They had a lot of friends and a lot of fun.

As nobody can do everything, I didn't know any more about "sports" than a hog knows about Sunday school. (I'm more the intellectual type.) Nevertheless I hauled teams of one sort and another around the city, went to all the games and cheered lustily although I had no clue what was going on. I listened to lamentation for losing, ecstacy for winning and future strategy on many long drives home. I would nod sagely like I knew what was going on and in my own dark heart would wonder why they would rather do this than become involved in a cause (I was kind of a hippie type in those days and had "causes.") The children pretty much ignored this and the only time they recognized my kind of alternate lifestyle is when they complained that they were embarrassed to go to church with me because my hair was too long.

There was one disciplining technique I will enumerate here.

My daughter Ashley was perfect in every way and never required any discipline of any sort ever. Josh was another matter. He was a regular type boy. Perfect, but flawed. One time his teacher, a woman I knew and trusted, called me to say Josh had done an unacceptable thing. I agreed and said that I would take care of it.

Josh and I discussed it and agreed that it was unacceptable and that he needed to be punished. When I was punished by my father I would get a lickin which mean I would get smacked on the butt with a willow. These sessions as I remember were not really frequent and not too memorable. The thing I do remember is that he would give me his pocket knife and send me out to cut a switch. Unnecessary cruelty, I thought.

It was a difficult choice. If the stick was too wimpy, he would send me out again. What I didn't tumble to until way too late is that if I had cut a huge one, he would never have hit me with it. Lickin was the punishment of choice in those days. All my friends got lickin's. Some got welts on the bonebutt and in one horrific instance a bone welt from a wire coat hanger (ouch).

Anyway, I thought this offence was a spanking item.

I explained to Josh that this was a spanking offence. He had no experience with such a thing. (He was about 10.) He had heard of it, of course, but had no real knowledge.

So we got the switch. (I did it myself.) In the garage he bent over and I gave him a swat. He screamed in pain and jumped up. I dropped the switch and held him in my arms. We both cried for a long time. He, because he was hurt. Me, because I was a hideous and cruel monster.

After it quit stinging he more or less forgot about it and never mentioned it again. However, I never forgot about it, never. I had nightmares for decades. Somebody hurt from this incident and that somebody was me.

Ok. So to recap.

1. Have a beautiful wife. (It does wonders for their appearance.)

2. Have lots of patience. (This is hard, but you can do it.)

3. Devote large blocks of time to child rearing. (A lot of this time seems to be taken up with foolishness. It isn't.)

4. DON'T HIT.

This is your recipe for perfect children.

Enjoy!

November 2003

Forgot my pants

I have designated myself as apologist for the elderly, infirm and senile of the community. It is a well documented fact that getting old is not easy. Well, boys and girls, you have no idea how hard.

May I cite an egregious example. Madam and I travel around sometimes and that entails packing up things. It has become a little joke with us. "What have you forgotten now."

One of the most memorable of forgets was when I forgot my pants. We had gone up to the "up North" to get a little culture. We were going to the opera with the uber cool and cultured ones and I forgot my pants. I ended up at the opera in my ratty old Levis and cowboy boots with the coat from my eleven hundred dollar suit, my shirt unbuttoned down to my belly button and a couple of gold neck chains.

I pretended that I wanted to look that way. Many people cast a look askance, as they used to say, and my wife stayed at least twenty feet away from me the whole time and only came to her seat after the lights were out. I wasn't too concerned. I don't know those people. I had hoped that they would think I was a fading Rock Star, but I could tell that they thought that I was a homeless person and what the hell was I doing in here.

Speaking of underwear, which we weren't but we are now. I went to a really cool Halloween party and everyone was in these glamorous outfits, me included. My daughter worked in Oman and she sent me an Omani Dish Dash. A dish dash for those not in the know is a long white dress, like the ones worn by the Afghan terrorists you see on TV except that mine is very high end, more like Prime Banclor the Saudi Ambassador.

The Arabs know how to dress for the climate. Resultantly these robes are very thin so as to keep cool. They are practically transparent. V.P.L. (visibly panty line) is not generally a guy problem unless the guy is wearing a dress, which I was, so to minimize my problem I wore my thong. Well it worked fine except that I made the mistake of telling some rowdy ladies at the party. Now I know how the girls in the fourth grade felt when we had "flip skirt day." I spent most of the party sitting down or leaning against the wall.

I did it for their own good try to visualize a 70-year-old man in a thong. The poor things would probably go blind. I was doing them a favor not giving them a peek.

This is another interesting underwear story. Do you remember your mother's or more probably your grandmother's admonishments about always wearing clean unraggedy underwear everyday in case a truck hits you and have to go to the hospital? They seemed to think that the hospital people would recoil in horror and be unable or unwilling to tend your wounds. They acted like it would be published in the newspaper and the whole extended family would have to move to a different town. I was so brain washed that the one time that I was rushed to the emergency ward I forgot my injury because all I could think about was, "Oh help me Jesus. Please don't let me have bad underwear."

When they pulled my pants off and I could see that I was wearing clean, almost new whity-tighty's I felt a huge relief and took the opportunity to pass out from pain.

October 2004

Halloween

It is a well-known fact that I have the prettiest and smartest granddaughter in this quadrant of the universe. Anyone who presumes to dispute this fact to my face had better be armed. That said, let me explain why I know this to be true, I have spent many, MANY hours with Kat playing Barbies, putting on and taking off outfits which range between magnificent and slutty (emphasis on slutty). We have spent many hours discussing current events, the world situation and how S_____ was rude in primary. We know each other pretty well.

Kat sailed into Kindergarten like the Queen Mary coming into New York harbor. All flags flying and all whistles blowing. She loves school and school loves her. But I want to take a different tack. Katarina's coolness factor is about the same as her Poppy's, which is 9. This is evident in her choice of a Halloween costume.

A little back-story here: As a schoolteacher in first grade I saw twenty Halloweens pass by. Parents don't know it, or at least they don't admit it, but Halloween is THE major holiday on the calendar. Everybody thinks that it is Christmas. Well, it's not. Nowadays children get presents everyday of their lives, coming in from all directions. Presents are no big deal. Dressing up, is. Trick or treat is collateral. Dressing up is major. Attention and discussion begin right after Labor Day. "What are you going to be for Halloween?" It is a serious and on-going debate, with decisions and revisions right up to the day.

Around Halloween begins (by adults) a lot of quivering and hand wringing about Devil worship and attendant silliness. The children don't know of it or care either.

The boys like to be as hideous and gruesome as possible with gouts of blood and eyeballs hanging on their cheek. The girls like to be princesses or something else glamorous (remember Barbie). Wal-Mart sells at least four million identical princess costumes every year. (Haven't you noticed when you go to the door for trick-or-treat that it looks like a Cinderella clone?)

Well, my Kat decided that she wanted to be a moose, yes a moose.

Her bemused parents asked me what I thought of her reasons for this unusual choice. (They sometimes ask my advice on parenting, which makes me feel wise.) And I said, "Who cares?"

It's the coolest thing I've ever heard of. Even in my own notions, which sometimes tend to be the bizarre, I have never thought of being a moose.

We are so excited. We have been making sketches and checking fabric swatches. (We have to make our own. Wal-Mart doesn't have mooses.) We even have an attendant. Her little brother Eric who is two and not all that choosy is going to be a flying squirrel, Rocky and Bullwinkle, get it? How satanic is that?

Halloween is not yet, but with all the attendant hullabaloo and excitement we are all on the verge of the vapors. This could end up as one of those times when it is better to journey hopefully than to arrive. But, I don't think so.

Love to All.

I used to be a Mexican

I have recently been checking out literature about how you can change your sexual orientation with therapy study and prayer.

I just hate it when I am forced to concur with positions that I consider untenable, but stuff happens.

I know how these guys feel and what they are doing.

I used to be a Mexican but I quit. Love figured in just as it has with the formerly gay men.

I had a girlfriend and I loved her dearly and she loved me, but her parents didn't love me. They hated that I was Mexican.

Well I wanted them to like me. I wanted to get along. So I bought the books, studied hard, did the therapy, took the test and passed. And became a white man.

I didn't mind being a Mexican except that I'd like to be taller. Well now I was taller, also sort of chubby and had really bad hair.

My girlfriend's parents were delighted. I was white, not a very prepossessing specimen, but white.

Now we come to the place where the law of unintended consequences kicks in.

My girlfriend didn't like me anymore. She said "If I had wanted a fat white guy with bad hair that is what I would have gone after. I didn't. I wanted a pretty little Mexican guy with sparkly teeth and shiny black curls. You ain't it, Porky, and you are over."

My heart was broken but there it was.

I have had an OK life as a white guy but you always think, What If?

I'm old now and preparing to be gathered to the bosom of Abraham. I have concerns about what will happen to me when I hit the pearly gates.

Many of the F.G.G. (formerly gay guys) quoted a lot of Christian scripture about abominations and vileness and other yucky stuff that they had overcome. OK for that.

What they didn't mention was the really important teaching from the Garden of Gethsemane, remember this? "Not My Will but Thy

Will be done." (Note this information is for Christians only who will understand it.) Well if God made us and God doesn't make mistakes, he must have done so because that's how he wanted us to be, right?

If we have changed ourselves into something that we liked better doesn't that seem a little presumptuous? Maybe he had a plan, and by thinking we could improve upon God's work we screwed it up.

What's he going to say about that?

Mumbly Peg

As the long train of ages glides by I remember things, important things, which have been shunted aside. No longer are the young instructed in these important and life affirming skills.

When I was small my grandmother taught me how to count to ten in Indian. (You are going to make a fuss about the huge generalization here, but I am going to ignore it.) It was thus: Eeen bum tag, Teen bum tag, Teather bum tag, Feather bum tag, Enoch, Een, Teen Teather, Feather, Fifth jack. No child should be forced to grow up without this important skill.

My grandmother also taught me that if you eat green apples you would get colliery marbles (Cholera Morbus) which sounds perfectly awful. I never did discover exactly what it was, but I stopped eating green apples.

Another important game was Mumbly Peg. This interesting past time faded away even before metal detectors in public schools. The primary requirement was a pocketknife. No boy, except the most blatant sissy, was without a pocketknife. The basic old timer pocketknife had two blades, sometimes three, was very heavy and had a loop on one end to fasten to a chain that was fastened to a belt loop. This knife had no corkscrew, screwdriver, bottle opener and/or scissors. These refinements came with a Swiss army knife, a whole different ballgame.

Mumbly Peg consisted of various moves, arcachic and difficult to describe. For example a move called Chin-zeez started with the tip of the blade held touching the chin. Then while swaying back and forth the player flipped up and released the blade so that it swung around and stuck up in the lawn. This game was played on the lawns. There were various other moves. The purpose was that the blade sticks up in the grass at the end of each move. The moves were difficult but not impossible, and much practice made a skillful Mumbly Pegger.

It occurs true that this game is similar to Jacks, an intricate and disappeared game of skill that was for girls. I can make this sexist claim because all this happened between 1942–1949, before equality was even dreamed of, for anyone.

Now we come to the peg part. As the game progressed and all parties had gone through the whole routine, the last man to finish has to "root the peg." A small stick was sharpened and tapped into the ground. So many taps were allowed to the winner to drive the peg into the ground. (Help me here. I don't remember how the number of taps was decided upon.) Anyway, the peg was driven far into the ground and the loser was required to pull the peg out of the ground with his teeth (root). A large mouthful of grass and dirt were obtained before the peg was finally pulled up. Is this a great game or what? A great skill was demonstrated by the winners and abject humiliation suffered by the loser, in the American way.

The clouds are back lit

The clouds are back lit and stately and white—
Sailing from blue day to
Star spangled night.
Conquistadors' ships bearing rich Inca treasures
To decadent kings with decadent pleasures

Since I have been inducted into the Pretty nearly Dead Poets Society of St. George, I have been thinking in metaphor. It's interesting and more fun than "really pretty" and "awesome."

These poets are old. I'm pushing 70 and they call me Gen X.

I received of the lord that which I also delivered (Corinthians 1:11,23)

The 4 major food groups in real time are:
Salt
Sugar
Chocolate
Grease—I'm gonna live forever.

What I did on my summer vacation

My summer vacation is somewhat bigger than some people's. It begins on May 28 when school's out and ends on August 27 when it begins anew. My summer vacation is broken up into segments. It is the only way that I have some control on the endless fun and foolishness. I am older than coal and slower than tar. Because of this I am an encumbrance and an annoyance to those more fortunate than myself and this includes everyone whose hair is not white. I endure a lot of pursed lips and toe tapping when it takes me five minutes to get out of the car.

My long-range revenge plans include living to be a hundred. (Of course I'm going to get revenge. "Don't get mad, get even," is my new mantra.) I am going to all the rest homes where the people who are now on my sh**list reside. I am going up to where they are strapped in their wheel chair and drooling in their lap and I am going to say, "Nanner, Nanner" and wiggle by butt in their faces. Revenge is sweet!

But in the erst while I am soldiering on. Last week I went to a family reunion. It was at Capitol Reef National Park, one of the most beautiful places on earth. As luck would have it, my wife had other business and my daughter-in-law is extremely pregnant so they came not. It devolved on me and Josh to pack up the stuff for us and two children, ages seven and four. Also, get the food for 32 people for lunch. (This was our family detail.)

Again prayers went up to heaven in thanksgiving for women. It came as a huge shock to my system that "somebody" had to buy food and pack-up. Always before I just rode shotgun with my feet on the dash. When we got there all this stuff miraculously appeared in the trunk of the car. My duties consisted of carrying it to the picnic table, after which I took a nap.

This trip was a revelation. It gave me the opportunity to expound a moral lecture to the children about responsibility. I quoted the story of "The Little Red Hen" and how she decided in the end, "If you want something done well, do it yourself." It has always been a part of my personal philosophy of life. The children were impressed I guess. At least they appeared to listen. The Little Red Hen is a compelling story. My son said later, "It is very interesting to learn from Poppy, that you learned your philosophy of life from a chicken."

It is difficult to be heavy with wisdom and ponderous with dignity with people who know you too well.

Uncle Robert, who is a professor of Geology and man who understands children, took us all on a hike to study rock formations. Most of the hike was in a streambed, and you know kids and water. There were 15 children under eight years old. (I can hear you gasping.) But really everything went pretty well and everyone got pretty wet. At the end of the journey was a waterfall. The more intrepid boys scrambled up the rocks and rode the waterfall down into a big pool at the bottom. My Katarina, seven years old and such a girl, surprised us all by taking the waterfall ride with the boys. Women, even very young ones, are a constant surprise to me.

Love to All.

Recently it has come to my attention

Recently it has come to my attention that life is not fair. I have not had time to observe this sad circumstance, because I have been zeroed in on my own life.

I'm OK. Not everybody is OK.

You hear, in the media, that some people are not OK. In fact, they are in dire straits (to put it mildly).

Everyone has regrets. It haunts me that I never brought the news.

Who wills the end wills the means. It was in another country and besides, the wench is dead.

Sometimes I think

Sometimes I think that I never was what I used to be.

Peter Peter Pumpkin Eater

Peter Peter pumpkin eater had a wife but couldn't . . .
_____. Poor Peter.
Every married man has had this unfortunate circumstance.
If they say they haven't, they are lying.

Old man Mose kicked the bucket.
Old man Mose
The Buck Buck, Bucket
Old man Mose kicked the bucket
Old man Mose is dead.

Numb hands

Numb hands are like blind eyes.

Generally I lead a pretty tranquil existence

Generally I lead a pretty tranquil existence. No strain, no pain. But of late there has been strain and pain and disillusion and disruption.

The long slow slide down the well-known tube has been disrupted yet again by medical appointments, therapy, and drug dependence. The only thing that makes it bearable is the drug dependence part.

Vestigia Flammae

"Vestigia flammae."
What the Queen of Carthage said when she first saw Aeneas,
"I recognize the vestiges of an old flame."

I wish that I was able to call up such cool quotes when the occasion demanded.

She knows things.
Things that she shouldn't know.
Things that she can't know.
She is too close to the ground, our Millie is.

The game's afoot!
Do a lot of stretching.
Old malignant and pathetic.

Ognib

I am not a pet person. I once had a dog when I was eight years old. She died when I was twenty one years old. I buried her under an apple tree. Her name was Ognib—that is a very cool name. It is Bingo spelled backward. I was eight years old and nowhere near clever enough to think of such a neat name. I think my mother did it. My mother was so funny. She helped me pick out Ognib from a litter of puppies, all of whom were cute and fat and loveable. Ognib was scrawny and lopsided and ugly. Of course, she was the one my mother chose. You should have seen our Christmas trees. Ognib was always ugly but popular with the boys. She had a million puppies. I loved Ognib and I loved my mother. One excellent mother and one excellent pet were enough to last me a lifetime.

Why are bears so lucky

A nimals have no concept of time. Does a bear go to sleep for months and wake up thinking it was a little nap and it is still Monday?

When I was little, time moved glacially. From one Christmastime to the next was eons.

Later—I'll never be sixteen. Still later, wow, I'm twenty-one. Now what?

Then life kicked in, the only time I thought about time was, is it time to go home from work?

After a time I began to pay more attention to time—my children were babies mewling and puking in their cradle. In time they were playing soccer in the park. Next time they were in caps and gowns. In a very short time they were gone from sight.

Why are bears so lucky.

In these hard times

In these hard times do you sometimes feel that it takes all the juice you can muster just to get up in the morning?

"What the hell's going on," you say. "I'm OK, my life is OK, why do I feel like this?"

I'll tell you why, you have a chemical imbalance. Go see a doctor and he'll give you a pill. You don't take pills, you say depression is a character disorder. Bullshit.

God inspires the sun to rise and the moon to set. God inspires scientists to discover insulin, polio vaccine, and Prozac. Give yourself a break. Cowboy up, tough it out, hang in there—The people who tell you that don't know how you feel. Tell them to stick it.

Every grandfather suffers growing pains

Every grandfather suffers growing pains, we're talking real pain here. Tending grandchildren is not for sissies. I may have mentioned that I have grandchildren (about 400 times). They look like stock grandchildren, pretty and sweet, but in fact they are real people, complex, fascinating, endearing and maddening.

I began my grandchild supervising duties when they were still diaper babies. That was a snap. Change their diaper, put them on a blanket on the floor with some kind of noise maker and read the paper. It became increasingly complex as time went on. Feeding with a spoon was an exercise in futility until I got wise to certain food groups. Applesauce, custard with bananas, ice cream, you are getting the picture. Anything green or remotely healthy was disdained.

Speaking of healthy, let me leap ahead a little. Last week Katarina told somebody (not me unfortunately) that trans fats had ruined her life. Pretty profound for a five year old, right? But it turned out that a ruined life for a five-year-old is not the same as it might be for you or me. It turns out that her parents won't take her to McDonald's anymore. The withdrawal of McGreaseballs and fries is what has caused her this grief.

My first real trauma began when we began to play Barbies. Everyone between three and 90 knows what Barbies are so I won't need to go into my blue stocking rant. Playing Barbies consists of changing the clothing on these dolls. The clothing varies from vulgar and ostentatious to semi naked and slutty. We change clothes to go for a walk, we change clothes to go to the malt shop to sashay around in front of a stunned looking Ken and his usually naked buddies (Ken isn't that much fun to dress). Interspersed with these clothing changes we play Night, Night. This is the part where you lay down on the floor and are covered with a blanket. I could love this part but it turns out to be the most maddening part of all. As soon as you get comfortable, it's over. "Ok, night, night is over. Back to the dressing room."

Eric is almost three now and has limited interest in Barbies. He does like to throw them at the wall. (He is not often asked to play.) What he likes is to shoot hoops. Just say "Park" and he is off like a shot to get his basketball and grabs my hand and tugs me toward the door.

I like shooting hoops even less than playing Barbies. Hoop shooting consists of standing under the basket, holding Eric up as high as possible (he is a very large 3-year old) while he takes a shot. If he gets a basket, we dance around then I put him down and he chases after the ball, brings it back and we do it again and again and again. Every Poppy of my age (71 last week) does not bend over and straighten up any more times than is absolutely necessary to be a semi functional adult. These basketball games take more bending over and straightening up than I would ordinarily do in two weeks. When they are over I am humped over and exhausted! That is why I try to introduce other fun things to do at the park, like shovel sand into a bucket while Poppy reads the paper. We all know, that was a big hit.

His other fun thing is rock throwing. This activity can occur at inopportune times and causes really dirty looks to be shot at me as if I'm the one throwing rocks.

He is amazingly accurate for 3. One day he was playing in the backyard unsupervised for a few minutes, you know how that goes. Everybody thinks that everybody else is watching the baby.

When I went in the backyard after they had gone home, I saw that the bird bath was full of rocks. The bird bath is twice as tall as he is and the rocks came from gramma's oriental pots clear across the yard.

We have recently advanced to more sophisticated play. Now we play cards. I love this new phase because we lay on the floor quietly, no running, no jumping, no lifting and stooping. It is my kind of fun, practically comatose.

The game is called UNO. It is basically very simple. I have never played it before with anyone but Kat and little man. The rules are extremely flexible. When I put down a S you are supposed to follow suit, Kat puts down an R. When I say "What are you doing?" she says, "Sometimes you can do that." Oh!

When I had one card and she had two cards (the object is to get rid of all your cards) on her turn she put down two cards and left me with one. When I questioned this, she said "Sometimes you can do that." Oh!

I don't win much but I am not required to do anything physical so I feel that it is a fair trade off. Little man plays too but his education so far consists of counting to ten in English and five in Spanish and singing "Quinkle, Quinkle Little Star." So he puts his cards down whenever he feels like, and declares himself the winner. "I win," he says and gets up and jumps on the couch until the next hand.

Another thing about being a Poppy that is so great: When I say something foolish or make a dorky mistake, Kat gently remonstrates me: "Oh Poppy, you silly goose." I am a fortunate man.

Kat is gone into organized fun now. She is on a soccer team. Poppy is not needed (except as pep squad). I hate it.

Love to all.

Illegal

"Illegal" has a long and checkered history—too often illegal has been lumped together with the likes of murder, rape, pedophilia, littering—there are many degrees of illegality. Coming to America to improve your life is not in the same category as serial murder. (Although to hear some people talk, you might think so).

The Cabin

When the high speed go-go stressful Big City life of St. George becomes too much to bear, I repair to the family cabin above Zion Park. There are huge pine trees, blue sky, wild flowers, and soft breezes. I lie on the lounge on the deck and listen to the sounds of the soft moccasins of the wendigo walking on the tops of the gently sighing trees. Heavenly.

Our family has been coming here since 1966. That is way back when. On the table is a journal that has been there since way back when. When anyone from our large extended family comes to spend some time they write in the journal.

I read through the journal from front to back when I was there. What tales it has to tell.

In the beginning God created heaven and earth and Grandpa created the cabin. R.W. Lewis, Grandpa's old missionary companion, had this cattle ranch up in the mountains above Zion Park and he wanted to quit the cow business and build cabins. R.W. said, "Help me Frank and I'll give you the lot of your choice." Grandpa was a building contractor in Los Angeles. He said OK.

Thus it was accomplished.

War Story

I was called into the Lieutenant's office. "Come in," snapped to and saluted, "as you were corporal, sit down."

Lt. Stewart was very young, very serious and very dorky. There were four Lieutenants in our unit all of whom were very young, very serious and totally useless. Our unit was run by the sergeants. Specifically, Master Sergeant John Doright Finny. The captain, the official officer in charge, was a famous suck ass and spent all of his time at 1st cavalry headquarters making political points.

Lieutenant Stewart checked the papers on his desk and without looking up said, "I see that you reported to the medic tent this morning with the clap."

"Yes, sir."

"I see also that I passed off on a request to attend a religious retreat in Seoul last week."

"Yes, sir."

"You went on a religious retreat and came back with the clap?"

"Yes, sir."

"Was it included in the religious festivities?"

"No, sir."

"You hear about Mormons being pussy hounds, but really. You are restricted to base for three weeks or until you are no longer contagious."

"Yes, sir."

"Dismissed."

Restricted, big deal. We were in the D.M.Z. in South Korea, there were no villages or towns or anything else for miles around.

When I left his office I went back to work. I was the Battery Clerk. Heavy Mortar Battery, First Cavalry.

I sat at my desk and tried to think if I should be ashamed, or at least embarrassed but I was neither. Why not?

I wasn't a callous and hardened veteran of many battles seeking forgetfulness and comfort from a carnal encounter. I was a draftee from Utah, a rube who knew as much about war as a hog knows about Easter baskets.

The war had been over for a year, the country was devastated and destroyed and had barely began to recover. Coming in I saw buildings blasted and in ruins, the train depot had huge bullet holes in the walls and tracks twisted up like silver ribbons of Christmas wrap. The people lived in shacks and lean-tos. It was dark and grim.

Where I was stationed there were no ruins or people at all. They had all been cleared out. The rice paddies had gone to ruin and the houses were abandoned.

So, the war, as a war, did not touch me. I lived in a tin shack with 25 other men, I owned a narrow cot and a wooden foot locker. I was surrounded, always, by men in various stages of undress, cursing, complaining, and polishing their boots. It was cold in the winter and hot in the summer and ugly all the time.

As I mentioned before, I am a provincial and only know people like myself. In heavy mortar battery were people as foreign to me as Martians. First of all, all the people in charge were mostly black. Where I came from, there were black people but they were black people like me. We went to the same schools, shopped at the same shops, drank from the same fountains. They were rubes just like me, only black, who noticed the difference. However, these black people were not like me. Their culture was different, their language was different, their perceptions were different. Outside of the fact that we all stood upright and had arms and legs, we were as different as butterflies are to harp seals.

There were also two minor ethnic groups: Puerto Ricans and hillbillies. The Puerto Ricans were, over all, an admirable bunch. They were serious, careful and conscientious, but kept to themselves mostly. The hillbillies were young, coarse, uneducated and silly, devoted to grab-ass, beer drinking, and anxious for sexual conquest. There were a few white guys like me, draftees, but they were silent, stunned by their misfortune and not of much use or interest.

Before this, at Camp Carson Colorado, I was trained as fire direction for heavy mortars, which I did not give a rat's ass about and paid no attention to at all.

On a bivouac the last week of boot camp, at Pike's Peak in snow up to a tall Indian's ass, we were standing in line to wash our mess gear all bundled up in field jacket, pile cap, scarf and gloves, when an immersion heater used to heat the water in the garbage cans where we washed our mess gear blew up, spraying flaming gas down the line of troops. The men at the front actually caught fire, those of us further back were sprayed with flaming gasoline. I remember my face being hot, but it was so damn cold that it felt good. I backed up and stood around like everyone else until the medics pulled me out and put me in an ambulance. I didn't even realize that I had been burned until I saw myself in a mirror at the hospital. The skin on my face was shredded and hanging in strips. My hand holding my mess gear was also burned. The hospital wasn't too bad, we had good food and a lot of free time to watch T.V., read, play pool, whatever.

When we began to scab up we looked like we had a farmer tan. A farmer tan, to those who don't know, is a tan face and a blindingly white forehead. When you see farmers come to church with a coat and tie and no hat, their faces are very brown and their foreheads are white above their eyebrows. That's how we looked. The pile caps covered our foreheads and were untouched.

When the scabs began to peel off, we were very pink underneath. One sad case was a black guy, a very handsome black guy who, as he told us, was very popular with the women. His scabs came off and he was pink, like the rest of us. He was horrified. The doctors told him that he would darken up after a while, but I don't know if he believed it.

It was not a big problem for me as I had been, in high school, a perambulating pimple farm. Zits galore. It hampered my social life, as you may imagine. As it was, I had deep pits on my face already, so a few scars couldn't be much worse.

When we were released from the hospital, I didn't look much worse than usual. A few dark scars, but what the hell.

Some of the men were not released when we were; the ones up close needed plastic surgery. The handsome black guy didn't come out either. I never found out if he turned out black and handsome. I hope so. I have always envied the handsome, but I hold them no ill will.

This has been a long digression, but I wanted to illustrate the circumstances at the time and, I hope, to give some insight to my feelings as this juncture.

I was alone and lonely, wounded, alien, and far from home from the first time, really, in my life. The young woman that I met at the Dai

Enko Tai hotel was kind to me and funny and someone I could talk to who was not coarse and ruined and bitter. The little hotel was in an alley away from the ruin of war. The neighborhood was not blasted and destroyed, and in that small space it was beautiful and peaceful, and I was happy for the first time in a long time.

I was not sophisticated but I was not a fool either. I knew what was going on. I didn't care. For three days I felt like a real person with someone to love. We can fool ourselves into thinking that things are not what they really are. We can ignore the bad shit and find some happiness in the small, good things around us. I did it then, and I do it now. I am not sorry or ashamed. What happened, happened, and it is a memory that I treasure.

Eccles Street Gang

A hem, ahem, my lecture today will be an elucidation between being a boy when I was a boy and being a boy nowadays.

The world in those days (1944 to 1950) bore no resemblance to the world of today. Not in any particular.

I was a charter member in the Eccles Street gang. There were 15 boys about my age, within two or three years. We lived in a neighborhood where all the collars were bluer than blue.

It was a time of large families. Most of the gang consisted of two brothers in each family, except me. I had a brother but he was too young to be significant. Everybody had two parents, the same two the whole time.

Divorce was unthinkable and undiscussed. The dads worked and the moms stayed home. Two of the guys' dad was killed in an accident and their mother had to go to work. It was horrible for everyone.

There were three gangs in the larger neighborhood. Us, the Oak Street gang, and the church gang.

We controlled the river. We had swimming holes and fishing spots. The Oak Street gang had the park with the playground, tennis courts, and ball field. The church gang had the church. We didn't have rumbles like West Side Story, but we were jealous of our territory and shared only grudgingly.

I remember one incident very clearly. We were playing touch football on the church lawn. The church guys didn't participate, all they ever did was ride their bikes to each other's houses and go inside and stay there. They were a creepy bunch.

Anyway, we were playing with the Oak Street gang. Now, for some reason that I don't remember, we would mix it up for these games. Maybe the older guys were trying to level the playing field by mixing up the skill levels so it would be a real game.

Dirt Newey, an Oaker, and about 17, was running with the ball. I was in the clear and called, "Here, Dirt." He threw a lateral pass which bounced off my chest. Somebody grabbed the fumble and ran with it.

Dirt really laid into me calling me all kinds of names, the most printable of them were: stupid, clumsy, and incompetent. Nobody stood up for me. I was humiliated and very hurt. (Dirt Newey was about 17 then, and I was ten, so he is probably dead now. I certainly hope so.)

This contretemp had two results. I never again played any team sports. I was clumsy and non-athletic and I didn't like sports anyway, so I quit. I would still do individual sports like running and pole vaulting, or swimming, but no more team anything.

Result #2: ever after that, when anyone did something stupid or screwed up somehow, I never chimed in on the resulting abuse. Sometimes, I even sided with the screw-up, but only to a certain point. A lot of times these disputes ended in blows, and I hated to be punched.

While athletic skills were much admired and studiously practiced, there was another skill that I really admired. Joe had a mouth on him, when provoked he could cut loose with a stream of invective that would peel the skin off your face. He was also small and very quick. So if anyone chased him, he always got away.

I sort of apprenticed myself to him. I didn't tell him so but I followed him around and watched and listened. In time I became a mouth myself. The "Mouth from the South," except that I wasn't vicious. I was funny. It is possible to be very coarse and insulting and funny at the same time. The victim would be furious but everyone else would be laughing. He would be hard pressed to punch me out when everyone else was laughing, so he would have to laugh too, reluctantly, and I seldom got punched, although I really deserved it.

As I said before, everybody had dads. My dad worked and came home and read the paper. Whatever else he did, I don't know. He had no hobbies, didn't go fishing or hang out with his friends. A big guy, strong, he did very physical work. Very good looking, everyone said so. Alas for me, I took after my mother who was beautiful beyond belief but not where you could see it. She was sort of a plain little sparrow, but my father adored her. He even told me once, "I had better apologize now," he said, "because if your mother and you were drowning and I could only save one of you, you wouldn't be the one." This is, of course, an apocryphal story. I could swim like a fish. What he was saying is that my mother was the most important thing in his life. He liked me O.K., but I was expendable and she was not. I was O.K. with that. I loved my mother too and if I drowned and she was saved, that was O.K. with me.

My father told me things from time to time. I remember one:

I had just gotten my first job. I was in High School. It was watering the golf course at night, dragging the hoses. It kept me up very late but that didn't seem to be a problem with him or me. I still had to get up and go to school in the morning, which I did. The thing that he told me was, "If a man hires you to work for him and trusts you," (I had no supervision at the golf course, I was there by myself) "you should do the best job that you can. You should be reliable and responsible. You will feel better about yourself if you give an honest day's work for an honest day's pay." I listened and I did that. All my life I did that and he was right. I did feel good about myself and there were even perks.

Even in the army, where goldbricking is endemic, I gave an honest day's work for an honest day's pay. The First Sergeant was so astonished by this peculiar behavior that he questioned me. "What do you expect to achieve by all this competence and hustle?" "I'm just trying to get along, Sarge."

For some reason I had very little yard bird duty (picking up cigarette butts) or walking guard in the snow. The other soldiers noticed this and when I would be coming from the mess hall with the Sergeant's cup of coffee, they would make sucking sounds to which I would reply with the silent single finger that we see so much with drivers of cars these days.

In those high and far off times, discipline was often physical. Mike and Jerry's dad used to lay into them with a belt for the slightest misdemeanor. No one was given a timeout or restricted T.V. Actually, there was no T.V. I used to get the switch every once in a while, but not all that often and I don't remember too many incidents, except one.

My mother had told me to do something or other, instead of that I jumped in the ditch with my clothes on. (I was always strange.) My mother told me, "Wait till daddy gets home." No idle threat. Well daddy came home just as I was getting out of the ditch. Well, my parents had a consultation and I was sent to get a switch. My father gave me his pocket knife and sent me to get a switch. My father did not view this as cruelty, but it was.

When I came back with the switch, he put me over his knee and whaled me good. The switching on my still-wet overalls was excruciating. I can't think that it taught me a lesson because jumping in the ditch was a peculiar thing to do in the first place, and was not likely to occur again. The thinking was that I had disobeyed my mother and that I should not do that again. I wish I could say that it worked, but it didn't.

The last time my father resorted to physical discipline was when I was 16 years old. I was in the kitchen and I was sassing my mother. He got up from his chair in the living room, put down the paper and came in and punched me in the face—hard—I slammed against the wall and slid down. The clock (an heirloom that had come across the plains) fell on top of me. It was undamaged, thank goodness. My father spoke not a word but went back to his paper. I put the clock back up and went silently to my room.

He never hit me again, and I never sassed my mother again. This time, it worked.

When I was 13 years old, I went to Junior High School. I had looked forward to this for a long time. Jr. High School was "Big Time."

About the same time as I was beginning to notice girls, I was struck by a plague. I became, in a very short time, a perambulating pimple farm. Every zit in the world loved my face, and they jostled and crowded each other for space.

I was a horror to behold. I was no jock, we already know that, nor was I an especially bright student. I had nothing really to recommend me and I had the face from hell. I was pretty sure that none of the pretty girls would want to come within a mile of me and I responded accordingly.

I vacillated between slinking around silently and alone and being loud and boisterous and vulgar (I still had the mouth). As strange as it sounds, I did have friends and most of them were girls, pretty popular girls. We hung out and did fun stuff and all that, but it wasn't boy-girl stuff. If you follow me, it was more like I was one of the girls.

They would talk about this cute boy and that cute boy and send me on spy missions into locker rooms and places that they couldn't go to see if so and so liked so and so, and who they talked about. I was a good spy. Listening in and asking leading questions and reporting this information to my masters. Many a young man had his head handed to him on the basis of my data. I had not a qualm about my treachery.

In time I fell in with bad company, of course. We smoked cigarettes, talked dirty and wore our Levis very low on our hips.

These stoners knew that I was in tight with all the popular babes in the school and were awed by the ease and casualness that I demonstrated. Little did they know that I was more of a house pet than a big stud, but I let them think what they wanted to think.

In those simpler times, before there was T.V. or on-line or video games, we still knew how to amuse ourselves. We had fraternities and sororities even in Jr. High School. A way to set yourselves apart and be somebody, they were just what you suppose them to be—nasty cliquey, snobby groups whose major function was to look down on everyone else, and I was all set up for that. I pledged to the baddest one. Delta Kappa, or D.K. My school was situated in such a way that we had the patricians on the Hill, the bourgeois in the middle, and the great unwashed down by the tracks.

I insinuated myself in with the rich kids mostly on the basis of my mouth (that mouth has taken me a lot of places). The sorority that was referred to as a Sister sorority was Auida Kai, or A.K. It wasn't Greek but I never knew what it meant then or now. I don't think anyone did.

Most of my lady friends were A.K. and we associated only (or mostly) with each other. The whole situation really didn't amount to much, all we did really was stand around in bunches in the hall and look arrogant and superior. (It doesn't take much to amuse some people.)

A couple of funny things happened in Jr. High. In the 10th grade, I was nominated for class president. We busily made signs and slogans and I glad-handed all about. Then one day we had to go have a fight with the "Ditchler" (another strange name) at a school about a mile away. One guy in the school had a car (this was 1949). He was a dork but we buddied up to him to use his car. (When I say we were nasty little bastards, I don't mean maybe.) So we went to get in this fight, when we pulled up the Ditchlers were already there. They were all huge and mean looking. We sat in the car and thought about it for a while. We were still thinking about it when one of the biggest ones, Malcolm Dalton, came over, opened the door and grabbed my shirt and pulled me out. All the buttons popped off my shirt and tore open. I was prepared to die, but I got my fists up and was going for an honorable death when who should appear (thank God) but Mr. Hawkins, a.k.a. Hawkeye, the truant officer. (I don't know if there are still truant officers nowadays or not. I don't think so.)

Anyway, that gave us all an excuse to flee, which we did. When we got back to the school we had missed two classes and on the front steps was the principal, Mr. Stark, and his weasely Lieutenant Mr. ____. Mr. Pack especially didn't like me, I don't know why. I was no more repulsive than the other DKs. But he could hardly suppress his glee when he announced that we were all suspended until we brought a parent in to be humiliated. "And you, Aikens, you are no longer a candidate for political office."

I was so terrified that I would have to bring my dad to school to hear the charges that my disqualification blew right past me.

In the end, my dad came (he had to leave work, he didn't like that) and I was re-instated. There was some talk of an insurrection and a walk out to protest my dismissal from the voting. I quickly disabused them of such foolishness. I had cheated certain death twice and I didn't want to go there again.

My dad, who had excellent, though off-center, child raising skills, said "What the hell are you doing now. Try to get some control of your life," (or words to that effect). This was 55 years ago, remember. And that was it.

Old age just goes on and on

Old age just goes on and on. There seems to be no end to it. (Well there is but I don't want to think about that yet.)

I just get saggier and baggier, weaker and leakier (we don't want to talk about that either.)

But I'm beginning to get the hang of it—I have decided to quit trying to be a regular person and fold into old age.

I am beginning at the bottom and working my way up.

When I was a small boy my grandpa had lace up boots. They were the greatest shoes I have ever seen. They went clear up to his calves.

I wanted some. Grandpa told me that you have to be an old person to wear those cool boots.

I decided that when I was an old person I would have some of those boots.

Well, you know, life takes a lot of attention so I sort of forgot about those boots, until I got to be an old person. I was about 65 and soon to retire when I saw the boots at Jolleys. They were black and shiny and just beautiful. I was 65 and believed what I was told—that 65 was an old person.

Well, I didn't feel old, I didn't even look old so I thought, hey this old age is not so bad. But the meltdown began pretty soon.

Family History

I recently had a birthday. Well, as a matter of fact, it was today. It is one of those birthdays that count. You know what I mean? Some birthdays are landmarks and the rest are a pain in the ass (unless you get a lot of really nice presents). The first counter is six, then you can go to school. The next biggie is eight, then you can be baptized. There is a long dry spell until sixteen, then you can drive. Then twenty-one so that you can drink in bars without fake I.D. After that there has been a lot going on (you hope) and the next really important milestone is sixty-five, then you can get your old age pension. Before that you can pick and choose which birthdays are important.

My fortieth birthday became one of those landmarks. It was a busy time in my life. I was soon to be a father, a little late in the game I admit but I was eager to commence. Also looming was a dark specter of serious unemployment. But all of that was put aside for a day when my excellent wife gave me a party like no other. She hired a hall, invited the known world and gave me a diamond ring with 40 on it, a diamond being the 0. I was flabbergasted, pleased, flattered and embarrassed. It was a surprise. The whole population knew about it but I did not. This means that either all my friends are good at keeping secrets or that I am very dense. Thinking about it later I realized that clues fell on me like rain. I picked up on nada.

The avowed purpose of this exercise is to write a history of my family. As luck will have it I am the oldest living person in my family on both sides, which means that I can hand out all kinds of bullshit and there is no one to contradict me. But I won't do that. I think what I will do is begin with what I know which is not everything, nor is it backed up with real evidence such as journals. What I tell you now is what I have heard, myself, from participants or second or third hand by trustworthy reporters.

Return Jackson Redden – My Great-Great Grandfather

I'll begin with my mother's side. In the beginning was Return Jackson Redden. Jack Redden was a river pirate on the Mississippi river. (If you can't have a horse thief in your background, a pirate will do just as well.) Jack and his gang appeared out of some caves in Memphis. In the 1830's and 40's there was, as now, a lot of commerce on the Mississippi flat boats and barges carrying all manner of things such as produce, livestock, manufactured goods, and paddle wheelers ferrying frivolous travelers with money. These boats and barges were lightly guarded, if at all.

The pirates would discover, by scouting around which boats had things that could be stolen and sold. Then they would row out heavily armed, take what they wanted and let the boat go on. In some cases they made the boat men come to shore and unload livestock or other cumbersome items and then let them go. There was not really much danger for the pirates because the Mississippi is long and mostly just uninhabited country with a lot of places to hide.

Jack had been at this for a while. When we take up our story he was in his late 30's. Jack Redden was a large man, tall and strong with dark hair and dark eyes. The most noticeable thing about him was that he was amazingly handsome. All the things written or spoken about him brought this up right away. This must be true because all the Reddens, even to this day are amazingly handsome.

It is told around camp fires that Jackson Redden was in Nauvoo, Illinois to scout up some pirating business and heard the prophet Joseph speak. He stopped being a pirate on the spot and offered his services to the prophet on a personal basis. It is not known what he told Joseph or what Joseph said to him but he turned up soon after as one of the prophet's bodyguards joining such illustrious company as Porter Rockwell and M. Hickman. At that time Joseph was the Mayor of Nauvoo, the Captain of the militia and about to run for President. The prophet Joseph had a lot of enemies and Jack had his work cut out for him.

Nauvoo was bustling and prosperous and for a time the biggest city in Illinois. At first the people of the neighborhood welcomed the Mormons. They were hard workers, made no trouble and contributed to the wealth of the countryside. Then the Mormons became more numerous. New converts poured in all the time. They became very powerful and as it is widely known then as now, they were a peculiar people who kept to themselves. They didn't make friends easily with the locals. Their new temple was a mysterious place where only the chosen could go, then as now. There were numerous multiple wives of polygamy. The local people began to think that maybe the Mormons were not such a good deal after all. They were strange and they had their own army.

It is a big Mormon thing to keep a journal, but it appears that Jack did not. At least none has turned up. There is the possibility that Jack couldn't read or write. This was not uncommon in those days. We have no knowledge of his childhood. He did appear in journals from time to time though not in any big way, "Jackson Redden and Porter Rockwell accompanied the prophet." Or "Jackson Redden and Bill Hickman were dispatched to Chicago to escort the new converts to Nauvoo." From this it appears that aside from bodyguard duties these men also ran errands for the prophet.

This brings us to an important place in the story. When the prophet Joseph was captured and taken to Carthage and killed, Jackson was "on an errand for the prophet." The reports were that he was devastated that he was not present to protect the prophet from the mob. It was his primary duty and he failed. It haunted him for the rest of his life.

Jackson quickly transferred his allegiance to Brigham Young, the new prophet, seer and revelator and leader of the Church of Jesus Christ of Latter Day Saints. The transition of leadership was not without problems. There was a power struggle. People took sides. It was a serious upheaval. The prophet Joseph had left no designated successor. When the dust had settled Brigham Young, one of the twelve apostles was in charge. Emma Smith, the prophet's wife, thought that one of her sons should be designated prophet. It didn't happen and Emma and some followers left the church to become the Reorganized Church of Jesus Christ of Latter Day Saints.

After a while the Mormons were declared Persona Non Grata by the state of Illinois and forced to move out. Brigham Young turned out to be just the man for the job. He shepherded the saints out of Nauvoo to Mexican territory, Utah, or as he called it the State of Deseret. The move and resettlement in Salt Lake City is a huge and fabulous story in itself, but we are concerned only with Return Jackson Redden. When

Brigham Young came across the plains in the fist wave of immigrants Jack was with him all the way. At the "This is the Place" monument in Salt Lake City his name is right there with Brigham.

Brigham Young was a powerful man, strong, smart, and very much in charge. He was the secular leader and the ecclesiastical leader in Deseret, which at that time took in Utah, Idaho, part of Arizona and California. He was the Boss of Bosses and how he wanted it was how it was. Everyone did as he said mostly out of love, respect and gratitude. He had brought the Saints to safety. No one was going to mess with them again and Brother Young would see to it.

The bodyguard job was not really necessary any more. They were in their own space and everyone around were friends. But still, there was work for the men who were referred to as Danites, Protectors of the Faith. They would go out on errands for Brother Young. No one knew where the Danites went and when they came back and no one asked why. There were rumors, whisperings, winks and nods but what the men did only Brigham and the men involved knew. One circulated family story tells of Porter Rockwell, Bill Hickman and Jackson Redden going up to Fort Bridger, Wyoming, a stop on the Mormon trail. Jim Bridger, a trapper and trader widely known in the territory, operated it. The Danites were sent up to talk to Mr. Bridger who was alleged to be cheating the immigrant Saints who stopped there. Bridger got wind of their coming and headed for the hills. Rockwell, Hickman and Redden waited a while and came home. Mr. Bridger heard the all clear and came back. There were no further reports of Saints being cheated. In fact they reported being treated with greatest respect and kindness.

We know the Jackson Redden was a river pirate, a criminal. We know that sometimes the people that they would rob would fight back or refuse to cooperate and that they were killed. How many we don't know, but I think it is safe to assume that Jack killed people. Enemies of the church disappeared without a trace. Those were different times and the frontier was a harsh and unforgiving place. If he killed as a pirate it was because it went with the job. If he killed for the church and his prophet it was because he saw it as his duty.

In the course of time Jack was retired from service. He was given a very large tract of land in Summit County in Coalville. He lived there and raised his considerable family. Only one photograph of Jackson

Redden exists. I have seen it once, very briefly. It is Jack and his five wives and an uncountable number of children. Jack is seated between his five wives all of whom are women of a certain age, all grim and work worn as were all of the women of the time. If they were young and beautiful once, it is all gone. Jack is central with a large grey beard to his waist. Surrounding them are their children. As I say I saw the picture only once and didn't have time to count, but other sources tell us that there were thirty-two off spring. All that I can remember is that the men were all tall with dark curls and beautiful smiles and all were very handsome. The girls were all demure, modest and unsmiling and it was difficult to tell if they were handsome as well. Jack died at a comfortable old age.

John-Henry Redden and Anna Maria Sargent – My Great Grandparents

Our story continues with John-Henry Redden, one of the sons. His birth order I don't know. John-Henry was a farmer and rancher and ran a hauling service transporting whatever needed to be moved to and from Salt Lake City and points in between. John-Henry was a solid citizen and a devout Mormon active in church affairs. I have seen a photograph of him and his family. You know the kind, sepia toned and everyone dressed to the nines and sitting stiffly. John-Henry seated with his wife Anna Maria Sargent (the Sargents loom large in this narrative) called Anna Marier by the family. John-Henry was a large, handsome man (of course) with white hair and a neat, white mustache. Anna Marier was a largish woman with her hair parted neatly in the middle and pulled back into a bun. They had five children.

Behind their parents were the two sons, Return James and Melvin Nephi. Jim was the image of his grandfather, tall, dark and handsome. Melvin was an anomaly. He was shorter, square and blond. His hair was parted in the middle and combed across with curls on the end. He was the baby of the family, maybe in his late teens. Seated on the end was my grandmother, Eleanor Alberta. Ella had dark hair with a little knot of curls on top. She was the eldest in the family and the most beautiful. She was calm and severe sitting up straight with her hands folded in her lap. Beside her and next to her mother was Inza. Also beautiful but smaller and not so striking as her sister. Next to her farther on the other side was Naomi Vilate called Daisy. Daisy was not beautiful. She was cute. She had cubby cheeks with major dimples and little curls all around her face. With huge eyes and a sweet smile she was a doll. She figures prominently in the story too.

Daisy married one of the dozens of Sargents living in the area. Moroni Lief Sargent called "Surrey" because he was a dashing man about town and came to call on Daisy in a very sharp surrey with two matching bays. Surrey was a sharp dresser too.

In the picture all of the women wore dark colored dresses with huge leg o' mutton sleeves and high necks. They varied slightly. Ella's had felt beads embroidered on the front. Inza had laces. Anna Marier had a lace collar and Daisy had an embroidered daisy. The men all wore three-piece suits with high collars and shiny cravats. They were a handsome and richly dressed family.

Daisy and Surrey lived just down the road and in time had a daughter, their only child.

My grandmother, Eleanor Alberta, married John Brown. My grandfather was sort of a hapless and mostly unlucky man who had a difficult life.

Inza married a salesman and moved to Tooele and passed off the screen. I can remember nothing told of Inza or her adventures. She was just gone.

Melvin was drowned swimming in the Weber River when he was 19 years old.

Going back to my great-aunt Daisy and Surrey. Daisy and Surrey Sargent had one daughter whose name I don't remember. I could look it up but the fact that she is so unmemorable fits in this story.

Daisy and Surrey's daughter had a baby out of wedlock, which, as you surely know, was very bad news in those days. The father's identity was not discussed, but he was alleged to be a married man of good repute in the community. The daughter had a baby and named him Denny.

Her parents were loved and respected by all and were not people who cast blame or shame on anyone. The daughter never married and lived always at home with her parents. She worked all of her life as a cook at the Summit County High School and if she ever traveled more than ten miles from home I would be surprised.

Denny grew up surrounded by love and kindness to be a big, strong, good looking boy with a head full of thick, dark curls. He was very smart and outgoing. He was a big jock in high school: football star, basketball star, high-speed runner and King of the Prom. Despite his having no father, there seemed to be no stigma attached to him and he was welcome anywhere.

His girlfriend, of course, was the prettiest girl in the school and also the daughter of the richest family in the country, Tonya Taggart. The Taggarts were big landowners and among their properties was Taggart's Camp, a sort of amusement park with camping and picnic grounds on the Weber River. Tonya worked there in the general store.

Tonya and Denny were married as soon as Denny returned from his mission. It was the custom then, but not so much now, to be married as soon as you came home. By now Surrey was quite old and Denny took over the farm. They built a house about a half a mile down the road from the old homestead and began their lives as farmers. Denny worked farmer's hours from can't see to can't see while Tonya stayed home alone. She was a pretty, young girl who had never been anywhere nor seen anything. She was lonely and bored.

So, Tonya went back to work helping her folks at the camp. At some point she met a man there. While Denny was at work she came and picked up her traps and left with this man to go to Salt Lake City where she supposedly lived the high life. This man was alleged to be rich and well connected.

Denny continued to work the farm, went to church and kept on as if nothing had happened. There were whispers, winks and nods, but Denny was liked and respected so nobody said anything. He appeared to make no effort to find her.

In time Tonya missed her family and came back with the man to visit her family.

A fatal mistake.

Denny turned up, put Tonya in the pick-up truck and took her home. A few days later a body was found a few miles down the Weber River. Depending on which story you listened to he was shot in the forehead or he had drowned. The Sheriff of Summit County who did the investigation was Jericho Sargent. The official story was drowning, death by misadventure (imagine that).

Denny and Tonya lived quietly for a while. After a time they had a child and eventually they began to appear at social functions, come to church together and melded back into the community. They had several more children and Denny was made Bishop. He took very good care of his mother and his grandparents, lived long and became a prosperous farmer.

One of his sons, in time, became Sheriff of Summit County replacing the now very old Jericho Sargent.

My Great Aunts and Uncles

Winding back to my great aunt Inza and great uncle Return James Redden (Jim). Out on the edge of the family that we are concerned with was an attractive young woman named Edna. She was a daughter of one of the many sons of Jackson Redden, a cousin. Edna was a special friend of Inza and spent a lot of time in great-grandpa John-Henry's household. Inza was a good Mormon girl and toed the line, but Edna felt stifled in the close, pious community and wanted to cut loose. Edna's dream was to go to Duchesne, a mining town over the mountain with a lot more going on, a "tent of wickedness" according to her family and way out of bounds.

The mines of Duchesne had attracted a lot of foreigners: Italians, Poles and Central Europeans of all kinds, Catholics mostly (gasp). There was dancing, singing, drinking and God knows what all. That is what Edna wanted to be a part of. She ran away and was there for a while before the anxious family discovered where she was. She was a beautiful girl of course (being a Redden) and very popular in the mining camp. She had a job in a grocery store and it is supposed she danced the night away in one of the many bars or taverns in Duchesne. When it was discovered where she was, a posse led by Jim Redden was displaced to bring her home, and he did.

It was a surprise to the family when very soon after Edna and Jim arrived in Coalville, they were married. Now, Jim was very well acquainted with Edna because she was a close friend of his sister Inza, but he was also her first cousin, and even among Mormons who married each other all the time this was unusual. Also, Jim had paid no special attention to Edna, but no explanation was offered. Jim and

Edna moved to Ogden where Jim went to work for the railroad. Soon after they arrived in Ogden, too soon, a son was born, Shandon. Shan was a beautiful baby and looked just like his dad, but remember, Edna was a Redden too.

Back in Duchesne, at some earlier point, a man was found out on the track with two bullets in his chest. This man had no connections, no family, and nobody knew much about him. He was a Boomer. They showed up in the boomtowns that sprang up all over the west. These men had no background, worked the mine and raised hell in the saloons. Boomers were rough and ready and fights were common-place, violent, and sometimes fatal. Finding a man dead was not all that uncommon. The Sheriff asked around to see if anybody knew any-thing about it. No one knew anything and the guy began to stink, so they buried him on the lone prairie and promptly forgot all about him.

In Ogden Jim and Edna bought a house across from the park where they lived in peace and serenity. (I guess.) They had several more chil-dren, two boys and two girls. One of their girls, Ardath, was my age and we went through school together.

Ardath was the youngest in the family, quite a bit behind every-one else, so she was still at home with her elderly parents when the other children were gone. Jim died and Edna held on for a while. In our family, there were some serious love matches and this was one of them. After Jim's death Edna just sort of wasted away. When she knew that she was dying, she told Ardath about the shooting of the miner in Duchesne. She was pregnant when Jim came to fetch her and the soon dead miner was the father of her child. She told Ardath that she didn't know for a long time about what had happened. She said that years later Jim told her that the drifter was shooting his mouth off about knocking up the pretty grocery store girl and Jim shot him to protect her good name. If anybody listened, or cared, nothing was ever said and nobody ever knew.

Why Ardath told me all of this, I'm not sure. We were in high school then and really never said much more than hi to each other. Maybe she couldn't bear to keep it to herself. She had to tell some-body. I was family and could be counted on to keep my mouth shut, which I did, until now. I don't know if I feel guilty or not, but Ardath is gone as are all the others. If I have any excuse for betraying her confidence, that's it.

John Daniel Brown and Eleanor Alberta Redden – My Grandparents

We can veer off here to John and Eleanor, my grandparents. Why Eleanor Alberta Redden married John Daniel Brown was a mystery to everyone. Eleanor was a famous beauty prominent in the local gentry and came from a first family prominent in the church. John Daniel Brown (aside—the story is told that John's family name was originally Delaplaine but it was difficult to pronounce and pretentious so they changed it to Brown.) was small, shorter than Eleanor, with a round face and a lot of golden curls. He was cute, but as nearly as I am able to find out, he had not much more to recommend him.

They were married in Coalville and John bounced around working for various ranches in the area, even for a time in the mines. He didn't like that. Their family grew apace. Virgil Paul was the oldest, Bessie Alberta was next, Claudia Aleena (my mother) was third and Letha was the baby. John and Ella moved to Altonah and John sharecropped for a Ute on the reservation named John Yesto. They had a little house and a steady job. The children went to the reservation school and all seemed to be peaceful.

John Yesto had a son named Feather Hat. He was 16 years old. There are no pictures, but Hat was described as tall, dark and handsome. The Utes as a people are tall and dark. Bessie was 14 years old at this time and beginning to bloom. Hat didn't want to be a tribal Ute. He wanted to be a white man. He had a white man haircut and wore white man clothes. He was paying special attention to Bessie.

It is one thing to work for an Indian. It is quite another to have one in the family. Grandma Ella made a huge fuss. Feather Hat and Bessie ran away to Duchesne, (that sink hole of sin and depravity) but were soon found and brought back. John and Ella packed up the kids and all their traps and moved to Ogden. At that time Ogden was a big rail hub and there were thought to be a lot of jobs. It didn't work out that way. John managed to work at this and that. It was coming upon the great depression and things grew ever more difficult. Mama told me about how they would rent a house and when the rent came due again, they would sneak out at night and put everything in the truck and leave. By now there were four more children, Yvonne (called Nonnie), Dale, Margie and Kenneth.

Mama's brother Virgil, by now had begun his career as a drunk (now called alcoholic). Claudia and Bessie worked as hired girls for rich Jewish families in Ogden. They did cleaning, cooking and child-care and lived-in. Grandpa John kept poking along.

Bessie, Claudia and Virg attended a new school about every two months. Nobody made it past the eighth grade. It was easier to quit than to struggle. Their attendance at church fell away too. With their transient life, they were unable to make many friends, so they became very self-contained. As I was growing up the "family" spent a lot of time together. No one seemed to have a friend outside of the family.

Clyde Walter Aikens and Claudia Aleena Brown – My Parents

In Ogden, at that time, there was a huge Ballroom called the "White City". A dome shaped building that looked like the Salt Lake Tabernacle. They had live music on Friday and Saturday nights and all the young people went there. It was the 30's version of a pick-up bar. All the Mormon boys and girls wouldn't go to bars, but they loved to dance.

Bessie and Claudia were working girls and had a little money to spend. They gave most of their money to Grandma because she had a lot of kids at home to raise, but they had enough for flapper-looking dresses. They had bobbed hair and spit curls. Mama was a blonde Redden, not a knock out but a cutie. Bessie (now known as Becky) was a dark Redden and gorgeous.

This is where they met Clyde, my dad. Clyde was a black Irishman, not too tall, but broad at the shoulder and narrow at the hip with shiny black hair combed straight back and big, brown eyes. He was a hottie. (Author's note—I spend a lot of time detailing how good looking everyone in my family is because I missed the boat. I'm not bitter but I wish it were different.)

Clyde paid special attention to Claudia who was cute. He was polite to Becky who was gorgeous. He could have had either one (I'm guess-ing) but he chose Claudia (thank God). They danced and danced. When I became a seminal being I knew that they were famous dancers. Ginger Rogers and Fred Astaire, stand back. All of my life, and all of theirs, their only recreation was dancing. They worked hard and had no hobbies or interests except dancing. Every Saturday night they went somewhere to dance. Their favorite venue was the Hermitage in Ogden Canyon. They were famous there. (aside) A long time later Barbara and I went to the Herm on Sunday night and danced the night away, only by this time it was Disco. We were famous too.

After while (not a long while) Clyde Walter Aikens, 21 years old, and Claudia Aleena Brown, 20 years old, were married by the Justice of the Peace in Farmington, Utah. They moved into a little shotgun house at 1035 20th Street where, 18 months later I was born. I was named James after my grandfather (of more we will hear later) and my Mother's younger brother.

This tiny house had three rooms all in a line, living room, bedroom and kitchen, with a shanty on the back. A large, empty field on the right and an irrigation ditch on the left. We lived there for six years. During that time a brother was born, Clyde Melvin after grandma's brother who drowned. Being a child I can't say much about what went on, but it seems now that we had a great time.

Becky (now Bessie again) had not married to everyone's amazement. At length my dad introduced her to his older brother Jack. John Lincoln Aikens was bald, coarse and inept but he was doing o.k. He began as a small building contractor and remodeler. He was smart and a very hard worker (a family trait that again passed me by). In time he built the Kaysville City Hall and the St. Joseph High School.

He and Bessie were married and about a week after my brother Mel was born they had a daughter, Janice. Mel and J.B. (Janice Bessie) were blonde, pale and frail and looked like twins, which they were often mistaken for.

John and Ella were still plunking along. Virg was now a serious drunk and as I heard later, a lot later, he blamed his father because he would not buy him a motorcycle. Margie and Nonnie married two brothers Sicilian Italians, Matthew and Carman. Margie was 17 and Matt was 32. Nonnie was 18 and Carman was 28. The men's parents Luke and Lucia were immigrants who worked hard and got lucky. They bought a farm on West 24th Street that was later bought out by the U.S. Government to build 24th Street Army Depot during the II World War. They bought a farm on upper 12th Street across from the new T.B. sanatorium (where my mother nearly died and where aunt Bessie did die, of T.B.). In time this farm was bought by the Weber

County School District for Ben Lomond School. Luke and Lucy fade from the picture.

Nonnie and Carm had five children Bonnie, Johnnie, David, Donna and Kelly. Marge and Matt had Patrick, De, Charlie, Elaine, Linda, Max and Lowell (Lowey).

Aunt Letha married Harry Rigley. Their children were Merlin, Kenny, Gene, Chris, Billy and Kathy.

Uncle Dale never married and was very strange. I don't think that he was queer, but he was very strange and helpless. His sisters took turns keeping him, much to the consternation of their husbands. It was rumored that he molested Patrick and Matt kicked him out and never spoke to him again but no charges were ever filed.

Uncle Ken married Sally and had two children, Kristy and Curtis. Sally disappeared and Ken gave his children to Sally's brother to raise and joined the Army in South Carolina. He met Jerry and they were married. He brought her home but she just didn't fit in with a sort of closed down, secretive family and went home. Ken then married Lida who had two children. He was a throwback to his father, cute with blonde curls and not much substance, but Lida hung in there and last I heard she was still hanging on.

The Redden family. From top left: Eleanor Alberta Redden (Grandmother), Melvin, Jim, Inza. Bottom row left to right: Daisy, John-Henry Redden (Great Grandfather) and Anna Maria Sargent (Great Grandmother).

Jim Aikens, late 1950s

1966

mid 1980s

POETRY

He believed in re-incarnation

He believed in re-incarnation
and came back as himself.

Not much progress there.

I have always worried about
being re-incarnated as a corncob.

that should give you a clue as
to the level of my self-esteem.

The great wheel of life rumbles apace
dragging all along with it.

In the deer park at Sarnath
Lord Buddha preached a sermon
Glorious in its beginning
Glorious in its middle
Glorious in its end.

Buddha also said____remember
what I have elucidated
and what I have not elucidated
Malunkyaputta

Whatever it was,
Malunkyaputta didn't write it down
or at least I couldn't find it
on the internet.

If l could, would it save me?

Imaginary gardens

Imaginary gardens with
real toads in them.

All praise to them
all praise

The drifting swan on the darkling flood
Ne plus Ultra

Rising stars and fading grandees

Swimmers not diving into clean water
but wading into blood.

Time is such a fleeting unsubstantial thing.
"I wasted time now time doth waste me."

decrepitude
Marie Antoinette

Unraveled thoughts

Unraveled thoughts in gathering night
unfocused intelligence: absence of light
icy fingers of dread
around your throat

cold winds of despair
unfazed
by a thin shabby coat

no charity
no hope
no help for pain

just the bludgeon of memory
again
and again

Anything can happen

Anything can happen in life
especially nothing.

The secret is,
that there is no secret.

It is a distressing thought that memory
constantly fills up with information
that is almost completely useless.

Who can know for sure
which way a life will turn
or dodge
or feint
or hide
or go silent?

There is comfort in planning ahead
but plans can go awry
[gang algae] as you can be pretty sure
that they probably will.

The success of an acceptable life
depends on flexibility.
Not inevitability.
Without it your options range
from disappointment to toast.

Being good for nothing

Being good for nothing.
Be wise.
Thus_____statesman like I'll
impose
and, safe from action
Advise
sheltered in impotence,
urge you to blows
and being good for nothing else
I'll be wise.

A consequence

A consequence which enabled me
to bring my life to life
was meeting you.

Before you came I was alive
but then,
So is a tree.

I was ok as a tree,
shedding leaves,
growing leaves,
you know,
like that.

I wasn't missing anything.
I didn't know that there was anything to miss.

I'm not a tree now
just standing there
growing rings.

I'm alive in a new way,
a better way.
I love you.

There are quite a few rings on me.
That could be a good thing.
I'm strong and steady.
No foolish wind can bend me.
I can be shaken,
but not toppled.

I have been shaken.
You have shaken me.

My leaves tremble.
My sap shoots out to my branches and roots,
Hot and thick.

But a tree in love is still a tree,
solid and silent.

Thinking many thoughts
but making few sounds.

Can you recognize my love song
in the sighing of my leaves?

I am, in fact, a man
but as mute as a tree.

How can I make you hear me?
How can I let you know that
I love you?

Help me.

A cautionary tale

The devil neither drinks nor smokes
nor does he engage in revelry,
But he is still the devil.

Would I know him if I saw him?

Is his moderation a disguise
to better lure us into the snare?

This is uncomfortable information.

We have been told that the devil
is handsome and has horns
and stinks of brimstone.

Easy to spot.
Easy to run away from.

Maybe not.

It appears that more vigilance is required.
The deceiver is as advertised

Clever devil.

Standing over the sink

Standing over the sink
Looking out the window
Choked with longing

"Why don't you walk your
goddamn dog in some other direction?"

I pull back
ashamed of the heat in my face
the swelling in my groin.

Leave me alone.

Everyday I get crazier
and crazier.

You are putting yourself in harms way.
You can't know who the crazies are.

Silver hair and a modest demeanor
can conceal a person
that I don't want to think about
and that you have reason to fear.

Leave me alone.
Leave me alone, please.

Little Orphan Annie's parents smoked

Little Orphan Annie's parents smoked.
I'll bet you didn't know that.

This was a long time ago,
before the Tobacco wars.
Smoking was just a thing that everybody did.

Do you remember
"Reach for a Murad instead of a sweet"?

The implication is,
sugar can kill you.
Oh really.
Anything else?

My grandmother and her eight daughters
used to sit around the kitchen table
and drink coffee and smoke.

My Mother, one of these daughters
died of smoking.
          as did Aunt Nonnie
          as did Aunt Becky
          as did Aunt Leah
             too Bad.

I wasn't the only orphan,
there were nine of us.
             too Bad.

In a world of choices,
can anyone be faulted for a wrong choice
based on faulty information?
       Yes.
           too Bad.

Of the nine orphans,
seven survive.
We all smoked.

None of the survivors now smoke.
We are all getting old
rather than dead.

Too soon old.
Too late smart.

Of my Grandmother's
thirty-three great grand children
      none smoke.

      How about that?

The captured pirate was skinned alive

Rigorously deny
that you see the guy
out of the corner of a
suspicious eye.

Who is that person?
in a long stinky bathrobe
carrying a farm implement
from century before last?

You know who —
and you know what he is here to do —
and you know that he is looking for you.

You knew he would show up sooner
(although you had hoped for later.)

So now what?
on a positive note:
you are tired.
Here is the rest you had hoped for
(desired)

Well, tho,
maybe a little nap would suffice
from all the information out there.
If you sleep with this guy,
it is the big sleep.
Really big.

(He's not even cute.)

Keeping with the positive:

The little woman would probably like to see you the
    hell out of here.
Annoying in the kitchen.
Peeing on the toilet seat.

Naught to fear at the judgement seat.
You have been working on your alibis for years.
They are perfect.

Think about it:
No more sore feet
No more Sal hepatica
No more senior moments
(when you forget your granddaughter's name)

Sounds better and better

"Hey Buddy. Yeah you in the nasty dress. Cummere.
    I wanna talk t'ya."

You didn't come and save me

You didn't come and save me
And I waited.
I waited a long time.

Things happened to me while
I was waiting
Bad things
I watched for you, but
You didn't come and save me.

The river of life flows down

The river of life flows down
around rocks into deep pools.

Things live in this river.
Things die in it.

In this river of life are warm shallow places and
dark cold scary places

It is possible to be washed
up into a back water and just
swirl around
            and around
      and around
going nowhere.

Some like that.
Smooth quiet, no surprises.

But later or sooner,
mostly sooner, you are pulled
back into the current.

An out of control life is scary
and dangerous and no fun.
But a subscription to the river of life theory absolves all blame
all responsibility.
I can't help myself. I must keep rolling along.

What was Chicken Licken?

What was Chicken Licken?
And why does Turkey Lurk?
Is he after Henney's Penny or some other dirty work?
Cocksey Locksey, Foxey Loxey
a similarity in name, was Cocksey a ringer?
Was he in on the game?

And what was Loose about the Goose?
His morals or his bowels?

We're lucky Foxey Locked around these
degenerate fowls.

I was at Lyme

I was at Lyme, right at the spot
Louisa Musgrove jumped off the cob.

I saw the swan of tuonela
undulating between life and death,
grieving all the way.

I knew early of the fate of Jugartha
and it broke my heart.
It still breaks my heart.

I know the questions of Socrates,
questions that curl back on themselves
and eat their tails.

I discovered that while I was waiting
for the gravy train my ship came in.
How does that make you feel?

Untitled #1

Twice and once the moon has onced around
and returned to find me here.
Patient, still, waiting.
What am I waiting for.
Wait with me and see.

Untitled #2

Save me, please somebody save me.
I'm sinking in the shifting, darkling sea.
When I skipped atop the swells
I never suspected these cold dark hells.
I looked no further than I could see.
There was no breadth or depth to me.

When, exactly did the lifeline break.
Where did I make my big mistake.
Did I outwit myself? I don't think so.
I usually go where I want to go.
What caused the problem,
What was different/wrong?
Was the problem short, or was it long.
How long has it been going on.

Why didn't I notice? Am I dense?
It has been noticed that I have no sense.

Untitled #3

It was only the next thing. Not the last thing.
Surely not the real thing,
Just one damn thing after another.

If it's not one thing it's another.

It is amazing how important "things" are in life.
To bring things to a head implies moving on.
Moving on to what?

More things.

Untitled #4

In the Dawnzer Lee Lite
(as Ramona has said.)
The tall still, very still inert reality.
Pines glow on the east side with golden light.
At the tips first then: all over.
The light is fine and new.
The sky has been pink and is now blue.
Hard blue, solid and impenetrable blue.
In the sunset (sometime later) the pines are gold again,
On the west side
Instead of the gold light coming in
It is going out —

But the light is different
It is harder, thicker
The light is not from the top —
But from the bottom
Less innocent.
More darkness
More shadows

The trees are recognizable but not the same.
A new complexion
Not sad — exactly — but darker,
Moodier — not coming alive but dying.
When the light is gone they are still there
But not as alive
More like still, dark monuments.

Untitled #5

Embargoed time doth stretch and pull.
Enough, enough
No going back.
No holding still.
Wrong done is wrong gone.
No calling back, fear, panic, remorse,
No use.
All is undone
Time is always cruel
Pulling everything toward death and still no rest.
Time goes on even if none is left to suffer it.

Untitled #6

"Wherever you go, there you are."
"But what if there is no there, there?"
What if you think that you are on the road to love
And when you get there you are there by yourself.

I know that she was with me —
I thought that she was with me.
Was she ever with me?
Maybe she did love me once — and now she doesn't.
"Like a bubble when it's burst, all at once and nothing first."
What the hell?

Untitled #7

The only reason
That you are still alive
Is because God don't want you
Anywhere near him

Tautology

Untitled #8

Waiting for the turkeys to come
Is a long and apprehensive wait.

The shadows are long and
The tops of the ponderosas
Are bright gold with the setting sun.

The tall snag at the end of the gully is waiting
As am I.

They have roosted there for ------------
A long long time.

Why don't they come?
Is it something I said?
Dark, Darker, Darkest
They don't come.
I have to go to bed
Empty and alone.

Untitled #9

Look out, not in and what do I see?
I see a stranger
Looking at me.
He has my lips, my hair, my eyes.
He looks like me
But in some cheap disguise.
I'm really better looking than the guy you see
But am I the illusion
Or am I me?

This causes a lot of people a lot of confusion.
Are you talking to me —
Or —
To the illusion.

There is really not much to me,
I'm a pretty empty shell.

Still, if you have gotten me, in a clutch,
You've got the real thing OK.
But it's still not much.

But, really what is important to see
A doppelganger or the real me?
I see myself as one guy.
A joy to my mother
But the actual fact
Might well be another.

San Francisco poemz #4

Sitting in the misty rain
Under the Bay Bridge
In the land of the ferries.
    Sliding silently in
    Loading up
    (It's commute time)
Slipping silently out
"Mare island"
"Mendocino"
"Tiburon"
The ferries come in through the mist to the dock.
People lined up like cows
At the milk shed.
"Del Norte"
When "Mendocino" left the dock was clear
Now it is full again
Everyone knows when
Their transport comes
It is not as if they come
Every fifteen minutes.
How cool is it to get on a boat
And float home
Through the fog, with gulls
Floating overhead
Most impressive is the muffled silence
The bubbling wake
Smaller, smaller, smaller, gone.

San Francisco poemz #5

In San Francisco, when it rains
nobody says "Well its good for the crops,"
they don't say anything.
They just pull out these huge umbrellas —
everbody has one.

I'm a Utah boy. I have never owned
an umbrella.
My mother used to have one but when she died
we threw it away.
So I was wet, me and the homeless guys.
It doesn't seem to bother them.
Nothing seems to bother them.
The appear to be only dimly aware that
they are alive.
Sad. Very sad.
But I am alive and I am wet.

In fact, I have no umbrella and no shoes.
You might could say that I'm not
right on top of it.

But, what the hey, I'm here
for adventure and a wet,
barefoot, smiling guy
attracts no attention.

San Francisco poemz #6

On the train
"I'm sorry this train is out of service."
        "What!"
"I don't live around here,
what is going on?"
        "I don't know."
We have all been kicked off.
A thousand people standing in a dark tunnel.
What will happen
Who knows.
Back on.
Nobody complains, no bitching.
These people just go with the flow.
One in four people on the train is talking
on a cell phone.
"I'll be late for dinner."

Is this fatalistic, or is it
just living the life?

If I didn't already have a life (sort of)
I would come here and live this one.

San Francisco poemz #7

How is it that tall
straight up and down cities
generate excitement?

I live in the desert where you can see
a hundred miles in every direction.
I love it.

Here you can't see a block ahead.
Streets come in
Go out

What's next? What's coming?
There is always something coming,
Something next.
Sometimes not so good stuff —
But more thrilling than scary.

I really couldn't live here.
Too over-stimulating
My head would explode.

It is a nice place to visit
I come here often

I love life in the fast lane
But I'm so goddamn old
That I can't live it.

But I remember
Loving In in Golden Gate Park in the
dark and fog

The "burning man" on Sunset Beach.

Janis Joplin at the Fillmore, "Me & Bobby Mcgee."

I was moving fast once, I guess that'll
have to be good enough.

A to Z

America is beautiful.
Best on all the earth.
Country of my heart.
Department of my birth.
Eagles screaming thru the air.
Flying high on high.
Greater visions
Higher hopes
Iron principles
Justice.
Kings need not apply.
Laborers and farmers,
Men and women of all stripes,
Need each other.
Often they do not know it until
Passions of war cause
Quickening of hearts and closeness is
Required.
Scenes of great beauty
Timeless mountains
Universal waves, crashing
Vigorous trucks rolling
Wild places, a little scary.
Young at heart, old in wisdom.
Zion in my heart.

From the poisoned well

From the poisoned well of hate, envy, revenge
    and disappointment comes sort of a foul odor

Let's get away—fast

The best poem written in the history of the world (my choice)
    is "Not waving, but drowning."

Daedalus moving through the labyrinth,
    kept one hand on the wall.

Ghost in the machine

Phan-todds (n.) as in Hoo Haws.
Irrational fears and anxiety.
Skin Walker—A zombie like creature formerly Human.
Runs on all fours very fast (as fast as a pickup truck.)
Kills as directed.

Suicide note

Why do I feel that I am disconnected from life?
Answer?
Things are the same
Nothing is different
Why?

I feel closed in upon (a convoluted description, but accurate)

Have I cut myself loose?
Or has someone cut me loose?

I have no answer.

Is there safety in silence?

Should I confide my suspicions to someone?
Who should I ask?
Has anyone noticed?
It is not all in my head
There are signs.

I would like to talk about it
But I'm afraid that nobody gives a shit.
I don't want to be a bother.

All swans are white

In the textbook example:
"All swans are white."
You could count white swans
for centuries and still not know
that all swans were white:
Not for sure.

No number of white swans could tell
you that all swans were white,
but a single black swan
could tell you that they
are not.

Who has proposed that
all swans are white,
when a black swan appears is not to say "Wrong again"
It is to say,
   "You call that a swan?"

One may sanctify the white swans
and send the black ones,
so to speak
to the gulag.

They are not now;
and never were.

In the batty moonlight

In the Batty Moonlight
Radiated universal death rays and bad karma
The wolf was always at the door
I dreamed in the language of elephants
It is better to be lucky than good

The necessary end

The roilings and toilings
are over at last
procrastincations are a thing
of the past.

Thoughts left unspoken will never
be said
There'll be much left unfinished
Because
I am dead.

I knew it was coming but I paid
scant attention.
It is only a move to another dimension.

Then, I perceived, with alarm and dismay
It was not at all like the way people say.

There were no pearly gates
no beating of wings
no golden stairways or
community sings

It was a dark and clammy place,
Not pleasant a bit
Instead of ambrosia
the place smelled like shit.

Crouching in darkness,
in fear and foreboding,
I heard a sound like
a coal truck unloading.

I caught a glimpse of heat and of flames,
What have you got yourself into now James?

What I did on my summer vacation

Rocks and Rills
abound around
bright hot sky
and scarlet ground
the mighty quiescient Colorado
slow, smooth, above
and cold below.

Skating upon its
undulating skin
our civilized veneer
stretching thin,
Hot, steamy visions
pour through our
brains
distant rapids roar
like trains
chocolate tongues
curling, lapping
jaws of monsters
snarling, snapping
into this inferno of
ravenous creatures
moves a boat load of
school teachers.

A boat manned by daemons
handsome and cruel
revenge themselves on
teachers of school.
They worship a bucket
full of stools
a ransome for
their ship of fools.
The time has come
the captain said
to make the Colorado
River run red,
break apart this
Sorry barque as
we plunge and dash
through streaming dark.

The sky with the
river in unwholesome
collusion fill the
sky with streaming
confusion of fiery
tracks and smoke and
silence
Breaking apart the
constellation.

Cassiopeia dying
cries one lost in the
immensity of Ink black
skies
(The pleiades meteor shower)

The teachers huddle and
shiver and quake
and wonder what
the configuration their
destructment will take.

Enter, Enter the daemons
who will carry
you through
this hellish hole.

Gather on board and hold on tight.
To be continued...

Hat

If a young man mislays his hat
he says, "I have mislaid my hat."
The old man says, "I have lost my hat."
"I must be getting old."

Mummy wants me to win $1,000 in a poetry contest. The entries must be 21 lines and uplifting . . .

How long is grief

How long is grief?
With its knots, and clumps, and
spirals and plunges.
It goes as far as the eye
can see and as far as the heart
can tolerate.
Will there never be an end?
Well, yes and no.
The darkness will lighten up
The wracking pain will mellow
to a dull throb.
Then after a long time it will
soften ever more and go back
Somewhere behind your eyes
You will ocassionally see it
and feel it but not in that
wracking and breathless way that
you remember.
How do I know?
Been there done that.
21 I'm sorry for your loss. Hang in there.

The devil neither smokes nor drinks

The devil neither smokes
nor drinks nor engages in
revelry, yet, he is still the devil.
The living remained
and suffered.
He made the moon
Made the sun to match
But not the stars
The stars came otherwise

We are all mad at night
When visible are the
Specters, who beleaguered the walls
of Prague
When demon eyes peer through
The slitted shutters.
When things go bump in the night.
When your fingers open and close
And itch to strangle.
The knife under your pillow burns
A blister on your cheek.
Macbeth hath murdered sleep
a long time gone
Unraveled thoughts in failing light
intelligence
Panic and fright
Icy fingers of dread around
your throat.
Cold winds of despair unfazed
By a thin shabby coat.
No escaping from the tangled skin
Just the bludgeon of memory again and again.

Rosemary

Rosemary is for remembrance
Blue roses are for forgetfulness
Rosemary is all over the damn place

Blue roses are hard to come by

Repentance comes before forgetting
It can happen but it takes
Forever

Bring me a blue rose
I need help in this matter
Forgiving is easy. Anybody can do that
I understand that.

But after I have been forgiven
How do I forget?
I have been forgiven, but
I can't forgive myself
Am I still on the hook?
A blue rose would do the trick.

It is hard to love

It is hard to love when your
Heart is bound
And tied with rope
And staked to the ground.

I know nothing of mermaids
Or why birds can fly
But I do know something about
Love gone awry.

Was it something I did?
Something I said?
I think of it often
Alone in my bed.

I had it all locked down
But then, maybe not
I appeared to have veered from
The right train of thought.

So alone and in silence, I linger all night
The moon washes my feet then
With silvery light.

I am a snout

I'm a snout, eh!
I listen and watch
I see things
I hear things

Sometimes I am dangerous
Sometimes I'm not.

I am unobtrusive and quiet.
Most of the time nobody knows
What I'm up to.
That's the plan.

I keep copious notes
If you see me coming, and you are up to no good
Be afraid.

If you are OK
Then
I am OK

My conceit is that I am the
Conscience for people who have
No conscience

Most of the time I am not welcome
Like the skunk at the picnic
But sometimes my efforts are
Appreciated.
Not always,
But.
Sometimes.

I do it because I am compelled.
Where the hell do I get off
Making myself the conscience of
The world?

You'd have to
Know me.

If you see me coming and you
Are just behaving strangely, for
Whatever reason.
Don't worry about it.

But if you are behaving badly
And causing harm and worry to
Others.
Be afraid.

We are headed down the river of no return

We are headed down the
River of no return.

Sometimes known as shit creek.

I don't think that you really love me.
I think you love the idea
of secret love.

But I am a man, what do
I know?

When we are caught you know
Who will take the rap—not me.

I am a man and men are pigs
No argument? I thought not.

I have been caught in this
Downward spiral before
Did I learn anything?
Looks like not.

It has been a concern of mine
With me all my life.
I have let the wrong head
Do my thinking for me.

Has this caused me grief?
Not much.

As luck would have it,
I am poster boy for the American Dream.
Do I deserve it?
Probably not.

I would be remiss if I
Didn't warn you how this will end.
Believe me, I know.

So this is your opportunity to
Call the whole thing off.

But I wouldn't be sorry
If you didn't.

What an asshole I am.

As the Cheshire Cat told Alice

As the Cheshire Cat told Alice, "We're all mad here."
A man of many abilities and no qualities.
A poor ill formed thing but mine own.
The chief mourner does not always attend the funeral.
Surrounded on all sides by held breath.
Nothing is just one more thing.

Sitting quietly

Sitting quietly in a still, flat, white place. No breath, no sound, no motion. (As idle as a painted ship, upon a painted ocean.)

Surrounded by faces,
Some Bewildered   and
Some Confused   and
Some demented   and
all insane.

It is as the Cheshire Cat told Alice, "We are all mad here!"

Surrounded on all sides by held breath.
Of
Loved ones
Unloved ones
Some ones
Other ones.

Crushed by the knowledge that nothing is just one more thing
and that the bottom line
is just the line on the bottom.

I am smothered by knowledge.
Trapped by its
Sticky
Suffocating
Useless
Weight

Oh for a little ignorance.
Oh for a little bliss.

PLAYS
AND
SCREENPLAYS

Sic Transit Gloria

EXT. MODEL LAUNDRY, 1950 – DAY

On a building's window a painted sign reads "Model Laundry and Dry Cleaning."

INT. MODEL LAUNDRY, 1950 – DAY

A rack of clothing, packages of sheets and towels, phones, and a desk adorn an office.

A MAN of about forty sits behind the desk.

A gawky BOY, sixteen years old with unruly hair and zits, stands in front of the desk.

MAN

Uncle Honey needs to have Saturdays off for the next month or so. You have your driving license now. How would you like to deliver his route for a few Saturdays?

BOY

Geeze Dad, that would be very mellow.

MAN

You are a big strong boy. You can carry the linen packages up the stairs with no troubles.

BOY

Yes sir, I can. This will be so mellow.
I have never been in a whorehouse before.

MAN

It would be better if your mother thinks that you are cleaning
machines and sweeping up, as usual.

BOY

Why?

MAN

Mothers, generally speaking, don't like their sixteen-year-old sons
hanging around whorehouses.

BOY

Okay, uh — will the ladies be there?

MAN

I don't know, maybe they have a union shop and get Saturdays off.

BOY

Oh man! I hope not.

MAN

Remember, you are just the delivery man. You bring the clean towels
and sheets and pick up the dirty ones. Mind your manners and keep
your mouth shut.

EXT. SHABBY HOTEL – DAY

The Boy parks truck in front of a shabby hotel.

He gets out bundles of sheets and towels and enters the hotel's front door.

INT. SHABBY HOTEL – DAY

The Boy eagerly hustles upstairs carrying his load.

His face falls when he sees a counter, unattended, and a long hall with many doors, all closed.

The place is shabby and dark.

His happy smile fades as he puts the fresh bundles down, picks up the dirty bundles, and descends the stairs.

INT. SHABBY HOTEL – DAY

The bundle-bearing Boy reaches the unattended counter at the top of the stairs. He sets down his burden and tiptoes to the hall.

He listens intently to faint moans emanating from behind closed doors.

INT. SHABBY HOTEL – DAY

Thoroughly disappointed, the Boy comes trudging up the stairs with his heavy bundles.

This time is different. There is a small lounge, with a couple of couches and easy chairs.

Of greater interest is a table with four LADIES in bathrobes sitting around drinking coffee and smoking cigarettes.

The bathrobes are of the type his mother might wear, not sexy peignoirs or diaphanous and revealing wraps.

LADY #1 points to a spot on the floor near the stairs.

LADY #1

Just put that stuff down over there.

The ladies glance idly his way.

The Boy puts the bundles down and fusses around with them in order to stall and take a better look around.

He picks up the dirty bundles and leaves.

INT. SHABBY HOTEL – DAY

The Boy arrives better dressed and as spruced up as possible. He flashes a big smile at the ladies.

BOY

(cheerfully)

Hi!

Again he stalls and fiddles with the bundles.

LADY #2

What happened to old Honey?

BOY

Well, Honey is my uncle, and he needed some Saturdays off for some reason, so my dad, who's the boss, told me to take over on Saturdays. I just got my driving license.

The Boy's charm and happy smile impress the ladies.

LADY #3

Would you like a cup of coffee, or are you one of those
Mormon boys?

BOY

(lying with conviction)

Oh, hell no. I'd like a cup of coffee.

He pulls up a chair and one of the ladies goes to the little bar in the
back and gets him a cup of coffee.

LADY #2

So do we call you young Honey, honey?

BOY

I call every Saturday, so call me faithful.

Everybody chuckles.

INT. SHABBY HOTEL – DAY

The Boy is greeted at the top of the stairs by Lady #1.

LADY #1

(pointing)

You come to the right place to drop your load.

The Boy sets down his bundles on the spot indicated.

The other ladies smile at the Boy from their seats at the table.

INT. SHABBY HOTEL – DAY

Once again the Boy is greeted at the top of the stairs.

LADY #1

(with a different emphasis on her words)

You come to the right place to drop your load, Ace.

The Boy begins to set down his heavy bundles in the usual place.

LADY #1

No, not there.

The lady steps back into the hall and jerks a thumb in the direction of the nearest closed door.

LADY #1

In here.

The Boy looks dumbfounded for only a moment. He begins to laugh.

Lady #1 laughs.

The other ladies around the table join in the laughter.

INT. SHABBY HOTEL – DAY

Five of the ladies and the Boy are seated around the table drinking coffee.

BOY

(to the oldest lady present}

You have some sort of accent — not foreign, but not from around here.

LADY #1

Boston.

BOY

Whoa, you are pretty far afield.

LADY #1

(slowly)

A long time ago Eddy came to Boston and convinced me that I needed to come to Utah and work at the Rose Palace.

BOY

Okay! That is pretty high end.

LADY #1

Indeed it is, and I was Madam Pompadour there for a long time.
Men lined up to visit me.

BOY

Why'd you quit?

LADY #1

I didn't quit. Eddy brought two new young girls up from Las Vegas
and someone had to go. That someone was me.

BOY

Oh.

The other ladies look at each other alarmed.

LADY #1

(good naturedly)

Yes, Tempus really fidgets when you're having fun, and almost before
I knew it, I was declared redundant. Now I'm just a two-bit whore on
Two-Bit Street. Sic Transit Gloria.

The other ladies look at each other sadly and then look down.

EXT. SHABBY HOTEL – DAY

The Boy is outside the door at the bottom of the stairs facing
Two-Bit Street when two of the ladies come out and join him.

The ladies greet him and smile, and one of them pats him on the
butt affectionately, as one might do to a little brother.

The ladies go back inside.

EXT. TWO-BIT STREET – DAY

A car crammed full of KIDS from the Boy's school cruises past the
hotel. Its male and female occupants are all staring at their classmate.

> KIDS
>
> (shouting more or less in unison)
>
> Ace, what are you doing?
>
> MALE #1
>
> You let those whores feel you up?
>
> BOY
>
> Why not?

The Boy ascends the stairs with a studied nonchalance.

INT. SCHOOL HALLWAY – DAY

Four eager MALES are questioning the Boy.

> MALE #2
>
> What's it like in there?

> MALE #3
>
> Do you do it with them?

> MALE #4
>
> You're sixteen — how come they let you in?

> MALE #5
>
> How much does it cost?

The Boy shrugs the questions off with a knowing smile.

INT. SCHOOL HALLWAY – DAY

Three concerned FEMALES are questioning the Boy.

> FEMALE #1
>
> What were you doing in that place?

> FEMALE #2
>
> Do your parents know?

> FEMALE #3
>
> What's wrong with you? You can catch a horrible disease.

BOY

(smiling)

I ain't doin' nothing. I just work there.

The Boy hurries down the hall until he is stopped by a friend.

MALE #6

Are they really cute, Ace?

BOY

No, not really. They look like everybody else.
A couple of them are fat.

MALE #6

What do you guys talk about?

BOY

The same old crap that my mom and her sisters talk about.
This hick town hasn't got a store where you can buy decent clothes,
or my boyfriend went to get his car fixed and got hosed. You know
what women talk about.

MALE #6

(nudging the Boy)

No hot stuff?

BOY

Hell no! I asked once, "How's business?" They told me it was railroad
payday and they did okay. Then they changed the subject.

MALE #6

Crapola.

INT. SHABBY HOTEL – DAY

The Boy and the ladies are sitting around the table drinking coffee and laughing.

A policeman, RALPH, comes up the stairs and takes a look around.

Ralph walks over to the table. All goes quiet.

RALPH

Well Ace, why aren't you in school?

BOY

It's Saturday, Ralph.

RALPH

What are you doing here on Saturday?
Does your dad know you're here?

The Boy points to the clean sheets and towels.

BOY

I am delivering the laundry for Uncle Honey.

RALPH

Oh!

Ralph looks around a little and leaves.

BOY

My goose is cooked.

LADY #1

Why?

BOY

Ralph the cop is the big brother of my best friend. I know that he will go home and tell his mother where I am. His mother will tell my mother and I'll be back sweeping behind the tumblers and shaking farts out of shirt tails.

The Boy gets up, walks slowly to the stairs, starts down, and turns to face the ladies.

BOY

(sadly, dramatically)

Sic Transit Gloria!

The Boy continues down the stairs.

FINIS

Barber Shop

SCENE ONE – Barber Shop

Barber with white jacket is dusting off the chair, in walks customer.

BARBER

Well Mr. Attorney General, how nice to see you.

ATTORNEY GENERAL

You know who I am?

BARBER

(Knowingly)
Oh yes, Mr. Attorney General, we know who you are.

ATTORNEY GENERAL

I'm here on business to have some meetings with the mayor. I was told that this is the best place in town to get a haircut.

BARBER

Oh yes sir, it is.

Attorney General sits down. Barber puts cloth things on his neck.

BARBER

Mr. Attorney General, while you're here getting a haircut, would you like a manicure? My wife does it. She is the best there is.

ATTORNEY GENERAL

Sure.

BARBER

(Calling over his shoulder) Utahna, you have a customer.

Utahna enters. She is a fundamentalist woman with a long dress and long hair (you know what I mean). Sits down next to the chair with a little table and puts Attorney General's hand in the water.

ATTORNEY GENERAL

I'm in kind of a hurry. Will this take long?

UTAHNA

Oh no sir, if you are in a hurry, I can get my sister to do your other hand. That will be twice as fast.

ATTORNEY GENERAL

O.K.

UTAHNA

(Calling over her shoulder)
Tiffany, can you come help me?

Tiffany enters. She is another fundamentalist-looking just like the first. She says "Hi" and puts down her little table and picks up the Attorney General's other hand.

The Attorney General is visibly uncomfortable. Everyone is working along when a third fundamentalist woman walks in. (Very young.)

She is dressed the same except that she is wearing a ton of makeup and her dress is slit up to the waist. The stomach is cut out of her dress and she is wearing a pierced ring in her belly button. She is wearing flip flops and chewing gum.

BARBER

Well hello, McKayla, how are things going at middle school?

MCKAYLA

Oh pretty good, Brother Jessup. But this bussing back and forth from Hildale takes forever and trying to fit in with the St. George kids is driving me crazy.

UTAHNA

What is the problem now, McKayla?

MCKAYLA

Oh it is just that I, like, don't know the language. I am, like, in the dark most of the time.

BARBER

The St. George kids speak English, just like you do.

MCKAYLA

You are totally wrong Mr. J. Totally, for instance, what is a "cheerleader?"

(Everyone looks at each other)

TIFFANY

I guess we don't know, dear. What is it?

MCKAYLA

I don't know either, yet. But there was a notice posted which called for cheerleader tryouts. All the girls were jumping up and down and squealing. It said to be in the gym tomorrow at 3:00.
I am going to scope it out.

UTAHNA

That's nice dear. Anything else that is new?

MCKAYLA

Oh yes, do you know what a baton twirler is?

OTHERS

No.

MCKAYLA

Well, this girl in the shortest skirt you have ever imagined, and without her garments too.

(All gasp)

And cowboy boots sprinting and prancing and jumping around, and she has this stick with a ball on the end and she waves it around and throws it up and catches it. She has this ghastly smile on her face that looks like it hurts. This all goes on for a very long time.

The other girls watching are all paying her compliments, like "Show it to us Miss Cellulite," "A billy goat would give up anything for a butt that size."

BARBER

Sounds strange but harmless.

Suddenly four small children rush in.

"Mommy, mommy."
She scoops them up and kisses them.

CHILD

How was middle school, mommy?

MCKAYLA

Boring . . .

McKayla scoops them up and starts to leave. "I'll go home and start dinner."

BARBER

Ok!

UTAHNA

Ok!

TIFFANY

Ok!

Exit.

Door opens. City council man Whatcott enters.

WHATCOTT

Oh goodness, you have a customer.

BARBER

Long time no see Mr. Whatcott.

WHATCOTT

I know it was clear yesterday. City Council meeting is tonight and
I need a shampoo blow-dry. I wanna look good for my fans—er,
constituents.

BARBER

Well we are giving the Attorney General the works right now.
(smiles)

ATTORNEY GENERAL

Oh, no, that's Ok, I am through.
(Tries to stand up but is handcuffed to the tables.)

TIFFANY

Oh don't wiggle around, Mr. Attorney General,
you'll smear the nail polish.

UTAHNA

You know, maybe we had better give him a Novocain shot.

ATTORNEY GENERAL

(panicky)
I've never heard of a Novocain shot for a manicure.

TIFFANY

We do it all the time.

A fundamentalist woman comes in quickly with a hypodermic and gives him two quick shots in his hands and leaves.

UTAHNA

The sharpened bamboo slivers don't seem to be in my table.

TIFFANY

I'll give you some.

BARBER

Mr. Whatcott we can take care of you.
I have hired a new stylist. He is really great.

BARBER

"Lance, we have a customer for you."

Lance flits in. Lance is obviously a gay man, a prancing gay man, with a floral smock, eye shadow and very limp wrists.

LANCE

Hello Mr---- oh my God, that hair is *ugly*!
It looks like it was frozen in time in the 70s.

Lance seats Mr. Whatcott and flings a floral wrap around his neck.

LANCE

(Touching his hair)
This stuff is ossified, what have you got on here, grout?

I suspect that the sunlight hasn't pierced this
bush since you were in 4th grade.

MR. WHATCOTT

Just a little off the top and trim the sides.

LANCE

Isn't that sweet, that's what my father used to say
but—(a long pause)—now he's dead.

I think a change is in order here.
(swoops around squinting at Mr. Whatcott's hair)
I see a smooth and shiny like Kobe Bryant and Michael Jordan.
It is so "Butch."

MR. WHATCOTT

(Horrified)
Oh I don't think so.

LANCE

Oh come on, you and Mr. Attorney General can be twins.

ATTORNEY GENERAL

What?
(begins to struggle with hand cuffs)

I don't really want . . .

Both barbers huddle over customers. When they come up both men
have bald shaven heads.

LANCE

Have a look.

The barbers hold up mirrors.

Both men scream loudly.

Fade to black.

SCENE TWO

Dinosaur Tracks National Monument.

Slabs of rock on the floor. Several people standing around looking at the rocks. People are wearing rain gear and hats.

Two people—one man, one woman—in dark very conservative clothing, talking to a man in a suit.

                         WOMAN

               Have you got the money?

                          SUIT

                     No, not yet.
                  (cups his hands)

                          MAN

               It's going to be too late.

                         WOMAN

              It will have been for nothing.

                          SUIT

          What about the city, have they got the money?

WOMAN

(Screaming)
They've got the money, they just don't care. The most important
thing that has happened in the world since the birth of George W.
Bush, and they don't care. (Begins to sob)

SUIT

I'm sorry. (cups his hands)

WOMAN

(Looking up) It's beginning to rain. (Screams) Throw your bodies
over the tracks, protect them with your lives.

People shuffle around.

One man sits on the rock.

WOMAN

(screams) No, no, you defile them!

Man jumps up.

FIRST WOMAN

What's the big deal, those rocks have been out in the rain for a
billion years, what's one or two more rain drops going to hurt?

WOMAN

Blasphemer!

FIRST WOMAN

Well, excuse me.

SUIT

Mrs. Johnson, please take it easy. (cups his hands)

WOMAN

You should have done more. You retired before the money was
certain. The curse will be on your head.

SUIT

I'm sorry (cups his hands)

Leaves with head down.

FIRST MAN

What's with this? (Cups hands to demonstrate)
Some sort of weird dinosaur prayer?

SECOND MAN

No. (cups his hands) You're in good hands with Allstate.

People shuffle around.

Man enters dressed in Safari gear, carrying a rifle.

WOMAN

Oh, Mr. _____ I'm so glad you have come.

SCENE THREE

Gunlock ward, rows of chairs and a pulpit in front. The people in
the chairs are a mix of old pioneer-looking people. Women with way
out of style dresses and men with cowboy shirts, thousand year old
double knit neck ties and cowboy boots. Also, interspersed are men
in $1100 dollar suits and women in ball gowns, tiaras and all kinds
of jewels, furs and scarves. Some children, mostly young boys.

The Bishop, a timid looking man in a suit comes up. Welcomes
everyone, blah blah blah.

Next speaker is Brother Bowler (a cowboy). Mustache, bolo tie, red
neck, white forehead.

B.B.

We are so happy that the state re-districting has moved the
wonderful people from Kayenta into our humble ward.

Nods and amens from the cowboys. Titters and blushes from the
Kayentas.

NEXT SPEAKER

I have an announcement—of ward business—We'll need ten elders
to go to the church farm to help castrate the new calves.

"Castrate" comes a scream and a very well dressed woman faints and
falls off her chair.

All rush around to help.

Pretty soon she is back in her seat with smelling salts and a fan.

SPEAKER

Brother Hemitt here will be outside on the steps to take
the names of volunteers.

Brother Hemitt has a bandolier of bullets over his shoulder and a
huge rifle. He gives a grim nod and a wave.

Sniffling and shuffling in the seats.

Bishop announces fast and testimony meeting.

First up is a garishly over-dressed lady.

LADY

Brothers and sisters, as I was telling my husband, a former CEO of
a Fortune 500 company and close personal friend of Vice President
Cheney, as we were eating dinner on our Spode china and Tiffany
silverware, "Dear," I said, "God has been good to us to send us on
an official mission to the poor benighted Gunlockians. God never
intended for women to wear dresses that were purchased at J.C.
Penny's in 1952. It is my mission to bring Tom Ford and Gianni
Versace to Gunlock for (Relief society cultural evening! What?)
Three thousand dollars for a nice Halston for Church is worth the
money. I say this in the name of Jesus Christ, amen.

Nest up, a severe military looking man in an expensive suit with four
general stars on his shoulders.

Speaking in a peremptory and loud military voice.

SPEAKER

I feel blessed that I have been called to be scout master
of the Gunlock ward. I hope to be worthy to shape up
these recruits (er) scouts.

Moans and shuffles from scout-age group in chapel.

I promise that discipline and training will shape up these
dog faces (er) boyscouts.

If the rumored war with Veyo erupts while I am in command
(becoming very agitated) we will crush those hillbillies
with a delta force. Trained, ruthless and inexorable
force of scouts from troop (   ).

(Recovering himself)
Or if not that we will work on merit badges
and community service. (Rolls his eyes)

Next up a small child.

CHILD

I believe that the Church of Jesus Christ is the true Church.
I love my mom and dad and I love everybody.
But my horse died and I am mad at Jesus.
Amen.

(Gasps)

Next up a young girl who beings to cry immediately.

GIRL

(Sniffles) I love being in young women,
I love all the young women, I love all the young men except
not all of them. That Jeremy is a snot. I love all the leaders.
I love the Bishop and his councilors and I love girls camp and
I love my parents. In the name of Jesus Christ, amen.

BISHOP

Thank you for bearing your testimonies.
We will close by singing on page 146.

"172" comes a bellow from the organist.

The Bishop flinches visibly. "172 I mean."

All Sing.

"Jesus wants me for a sunbeam."

New words to be written at a later date. Such as to bring all the prior events together and point out that this has been all in fun and if anyone has been offended they can kiss my ass.

LETTERS

Dear Barbara and Squire

Dear Barbara and Squire,

I hope that sufficient time has passed for the shock of that appalling photograph to dim in your memory. You know the one on the family page of the two hooligans who appear to not have a notion of how inappropriate they look.

I must take the lion's share of the blame because I should have been setting a better example for one who seems to have the potential for being the newest member of the family. (In my defense I must say that he was a willing co-conspirator.)

My excuse is that I am dignity impaired. It has been a problem my whole life. You can't imagine all of the problems that it has caused me. I had hoped that age would temper this unfortunate circumstance but, alas, it has not been so.

So. It is my hope that (as you suggested Barbara) all of the <u>grownups</u> were in bed and all of the more civilized guests gone home and only the family is aware of this shocking aberration and families must put up with it because they have no choice. Right.

But if by some awful mischance a regular person was offended, please let me know who and I will write them a humble, groveling and abject apology and they will forgive me, they always do. (This has happened before.)

Please don't be mad at me.

On a happier note, I enclose my newest commentary. It will reinforce the image that I wish to employ—that of a benign and caring old grandfather which I really am. (Except for sometimes.)

Have a nice life.

Love,
Jim

Dear Bone Person

Dear Bone Person,

I hope you don't mind the P.C. version of your name. I got in serious trouble with P.C.-ness and I vowed that it wouldn't happen again.

I called a friend of mine a stupid cunt. She got mad, not because of the name calling but because it was sexist. Had I referred to her as a stupid asshole that would be OK because of the universality of assholes. She also said that I was a dickhead but that she would never call me that because it was sexist. She settled on a piece of shit. It is pretty obvious that my friends and I are vulgar and coarse beyond imagination. But confession is not the purpose of this letter. This is a fan letter.

"Don't give a Shite." You are too cool for school. I had intended to write this letter some time ago. I realize that it is a long time since you wrote that but I am immensely old and many things slip away to some dark place in my head, never to be seen again. But sometimes something surfaces. "Better late than never."

I am a huge fan of your work. It makes me laugh and laugh and laugh. It also has some trenchant observations embedded which I like to look for.

It also lines up with my own Weltanschauung and everybody likes to be agreed with.

Keep up the good work.

Dear Dave

Dear Dave,

These are times that try men's souls ----------. By this I mean birth-days. It is difficult to be totally out of control and find yourself being dragged behind the great wheel of life toward cold death. No way to get off.

You poor bugger. Welcome to the club.

Happy Birthday.
Jim

Dear Derrick and Barbara and Geraldine and Elliot

Dear Derrick and Barbara and Geraldine and Elliot and any other strays who might be around. You run the openest of open houses and make everyone feel so welcome including, but not limited to, me and BJ, Ashley and Ruskin, Nellie and Roland, the lads and on and on and on.

I am sending you my column "What I did on my summer vacation." If you find yourselves referred to as animals, I meant it in the kindest way.

In truth I wrote so much that the editor told me, "We don't print novels."

It has been much pruned down, No Burren, no cottages, no adventure by the sea. The cultural stuff was left in—offal (tee hee.)

Say this three times: The sheiks, sixth sheep is sick.

Love to all,
Jim

Dear Emerson

Dear Emerson,

Your old Poppy doesn't have a bag of gold to give you or even some words of wisdom (wisdom seems to have passed old Poppy by.)

But what I do have is a lot of good luck which I will gladly share with you. The wise old saying goes, "It is better to be lucky than smart."

You are already a cinch for smart. Your parents have seen to that, but to be lucky AND smart is a good way to go.

No matter how it shakes down you will have love and kindness and comfort from all those around you and you can't do better than that.

With much love,
Poppy

Dear Kari and Dave

Dear Kari and Dave,

As I slide deeper down the dark tube of senility and decay, I forget more and more things. This is not a bad thing, if you think about it, but it can be embarrassing.

Example: Have I written you to thank you for having us stay with you, and without you, in Park City?

Well there you go!

It is very hot here. I am going to Ireland sometime soon. I have a new drug dealer, an inside man. But I will always remember your kindness and generosity to me, David. Or not. Don't count on it!

Thanks again for letting us stay in your pretty place, a welcome change from the hassle and stress of retirement.

See you soon?

Love,
Jim

Dear Kathy

Dear Kathy,

On my next birthday, in the spring, I will be 70 years old. Officially an Old Man. (I thought it would never happen.)

And so, I have been taking stock of my most excellent and fulfilling and fun life. I have been remembering the people who have been there for me, who have taken a large role in making my life a great life, the life that it was (is.)

While I don't yet have one foot in the grave I can see it out there in the middle distance. So while my switches are up and my lights still on (mostly) I want to acknowledge and thank you for your very essential actions on my behalf.

Of course we have been close friends and disco buddies and sharers of life so you may not have even noticed the impact you have had on my life.

Thing one: When you decided to shift your own life onto a different level, quit your job and go back to school to fulfill a dream of being a nurse I was impressed. But when I lost my job, rather abruptly, and was practically rigid with fear for my future and the future of my family, you gave me counsel. Go back to school, set your goal, follow your heart.

I did as you advised me to do. I made it. I became a school teacher in the first grade. I had 20 years of fun and accomplishment and satisfaction and without your support I don't know if I would have made it or not.

That is moot now but the real fact is I watched you carefully. Your example was in front of me the whole time.

I was like the little engine that could. "I think I can, I think I can, I think I can." If Kathy can and you could, and towed me right behind you the whole way.

I have always known how important you have been to my life but I probably never told you. Now I'm telling you.

When I had cancer. Cancer is scary. You volunteered to assist Drs. Grua and Harline.

They say people who are very ill or seriously injured sometimes hear the flutter of angel wings. I had an angel actually speak to me. I remember after the operation and I was in my room still not out of the anesthesia. You came and leaned over me and whispered in my ear. I don't remember words but something like "everything is all right" or "you are fine." I do remember your beautiful face and your soft voice and I remember that I never gave cancer another thought.

If you have been told by an angel that everything is OK, what more is there to say?

I know this sounds so mushy and maudlin but it really isn't. You loom very large in my life. What you have done for me is no small thing. I want you to know that I appreciate it and I thank you.

On a more cheerful note, I enclose a commentary which I write for the St. George paper. The Spectrum. I can write anything I want to so it is mostly silly stuff but I hope it makes people laugh.

It keeps me off the street and out of bars (for a while anyway) and I'm having fun.

I would love to see you sometime but just because we are apart doesn't mean that we are absent. Say hi to fireman Hansen and David and Kelly and your whole raft of grandkids.

Love,
Jim

Dear Lizzie

Dear Lizzie,

We both offer you our unconditional love and support in your pursuit of the sybaritic life and we pray that it goes on forever.

Love, Jim and BJ

Dear Mr. Smith

Dear Mr. Smith,

You are cutting into my territory. I'm the funny guy here. "The orbit of Pluto" indeed.

I may as well say right off that I am a world-class, freestyle plagiarizer. My fan base is people like myself. Real Old. And in a couple of weeks they will have forgotten that they ever read such a thing and I may use it again to great effect. (That is if I have written it down and not tossed the paper myself.)

I have the first question for Mr. Answer person. (Dave Barry will be sure to hear about this – I can steal from others but I am adamant about not letting others get away with it. This is called Ethics. (Har))

If it takes a chicken and a half a day and a half to lay an egg and a half, how long does it take to teach a maggot to sing? I know the answer. Marilyn Vos Savant told me (she returns my calls) (nanner nanner).

Respectfully Submitted,
Jim

P.S. You might try radical politics. Tony Van Hemert told me personally that he has gotten death threats. What could be more fun than that?

P.P.S. If you plan to exacerbate Episcopalians may I offer, to a colleague, a word of warning? I know only one Episcopalian and she is a formidable and powerful woman and I'm guessing that she would not take to being exacerbated very kindly and you could end up with a punch in the nose. And if you turn the other cheek you could get a punch there too.

She could, of course give you a wussy first amendment sermon but in her heart she really would rather give you a purple ear.

P.P.P.S. As a decent Christian gentleman (not Episcopalian, Mormon), I have been exacerbated by experts long and often and it rolls off like criticism of the present Administration.

I digress. I really am concerned with your welfare if you mess with me. Not from me because I am non-violent (a synonym for that is "chicken"). But from a legion of supporters at "Shady Pines" and other relevant facilities. They are incensed at your trespass on my turf and have offered to stone you (if you'll get close enough and stand still enough.)

Be warned Mr. Smith.

I'd also like to take the opportunity to distance myself from the rumor that I am involved in the plot to throw a dead cat on your porch. It's not that I particularly like cats but that I go in terror of those P.E.T.A. people. I stay far away from dead animals (except for the ones cut into small pieces and placed on plastic trays and wrapped in cellophane. (Did I say cellophane? Do you know what cellophane is? You are older than you look.)

Dear Norm

Dear Norm,

Happy Birthday to you
You live in the zoo
You look like a monkey
And you smell like one too.

This bit of doggerel is much beloved of six year olds. (that's me)

It is not, however, to be taken at face value. You don't live in the zoo and you don't look like a monkey. I am not cognizant enough about monkey hygiene to comment on the smell part.

Which is neither here nor there. This is to wish you a very Happy Birthday. You have already had more birthdays than the Planet Venus and if we are lucky you will have many more. We love you Normie and rely on your wisdom and stabilizing influence in these difficult times. (That warmth that you feel behind you is smoke being blown up your ass.)

Happy Birthday.
Love J & B

Dear Peacocks

Dear Peacocks,

I enjoyed the evening of serious politics a lot, I enjoyed even more the pleasure of your company. It appears that you know all the really fun people in Kayenta.

"If you meet four Democrats you are sure to meet a fifth"—this is not me, this is Katie's observation.

However!—the three buck chuck certainly enhanced the festivities.

Thank you for the invitation. I am a big supporter of the Democrats and I am so happy to know who my co-conspirators are. Thank you.

Jim

P.S. I'm sorry I ran over your dog.

Dear Preston

Dear Preston,

Enclosed please find my latest commentary as well as some rebuttal letters to the Editor.

I have no information of your politics but I know that you enjoy a little shit in the game . . .

. . . Pause here and read the commentary . . .

Now you know where my sympathies lie and you have read the response of the Arch Villainess Phyllis—a careful and measured response, not shrill or defiant and a little incoherent. I did enjoy the clever spin she put in: "I see that you agree there is a problem. Not."

It makes me sad to realize that I have fallen into such disrepair that I stoop to recreational harassment of old ladies, a shallow and sorry excuse for a life.

I felt very sorry for the man in the other letter, he just didn't get the point. I was tempted to call him and explain but couldn't think how to go about it without insulting him further. So I let it go.

Say "hey" to Miss Susan and I hope she is riding her bicycle around safely and having a nice time with her grandchildren.

Jim

Dear Ray

Dear Ray,

Being old and frail, senile and insane I have a lot to deal with but it is no excuse for bad manners.

I am very tardy in thanking you for your excellent doctoring skills and your generous help with my medication.

Dear Richard

Dear Richard,

Enclosed is the shirt that was assigned to you in my will.

Due to circumstances there will be a delay in the Viking funeral.

I surveyed the Ivins reservoir recently (the site of the festivities) and it is not only dry as a bone, there are six foot high trees growing in the bottom. It may not fill until the retreat of the next Ice Age.

To compound the difficulty, I feel great. A recent physical turned up nothing but senior onset senility (what else is new) and incipient hypochondria. This means I could live until the next Ice Age. Sorry.

In light of these sad developments I am going to give you your heritage now. You can wear it to school and demonstrate to your students what a cool Dude really looks like. It could possibly inspire the little bastards to turn in their homework on time.

Don't become too personally involved with serial killers and vote for the Democrats.

Love to all,
Jim

Dear Robert and Trisha

Dear Robert and Trisha,

I have to say that the much anticipated camporee was even better than I had hoped. The camp space alone was a dream. The food, the food preparation, geological information, wild life itself and especially the sunsets, unbelievable. Organization and logistics alone are staggering.

But my favorite part (I'll be you can guess? Yes!) "Indiana Eves and the creek of death." What a thriller. We have photos already of Jennie and me defying death going over the falls.

I can't thank you enough for a weekend to go in the memory book (or better a scrapbook). Memory at my time of life is unreliable. In fact I'll probably have forgotten the whole thing by Wednesday. (Just kidding).

I speak for us both when I say thank you very much.

I hope it won't embarrass Robert when I say that you are my favorite, most fun Uncle.

Love,
Jim

Dear Uncle Robert

Dear Uncle Robert,

As a person well placed to expound upon the vicissitudes of growing older, I was planning to offer some sage advice. Except I forgot what it was (another benefit of old age.)

Wandering around in a daze is annoying to those around you but will keep you from hurting anyone, recalling painful mistakes, making wrong decisions (making any decisions) and telling jokes (which everyone will appreciate.)

Happy Birthday (if it is your birthday. I think that's why we're here.)

Love,
Jim

Precious flower

Precious flower,

I just finished "Stiff." It is a hoot. That woman is funny in a way that I aspire to. If I could get as good a subject maybe I could write a book as informative and funny as this one.

Tell Beth thanks!

Love,
DD

To Whom It May Concern

To Whom It May Concern:

In response to the advert in the City Weekly, I would like to put myself forward as a candidate for employment in your august and scintillating journal (what is that great sucking sound).

I am no professional. I do not have a resume to offer. I am one of Dr. Johnson's harmless drudges.

I am a retired person of immense age. My sole claim to being a writer is that I have a published column in the St. George daily Spectrum (see enclosed).

I mostly represent the curmudgeon population, which in St. George is vast. I am bad tempered and foul-mouthed. I am just left of Mother Theresa and was on the barricades with Madam Dafarge. My liberal credentials go way back.

I am a Utah native and I can speak and write L.D.S.

I am a retired schoolteacher, but that really won't resonate in this line of work. I taught first grade for 20 years. We learned periods and capitals and that is about as far as it went.

Now for the rat in the buttermilk. I live way out in the desert near the Shivwits Piute reservation and I am locked down. I almost never get further north than Panguitch and I am sure that if a snowflake fell on me it would burn through to the ground like hot lead.

Your ad says "wider" community. Much would depend on how wide, but I figure that the human condition is the human condition and that is what I look at.

What I propose is that if you are interested I could be a stringer covering the south end beat. "Is Kanab turning into a meth capital?"

"What are the Hildale ladies smuggling out in those lovely quilts?"

Shit like that.

I have no computer skills and I have no intention of getting any. (It's a curmudgeon thing.) However, if machine skills are required I have people who can handle that as you can see. Ordinarily my correspondence is written with a quill on off-white letterhead paper and sealed with wax. Miss Manners has commended me for holding down the fort.

I want to be up front with you. I am incredibly old and my activity levels range from inert to comatose, but I am able to stir myself into action for something as interesting and fun as this job looks to be. Am I correct in assuming that this is not a 9 to 5 with weekly deadlines? If it is once in a while when something hot turns up I would like to be your mole in Dixie.

Dear Sir

Dear Sir:

I have been writing a column for the St. George Spectrum for about 2 years. (Enclosed).

The background that you preferred (as noted) is in newspaper writing and journalism. In this I do not qualify. I was a day laborer for 25 years in my first life. Due to circumstances, I was then a first grade teacher for 20 years. I have been retired for 5 years.

If you do the math you will note that I am immensely old.

I had spent the earlier part of my retirement laying around the house and hanging out, but that sort of thing was unproductive and eventually boring.

I needed something to do. I sent a resume and sample of my work to the Spectrum and was put on staff in the Writer's Group. I write a column monthly on whatever subject I choose.

I presently live in St. George, Utah, and have no plans to live elsewhere. (Come here for a while and you will see why.)

I was thinking, that, if you like my stuff, that maybe you could like, put me on as a sort of "Reporter from the fringe." There is a lot of fringy stuff going on here in rural Utah, and I am as fringy as they are and able to ingratiate myself and turn treacherous and sell them out. (Like that?) Think secret, sinister, polygamous machinations. Think Virgin gun laws. Think La Verkin anti-U.N. ordinance. Who knows what kind of shenanigans and undercover merriment goes on in Panguitch? I can find out.

That cliché about old age and treachery is truer than true, and I can prove it.

Waiting to hear from you.

Love to all,
Jim

Dear Dave

Dear Dave,

These are the times that try men's souls (Birthdays).

If you have worked hard and sacrificed and attained your goals, well, la-te-dah.

If you are like the rest of us, you are just glad to be hanging on.

The council I give as one who has hung on longer than anybody is: Don't hike up narrow canyons when it is rainy and drink enough red wine and keep your arteries unclogged.

Works for me.

Happy Birthday!

Dear Preston

Dear Preston:

I didn't know that you lived in "Bucks County," a cool place, like Kayenta is a cool place although on a much diminished scale.

For some reason, that I cannot explain, due to my diminishing mental faculties, I know quite a lot about Bucks County and about the Algonquin round table and Edna Ferber and Alexander Woollcott and Dorothy Parker.

I have long been a theater buff but even I don't go back to 1920---. But I am familiar with most of his plays.

As word would have it, I too have written a play. It was in the 6th grade and it was about the Mormon Pioneers. It was called "The Broken Wheel," and it was about a broken wheel which is about all I remember about it. I also wrote a song for the play. Something about overcoming adversity. It was a very high minded production.

It was a huge success. I dined out on my celebrity for a long time after that.

I was a bright kid with a fine future until I fell in with bad company and I just loved it. I soon *became* the bad company until I escaped just before the drag net went out.

But that is a different story.

Thank you for thinking of me and since I know that you appreciate fine literature I am sending you my last two commentaries. I got into some difficulty for making light of the flood victims. It was not my intention but what can I say.

I have made a careful perusal

I have made a careful perusal of all the letters to the editor and the stated aims of the Citizens Council on illegal immigration and I have concluded that the overwhelming rational for their dismay and discomfort over our new citizens is *money*. How much it is costing them personally.

I have been mistaken for a homeless person before. I guess that there is something threadbare and woebegone about my person and that causes this to happen. It always takes me by surprise and I always go to a mirror and check myself out. I look O.K. to me, but there is just something that I am missing.

Being a hard driving investigative reporter is a lot harder than being an old nuisance. You have to actually have to get up off your duff and do something. I may not be able to continue this sort of arduous labor. I actually went to a public meeting right at my nap time, so talk about sacrifice in support of the First Amendment. The First Amendment guarantees life, liberty and the pursuit of happiness. A lot of the discussion seems to center around Mexicans who live in Utah getting in-state college tuition, while my children (from California) don't (what!).

Speaking of California, as we were, a lot of Californians are fleeing the sinking ship and coming here (oh goodie). They are taking some offence to the Mexicans reclaiming California. If you hark back a ways, and not all that long, Mexico owned California. But an overwhelming crowd of miners, boomers, gamblers, homesteaders, prostitutes and thieves drove them all away. Well now they're baaaack in sufficiently overwhelming numbers. How does it feel?

I was told to check the "Care and Share" because those people are sucking up all of the charity. So I did. I talked to this nice but gimlet eyed lady who told me, in no uncertain terms, that charity is for people who need a hand, no matter who. "And why do you ask?" I tried to explain myself even as I edged toward the door. I agreed with her whole-heartedly but she scared me anyway.

Care and Share
Unemployment office
Welfare Department

"You would think that a person in your situation would not be-
grudge helping someone who needed help. My situation----

At the Social Welfare office I asked the lady there if when small
brown people without drivers licenses come in they are automati-
cally given a small wheelbarrow full of money with a packet of food
stamps, a medical card, new glasses, and a bus pass? She said no.

I thought that, while I was right there, I might see if I could cadge
a hand out, so I put on my most winsome homeless person smile and
asked if I qualified for some government largess. "Probably not," she
said, putting on a snarky smile. It is easier to get blood out of a turnip
than to get money out of me. With my smile frozen in place, I backed
slowly out the door.

Those of you worried about money can take comfort in the fact
that this cheerful lady is taking good care of your tax money.

Two scary ladies in one day. I was feeling a little stressed. It occurred to me that I wouldn't have these problems if I minded my own
business. Well I don't like to mind my own business, never have. But
upon cooler reflection I can see that this immigration thing is going
my way so why give myself heartburn. I should go back to complaining about my health problems. I'll bet that you are looking forward
to that?

Love to all!

Dear Roy,

Dear Roy,

I know that I am way tardy with this and I have a shit load of alibis . . . but better late . . .

Thank you for your excellent repair and installation of my fountain. It works like a champ. I really appreciate your doing this, not to mention saving me a ton of money.

I'm sorry that I am so slow.

Thanks again,
Jim

Dear precious flower of all the universe and Mr. Hartley

Dear precious flower of all the universe and Mr. Hartley,

Greetings. I am, at this moment, lounging (with cocktail in hand) at Richie's pool in Lake Havasu. I am still in awe of people who have their own swimming pools.

Mummy and J.P. (Judy's new name) have gone to Phoenix to go to art shows (yeah, right). So far all the conversation seems to indicate lengthy visits to Target, Dillard's, Home Depot, Costco and other high end boutiques.

We have been here for a week now and as it is a well-known fact that fish and guests begin to stink after three days. We are in the putrefying range by now but no one has suggested that we get the hell out.

I have been wearing my African jewelry everywhere. It is so cool. Thank you again for remembering me.

Dear Barbara and Derrick

Dear Barbara and Derrick,

Where should I begin? You were, as usual, perfect hosts. The misty green dells complete with rock walls and woolly sheep are a happy memory.

As we speak I look out the window and see a red mountain, a brown valley, a hard blue sky. Temperature 106°. That is really hot.

Speaking of hot, we had a hot time at the latest High B. Wedding. We all welcome the newest edition to your international family.

We are very much looking forward to giving you a payback in September, the weather is beautiful there and one option is, Uncle Robert whom you have met has reserved a camp ground at Capitol Reef National Park, a really beautiful place for a week in September for a family reunion. We all camp out in tents, (even Barbara Jane). It would be great if you could come to and meet our very large but very nice family.

Dear Rusky

Dear Rusky,

I need to thank you personally for the great kindness and generosity that we find at your hands.

The trip to the redwoods was out of the kindness of your heart and for no other reason.

You make our Ashley happy, you're good, and funny and interesting, and she loves you and for that we love you too.

The most fun that we ever did was being parents, you'll love it too, just relax and go with the flow.

Love, Jim

Dear Friends

Dear Friends,

We have re-settled in our (almost) new house. Our company has come and gone and we have been invited to visit next year for a couple of weeks in the great Northwest.

It is a really beautiful time of year here and it is nice to just sit down for a few minutes.

We had a lovely time at your house and pool. We really don't get to see enough of each other. We can't wait for disaster to bring us together. We should control our own destinies. (How is that for high minded.)

Enclosed please find enclosures.

Have a nice life.

Love to all,
J.

Dear Judy

Dear Judy,

As the long train of ages glides past memories fade in and out some are bright and happy some are darker and not so welcome.

But old Larry evokes only happy remembrances. He was cheerful and caused no offense. He had some wild and crazy ways but that was just him.

The kid had a good run and did pretty much as he pleased (we should all be so lucky). So we should think of him as he thought of himself.

Just let it all hang out.

Just think, Larry has joined "Elephant!" They should have many memories to reminisce about!

Dear Rocket

Dear Rocket,

I need to propose an enigma:

One man, trim, athletic, watches his diet, doesn't drink too much and prays daily and has a heart attack.

A second man very old and hugely fat who thinks the four food groups are salt, sugar, beer, and grease, who could not outrun a herd of blood-thirsty turtles, and hardly ever draws a sober breath has a heart like a pile driver.

Deduction: life is not fair. If you have ever thought so you are not attentive (possibly in need of stimulants).

But in the end we are all alive (after a fashion) which we must all agree is better than being poked in the ass with a sharp stick.

When you behave yourself (or not) your chances of having another birthday are fair to good. Congratulations on the last one just passed. Happy Birthday.

Dear Razor

Dear Razor:

I am so sorry that you have had a heart attack, major surgery, pain and misery, not even to mention scaring the hell out of yourself and your large circle of friends.

However you are not dead and all the recovery details can be worked out slowly and carefully. You will be as good as new.

However you can never be held over the heads of big fat couch potatoes ever again as an example of what they should be. But I think you can live with that, "Live" being the operative word.

Please get well soon so that Rocky can have his damn birthday party before the beer goes flat.

Love, Jim

Dear Norris and Di

Dear Norris and Di,

We made it home after a long, long, long, long drive. It grew steadily hotter as we got further south. 108° and blinding sun. I long for the whispering pines and gentle rain drops.

You are very lucky indeed and we are lucky too, to have such generous and gracious friends as you.

We enjoyed ourselves very much. We felt comfortable and very much at home. It was great.

I am enclosing my latest commentary. Because I like to show off and because maybe you will find it funny.

Thank you again, we look forward to seeing you when the earth cools down.

Love to all,
Jim

P.S. A package will be coming soon with a sexy garment and some other stuff.

J.

Dear David and Kari

Dear David and Kari,

I am a little slow going with my letter writing chores. But as you know I am real old.

We had such a great time staying with you during the Arts festival. It was really great to see Joe and Marsha and Sandy and Bert and old once-in-25-years Gary . . . . you know I'm thinking that maybe we didn't stay with you, we stayed in a hotel. Oh well, you probably offered, you always do. You are so kind and generous so thanks for the offer anyway.

(I tried ginkgo biloba for memory enhancement but it gave me the shits.)

Love to all,
Jim

Dear Precious flower of all the universe and light of the world and Ruskin

Dear Precious flower of all the universe and light of the world and Ruskin,

I hope this finds you in good health and more importantly good spirits.

We have all suffered mightily from the terrible tragedy and I try not to think about it because it makes me cry.

Enclosed please find "What I did on my summer vacation." No names are mentioned (except for Louis XVI and he won't sue, he's dead.)

Mummy and I had such fun going on holiday with you we must do it again. (Barbara's birthday, Tuscany, whoa.)

Write me all the dish on the girl friends.

I love you and I'll see you soon. Thanksgiving?

Love to all,
DD

P.S. Is it true that Kathy and Debbie are on the dole?

Having birthdays is a lot of fun for young kids like yourself

Having birthdays is a lot of fun for young kids like yourself. You get lots of toys and cake and can stay up late.

Enjoy it while you can. Soon the only toy you will get is a Zimmer frame and instead of cake you get Metamucil and you will be up late every night for your six visits to the bathroom. But that's a long way off.

Isn't it?

J.

Dear Joyce

Dear Joyce,

Where would my sweet tooth be without you? (Probably still in my head.)

Just kidding. I have two teeth left and all the candy in the world can't hurt them. All my other teeth are made of the same material as toilets. Impervious to harm. I can eat all the cookies and candy in the world.

Thank you very much.

Love,
Jim

Dear J & J

Dear J & J,

Now that I have my fashionable vests, and can flounce around and show off throughout the metro area, it has gotten too warm. I could wear them with no shirt but a brief visualization of this grievous mistake would make a hog vomit. As a compassionate person I would never subject any human being (or extraterrestrial) to this horror.

Well, maybe it will cool off.

Thank you, I love you and I love Nuts & Chews, but not in the same way.

Happy New Year.

Dear Maurine

Dear Maurine,

Homemade Biscotti, how cool is that? You have long been one of my coolest friends. Stemming lovingly, I think, from your steadfast faith and serious compliance with the policies of Jesus Christ which makes it possible for you to overlook my dilapidated and sorry ways. "Of all the virtues, charity is the greatest of these." If not for the charity of my friends I would be a sorry and lonely man. But as it is I'm covered (at least for right now.)

Thank you for the Christmas presents of the biscotti and generosity and kindness.

Love,
Jim

Dear Derrick and Barbara

Dear Derrick and Barbara,

To suggest that I am in the same league as Alistair Cooke is a huge compliment but I think due more to kindness than true fact.

I am enclosing my latest article, which I am sad to say is terrible.... I have a new editor who is a young woman of 25 who is not familiar with my work which consists of mostly silliness, and has tried to clarify (her words) my message.

The message is that there is no message. I called her a high dudgeon and she thought that "high dudgeon" was an address in Cumbria. Good grief.

Thank you for the book. It is very enlightening, so far, I had no idea that the English thought of Americans in that way. (Too generous if you ask me.)

Thank you,
Jim

Animals have no concept of time

Animals have no concept of time. A bear goes to sleep for months, wakes up, thinks it was just a little nap and it is still Monday.

Time is a concept devised by humans to irritate and annoy. You will be better off to pay no attention to it.

It works for bears!

Happy Birthday.

Dear Friend

Dear Friend,

It is incumbent upon me to prophesy, to look into your future and see how it shakes down.

You are a brave man to begin a whole new life at the age of 60. I can relate, I did the same and it became one of the shining parts of a mostly excellent life.

If you put your whole self into this new life and retain the good humor, generosity and kindness that have made you famous in the community, you cannot fail.

I promise.

Love,
Jim

Dear Gordon

Dear Gordon,

Now that I may address you as an equal, that is to say an old bastard, I welcome you to the brotherhood. It may seem like fun now but it is all downhill from here on out.

The first 10 years are not so bad. You slow down a little and forget things but nothing much. It's the next ten are when it begins. You go down that slippery slope like a greased pig on an inner tube.

On that merry note, I want to take the opportunity to wish you a very Happy Birthday and lament the fact that I missed the party of the year.

Everybody in town sneaked in your house and surprised the shit out of you. I love that kind of carrying on.

I couldn't be there but my warmest wishes were.

Happy Birthday.

Party on Bro.
J.

Dear beloved Zora

Dear beloved Zora,

Once again the tiki bar was at the apogee of coolness. Anybody who is anybody was there. Quatro De Mayo has never seen such a party and not a Mexican in sight.

Where would we be without party central? Where would we be without you?

Up the well-known creek is where.

Don't let this happen.

Dear Josh

Dear Josh,

We all pride ourselves on our together family. We all love and respect each other from the top, me, to the least rugrat. We are blessed.

Mama and I are blessed by having such an excellent son. We love you very much, which is easy. You make yourself easy to love by your actions. We admire you for the way you look after your family, putting them first and all else second.

We want to take the opportunity of your birthday to thank you for 33 years of interesting, exciting and fun times, and hope for many more of the same.

Love.

Dear Charlie and Joyce

Dear Charlie and Joyce,

I'm sure that you know how much your friends and neighbors appreciate all the time and effort that you put into "trips and trails."

It is a high point in our lives and we are excited before we go and thrilled when we come back. And the trips are a topic of conversation all the time.

You surely know what high esteem we all feel for you both but it doesn't hurt to say so.

So, I'm saying so.

Thank you very much and keep on keeping on. I'll be there as long as I can stagger around (and catch a ride).

Love,
Jim

As friends of long standing

As friends of long standing you know my problems with diminished intellectual capacity. I have only the briefest spans of coherence. Sometimes only lasting a few seconds. (Be patient, this is going somewhere.)

I am presenting this back story as preparation for my alibi for not writing thank you notes promptly.

I really loved your Christmas present and thank you so much. I love presents and don't want to make you mad so I don't get any more. I love Christmas. I love presents and I love you. Thank you again.

Happy New Year

Love,
Jim

Dear Derrick

Dear Derrick,

In these difficult days of international strife the mail has become erratic.

-------------No it hasn't. I am ashamed to present this pathetic excuse for not writing to thank you for your excellent Christmas gifts. My little belt loop whisky flask is the envy of all. Thank you so much for your thoughtfulness.

You guys zipped in to San Fran and out again before we could get it together. I hope to see you all soon. We have a lot of fun together. What else is there but good times, red wine and rock and roll?

Thanks again.
Jim

Excuse me, why

Excuse me, why does Randall Smith get an article in your magazine when I am ignored? Is it because most of my stuff is silly and self-serving? I can write grim and doom-oriented stuff (well, no I can't but nobody wants to read that stuff anyway). I can write heart warming and uplifting stuff too (no I can't that sort of thing is inimical to my curmudgeons orientation and just thinking of it makes me woozy.) But I could think of something of interest to your intelligent, sophisticated and discerning readership.

Writing an article for a high status slick magazine with my picture (I'll get a new picture) and a bio and all that would be cool beyond belief. And it would improve my gravitas which needs a lot of improvement. I have allowed by dignity to slip so far, so often, that now the young men of the family feel free to play grab-ass with me at large gatherings. My dream of being a wise and respected patriarch is going down the tubes. I need your support.

Thanking you in advance.

Love to all.
Jim

Every once in a while

Every once in a while it comes to me (not often enough) that there are people who are very important to me. People who have done me a kindness or service which I have promptly forgotten. Since I am very old, most of these people die before I get around to thanking them.

I miss them when they are gone, and realize how important they were and am mad at myself for missing the moment.

I do, however, keep a list, and when I too am dead I will look them up and thank them. Unfortunately probably not too many of these people will be where I am (not to put too fine a point on it) so I'll be out of luck.

However you are not dead, fortunately for me (and you).

So I get to assure you of my gratitude and good will and welcome you back to your new home (new home, old friends).

I am always in need of your scholarly services. I'll be BAAAAACK.

Affectionately,
Jim

Made in the USA
San Bernardino, CA
18 June 2020